THE LEGAL SYSTEM OF THE PEOPLE'S REPUBLIC OF CHINA

IN A NUTSHELL

SECOND EDITION

By

DANIEL C.K. CHOW

Joseph S. Platt-Porter Wright Morris & Arthur
Professor of Law

The Ohio State University
Michael E. Moritz College of Law

WEST®

A Thomson Reuters business

Mat #40766983

Nutshell Series, In a Nutshell, and the Nutshell Logo are trademarks registered in the U.S. Patent and Trademark Office.

© West, a Thomson business, 2003
© 2009 Thomson Reuters

    610 Opperman Drive
    St. Paul, MN 55123
    1–800–313–9378

Printed in the United States of America

ISBN: 978–0–314–19882–2

TEXT IS PRINTED ON 10% POST
CONSUMER RECYCLED PAPER

To my wife Ching and our son Alan

*

PREFACE TO
THE SECOND EDITION

I am grateful that this book has warmly received and widely adopted for use in law schools and other academic departments in the United States and abroad. This second edition has been thoroughly updated and revised. I have been fortunate to receive the support and guidance of Dean Alan Michaels and Associate Deans Josh Stulberg and Donald Tobin of the Ohio State University College of Law in this project.

This edition greatly benefited from the able research assistance and critical commentary of Xing Na, a doctoral candidate in International Law at the Wuhan University School of Law in Wuhan, Hubei, China and a visiting scholar at Ohio State during the 2007-2008 academic year. I am also indebted to Melanie Oberlin, Research Librarian at the Ohio University College of Law, and Chao You (Phoebe), an LLM student at the Ohio State University College of Law.

I owe the greatest debt in this and all other endeavors in my life to my wife Ching. This book is dedicated to her and to our son Alan.

DANIEL C.K. CHOW

April 2009
Columbus, Ohio

*

V

PREFACE TO
THE FIRST EDITION

This book is based upon several years that I lived in the People's Republic of China in the late 1990s when I took a leave of absence from my academic duties at the Ohio State University College of Law to serve as in-house counsel for a multinational enterprise with substantial China operations and ambitious plans for expanding its China business. I lived and worked in the busy southeastern port city of Guangzhou, one of the first areas open to foreign direct investment, and a vanguard for bold change and progress.

As a busy lawyer in an understaffed legal department, I had many different responsibilities and opportunities to meet with high-level officials of China's many different governmental organs. I also had regular contact with judges, prosecutors, security officials, party cadres, foreign and local lawyers, and academics. In addition to my contacts with China's mainstream legal system, I also had many opportunities to learn about China's illegal underground economy with its many dangerous and nefarious characters. My work in protecting the company's intellectual property led me on investigations and raids of underground factories, markets, and warehouses dealing in pirated, counterfeit, and smuggled products. Working with professional private investigation agencies and through the use of various subterfuges and assumed identities, I was also able to have direct contacts with suspected counterfeiters, pirates, and other criminal elements in China's illegal economy. These stark experiences gave me a sense of the many enforcement challenges that lie ahead for China's earnest law reformers who seek to enact effective laws protecting the interests of legitimate business and property owners. My contacts with both the mainstream legal system and the underground economy gave me a realistic sense of China's progress and the serious issues and problems that remain.

Outside of work, I benefited from many opportunities to learn about the life of China's people and to interact with many associates, colleagues, and friends in social settings. Some of these opportunities led to lasting friendships that I renew on the regular occasions that I travel to China for professional or personal reasons. During my years in China, I had many frank discussions with Chinese from all walks of life about China's problems and prospects and the complex relations between the United States and China. Not all of these discussions were amicable nor were all of my relationships harmonious, but I learned and benefited from them all. I absorbed a sense of the conflicting attitudes of admiration, respect, distrust, and resentment that are simultaneously held by many contemporary Chinese toward the United States. When my China assignment was over, I returned to the United States and my academic career with a sense of China's many challenges and issues that lie ahead as well as a sense of the nation's hopes for the future. These invaluable experiences have enriched and deepened my understanding of China and of the role of law in modern China. These experiences form the basis for this volume.

DANIEL C.K. CHOW

October 2002
Columbus, Ohio

*

Map of the People's Republic of China and Taiwan

*

OUTLINE

XIII

THE LEGAL SYSTEM OF THE PEOPLE'S REPUBLIC OF CHINA
IN A NUTSHELL

SECOND EDITION

*

CHAPTER ONE

INTRODUCTION

This book is written for an audience of lawyers, academics, students, and others who seek an overview of the legal system of the People's Republic of China (PRC or China) but who may come to this study without specialized knowledge about China. This book will examine China's legal system in the broader context of the historical traditions that have shaped modern China and the social and political institutions and economic policies that are propelling the nation forward in the new millennium.

A. UNDERSTANDING MODERN CHINA IN ITS HISTORICAL CONTEXT

The remainder of this chapter is devoted to an examination of modern China in the context of the vast changes and political upheavals that have occurred in that nation during the course of the twentieth century. As the discussion below sets forth, the sporadic development and retrenchment of China's legal system in its recent history mirrors China's larger fortunes. During the many periods of chaos during China's recent history, China's legal system and the rule of law all but ceased to exist altogether, if they ever took hold. As soon as a government was able to establish its position with

1

relative stability, attempts were made to establish or to resuscitate a legal system in China. This same pattern was followed by the vastly different regimes that assumed power during this period, including the Qing (pronounced "Ching") government, the last imperial dynasty, the Nationalist government (*Guomingdang*) that briefly established a republican form of government from 1912–1949, and the current government under the control of the Communist Party of China (CPC or Party) since 1949. It is no coincidence that the inception of the current legal system dates back only several decades to the 1970s and corresponds with the beginning of China's modern economic expansion and reform after the political terror of the Cultural Revolution. Understanding the relationship between political stability and law in China, across different regimes, helps to illuminate the role of law in Chinese society today. China's current level of political stability and economic development is the result of a long journey from some of the nation's bleakest days to the present period of optimism. This journey is the subject of the next sections of this chapter.

IMPORTANT PERIODS IN MODERN CHINA

Imperial China

Ming Dynasty	1368–1644
Qing Dynasty	1644–1912

Republic of China

1912–1949

People's Republic of China

1949–present

1. THE UNDERPINNINGS OF MODERN CHINA AND ITS LEGAL SYSTEM

At the beginning of the twenty-first century, China stands as a nation on the rise. China is now firmly within the control of its own people, its sovereignty free from the domination by external forces that marked its history in the nineteenth and the first half of the twentieth century. The nation enjoys a stability and relative prosperity unknown in its modern history and scarcely imaginable during the many dark and chaotic years of the twentieth century. Two recent events are symbolic of China's new prominence on the world stage. In August 2008, China played host to the Summer Olympics amid unprecedented anticipation and controversy. Although China did not satisfy the many critics of its human rights record, China astonished the world with a lavish spectacle made possible by seemingly unlimited resources and a sea of people that appeared cheerful, loyal, and deeply patriotic. For China, the Olympics announced its arrival on the world stage as a leading nation, vindicated the legitimacy of its ruling government, and rebuffed its critics of its record on human rights. On November 11, 2001, China was granted full membership into the World Trade Organization (WTO) by the Fourth

Ministerial Conference by consensus. China is now a member of the world's most important commercial law regime and has the opportunity to become a leader in shaping the law of international commerce for the future. These two watershed events mark the world community's acknowledgement of China's arrival as an important nation in the mainstream world community less than two decades from the events of Tiananmen Square that led many countries to label China as a renegade nation. WTO accession also marks China's commitment to and respect for the rule of law. It foreshadows a more important role for law in China for the future.

The contrast between China's status in the world today and its position just one hundred years ago at the beginning of the twentieth century could scarcely be more stark. Racked by internal decay and the external pressures of foreign domination, China was a nation in decline. The moribund Qing dynasty, the last in a long line of imperial governments dating back over 2,000 years, was paralyzed by greed, ignorance, and incompetence. Content with China's innate superiority, the senescent Qing emperor in the late eighteenth century had steadfastly refused to lift restrictions on foreign trade, secure in the view that a superior China had no need to engage with foreign nations. Confined by restricted trading rights with China, England sought to expand its trade with China, especially the lucrative but poisonous trade in imported opium from India. When China resisted and destroyed opium stocks in the southern port city of Guangzhou in a move reminiscent of the bold dumping of tea into Boston harbor by American settlers in 1773, British gunboats set sail from England on a mission to inflict punishment on China during the Opium War of 1839–42. The antiquated and ill-equipped armies of the Qing were no match for the superior technology of the British gunboats. After a series of humiliating defeats, China capitulated in the unequal Treaty of Nanjing in 1842. A second war with the French and British resulted in a new set of unequal treaties at Tianjin in 1858, and a punitive Anglo–French expedition in 1860 resulted in the occupation of Beijing to secure the final acceptance by China of the unequal treaty system that lasted for more than a century from 1842 to 1949.

The treaty system was imposed by foreign nations to force greater access to China's markets. Although the treaties were signed as between equal sovereign powers, they were quite unequal and forced China into a weaker position against its will. The treaties all exhibited some common traits. In addition to requiring an indemnity to be paid by China, the treaties granted numerous special privileges to foreigners who were to be treated better than native Chinese, and imposed the principle of extraterritoriality exempting all foreigners in the treaty ports from Chinese law and allowing them to enjoy foreign consular jurisdiction under their own nationality. Extraterritoriality was justified on the ground that China's laws and legal system were barbaric and lacked a developed commercial law regime. In all there were more than eighty treaty ports, consisting of most of China's prominent cities, which became subject to foreign domination and control. To ensure that tariffs under the treaty system were properly collected and not dissipated because of corruption in the Chinese system, foreign treaty powers established the Imperial Maritime Customs Service in 1854. When the Englishman Robert Hart assumed his post as China's Commissioner General of Customs, China considered the appointment of a foreigner to supervise the collection of its own duties to be a symbol of its weakness in the face of foreign power.

Additional military disaster took the form of the Sino–Japanese war of 1894–95. Under the pretext of intervening in Korea to quell rebels, Japan's modern navy crushed the antiquated Chinese fleet. Forced to pay a huge indemnity as the price of defeat, China funded the indemnity payments by going into debt with European bondholders. The increasing debt to Europe and Japan expanded their spheres of influence in China. By end of the nineteenth century, Britain, France, Germany, Russia, and Japan all held control over a major naval port and over railways leading to mines in China's interior. The growing foreign influence led to a local backlash in the form of the Boxer Uprising of 1898–1901, which incited punitive measures by foreign nations that only compounded China's misery. One of the best known events of the nineteenth century because a large number of foreign diplomats, journalists, and their families were besieged in the legation quarters in Beijing, the Boxer Rebellion was a peasant-based uprising based upon principles of spirituality and martial arts and fueled by a fanatical hatred of foreigners. The Boxers killed at least 250 foreigners before the Rebellion was crushed by an alliance of eight national armies. To punish China, the alliance of foreign nations imposed the draconian Boxer Protocol of 1901 on the Qing government. The Protocol required the destruction of some twenty-five Qing forts and the imposition of a crippling $333 million indemnity. The Boxer Protocol further weakened China just as foreign nations seemed prepared to launch an all-out race for imperialist conquest of China. Like a ripe melon, China was about to be carved up by foreign nations eager to stake their claims. By the beginning of the twentieth century, the future of China as an independent sovereign nation was in peril. Whether China would survive or perish was unclear.

For the Chinese, these initial encounters with foreign nations and international trade and commerce in the nineteenth and twentieth centuries proved costly. In terms of lives lost there were a number of internal peasant-based rebellions that were far more damaging. Millions were killed in the Taiping, Nian, Muslim, and smaller rebellions that racked the nation in the mid-nineteenth century. Compared with these domestic rebellions, the foreign incursions inflicted minor damage on the nation. But while the internal rebellions cost many more lives, the damage inflicted to the spirit of the nation was superficial by comparison. By contrast, foreign intrusions were a source of great humiliation and demoralization for China. In the Ming and early Qing dynasties, China was at or near the peak of its glory with remarkable achievements in culture and the arts and a civilization that was the equal or superior of any other on Earth. The military defeats suffered by China at the hands of superior foreign military forces once and for all debunked the myth of Chinese superiority and began the legend of foreign superiority, vestiges of which are still present in China today. Foreign control of China's treaty ports, exemption of foreigners from Chinese law, and the installment of foreigners as officials to run China's own maritime government further added to the sense of the breach of the nation's sovereignty. The imposition of the insidious and debilitating opium trade by England on China against its will increased the nation's sense of desperation and helplessness. As an indication of the nation's loss of self-confidence and increasing demoralization, by 1900 China was a nation of 470 million people of which some 40 million were consumers of opium and of which 15 million were addicts.

For those who encounter China today, it is important to realize that the results of these foreign incursions into China that seem so distant are still felt today. The preamble to the 1982 PRC Constitution begins with a reminder that "[a]fter 1840, [] China was gradually turned into ... a semi-colonial country" and that "the Chinese people waged many successive heroic struggles for national indepen-

dence and liberation." *See* PRC Const., Prmbl. at
¶ 2. Moreover, the symbols of Chinese weakness in
the face of foreign aggression are not all to be found
in the distant past. For many Chinese, Hong Kong
stood as an enduring symbol of western imperialism
until just a decade ago. An island off China's southern coast, Hong Kong was first ceded to the British
as a spoil of war at the end of the first Opium War
in 1842 and ruled as a British colony on China's
front step for over 150 years until its return to
Chinese sovereignty in 1997. Many Chinese today
use the term "Treaty of Nanjing" to refer to any
unequal agreement or relationship between China
and a foreign nation or between Chinese and foreigners. Many in China believe that Taiwan, regarded as a renegade province since the end of the
Chinese civil war in 1949, would have long returned
to Chinese sovereignty without the prospect of a
United States intervention if China were to use
military force against Taiwan. In Beijing today,
school children visit the massive ruins of the Summer Palace, sacked by Anglo–French forces as a
punitive measure during the second Opium War
over a century ago in 1860, and are told that the
ruins are preserved to stand as a reminder and a
warning of the results of China's weakness in the
face of foreign power.

2. CHINA'S TWENTIETH CENTURY JOURNEY TO MODERNITY

As the Qing government proved incapable of dealing with foreign intrusion from without and moral

decay from within, revolutionary forces led by Dr. Sun Yatsen and his Nationalist Party began to plot its overthrow and the installation of a republican form of government. When the end for the Qing dynasty finally came, it was less of an overthrow than a weary implosion. In 1911, an uprising in Wuhan, a city located in central China, led to a defection of most of China's provinces, which declared their independence from the Qing government. In 1912, the Qing emperor abdicated and the reformers set up a provisional republican government in Nanjing ending over 2,000 years of imperial rule. Efforts to establish a parliamentary system for the fledgling republic failed when Yuan Shikai, the new president, assumed dictatorial powers and attempted to have himself declared emperor but died without success in 1916. Thereafter, China descended into the era of warlordism as various successive governments of the northern warlords, local strongmen with their own private armies, competed for power. Both the newly formed Communist Party and the Nationalist Party, led first by Dr. Sun and then his successor, the military politician Chiang Kai-shek, cooperated and competed to defeat warlordism and to limit foreign imperialism in the 1920s.

The decisive event that consolidated the power of the Nationalist Party was the Northern Expedition in 1927, a military campaign led by Chiang that defeated or absorbed warlord forces into the Nationalist government. Turning against the Communists who had collaborated with him, Chiang began a campaign in 1927 to hunt down and exterminate all Communist supporters and sympathizers. Many historians believed that Chiang would have succeeded if Japan's aggressions in China did not force the two rival groups to assume a second united front in their war of resistance against Japan. In 1931, Japan seized the northern region of Manchuria and began an all-out invasion to conquer China in 1937. In his war efforts against Japan, Chiang enjoyed the strong military and financial support of the United States. His wife, the Wellesley-educated Song Meiling, captivated American audiences and both houses of Congress during her triumphant tour of the United States in 1943. With her fluent English and oriental charm, Madame Chiang helped to secure millions of dollars in unrestricted aid and equipment from the United States. One indication of the close ties forged between the United States and China is that at one point, the American General Joseph Stillwell was allowed by Chiang Kai-shek to assume command of all Chinese forces within China in order to direct the war against Japan. Stillwell was one of the few observers at the time to understand that Chiang had no real intention of fighting the Japanese. Chiang believed that Japan would eventually be defeated by the Allies during World War II without his help. Chiang's strategy was to engage in a stalemate with the Japanese, to hoard weapons, equipment, ammunition, and to save his best fighting forces for the inevitable conflict with the Communists that would occur after Japan was defeated.

The war with Japan from 1937–45 was a cruel and destructive all-out fight in which no mercy on the battlefield was asked for or received. International rules of engagement in modern warfare were ignored as blood lust resulted in some of the worst and most sadistic atrocities in modern warfare being inflicted by the Japanese army on China's civilian population, adding immeasurably to China's desperation and the misery of its people. But though China suffered horrendous initial setbacks, the Chinese were able to endure in a drawn out war of attrition against the Japanese. The stakes were the survival of the Chinese nation for China would have ceased to exist and the Chinese people would have been enslaved if Japan had achieved victory. By some accounts, China lost some 25 million lives in the conflict with Japan.

With Japan's defeat in China at the end of the Second World War, Chiang's Nationalist government and the Communist Party, now under the leadership of Mao Zedong, ended all pretense of cooperation and all-out conflict was soon to break out. Although the United States sent Secretary of State George Marshall to help broker a peaceful solution to the rivalry, there was never a realistic possibility of reconciliation. Implacable enemies to the end, both Chiang and Mao would be satisfied only with the complete destruction of the other. The rivals soon plunged the war weary nation once again into bloody conflict. Although the Nationalists had armed forces twice the size of the Communists at the beginning of the conflict and the advantage of American equipment and backing, the Nationalists managed to lose the civil war due to incompetence in the battlefield and corruption in command and governance. By 1949, Mao had vanquished Chiang and the Nationalists to the island province of Taiwan where Chiang set up a government in exile and where the Nationalists continue to exert power today. With all of his enemies vanquished or dead, Mao formally declared the founding of the People's Republic of China on October 1, 1949.

The loss of China to Communism triggered a wave of bitter recriminations in the United States. The end of World War II led to the beginning of the era of the Cold War and the fear of Communism would soon reach its peak in the 1950s. The United States had great hopes that the Nationalists would lead China to democracy and that a strong republican China would counterbalance the growing menace of the neighboring Soviet Union and its eastern sphere of influence. United States' hopes were crushed when the Nationalists were routed and had to flee to Taiwan where they continued to enjoy the support of the United States. These events help to explain the United States' longtime support for Taiwan, where the Nationalists eventually allowed a real democracy to grow and flourish. The United States also continued to recognize the Nationalists as the legitimate rulers of China until President Jimmy Carter switched formal diplomatic recognition to China in 1978. But while the United States no longer maintains formal diplomatic relations with Taiwan, the United States still continues to support Taiwan with arms and with the prospect of military support in the case of an unprovoked attack by China. The role of the United States as Taiwan's protector and savior continues to rankle China's leaders who regard the Taiwan issue to be an internal affair and subject to no interference from external sources. These events also explain why Taiwan continues to be the single largest issue of contention in the relationship between the United States and China.

IMPORTANT EVENTS IN
THE PRC, 1949–1978

Founding of the PRC	October 1949
Anti–Rightist Campaign	1957–1958
Great Leap Forward	1958–1960
Cultural Revolution	1966–1976
Death of Mao Zedong	September 1976
Deng Xiaoping wins power	late 1978
Economic Reforms	1978–present
Revival of the Legal System	1978–present

3. THE PEOPLE'S REPUBLIC OF CHINA

The years immediately after its establishment were ones of euphoria for the new nation. For the first time in over a century, mainland China was free from foreign intrusion and its sovereignty firmly in Chinese hands. The nation was finally at peace after more than a century of intermittent and disastrous military defeats. All of its enemies, internal and external, were destroyed or vanquished. China's people had endured prolonged periods of immense suffering and misery, all of which appeared to be at an end as the nation seemed to have entered a new era of tranquility and optimism.

Any hope for a prolonged end to conflict and turmoil was soon dashed when Mao launched the Anti–Rightist Campaign in 1957–58, which marked the beginning of what some have described as a twenty-year lost period for China in which all progress was stalled in the face of social and political chaos that ended with Mao's death in 1976. The Anti–Rightist Campaign was a rectification movement directed against some party members and intellectuals who expressed their criticism of the Communist Party regime during the Hundred Flowers Campaign of 1956–57—so named for the phrase, "Let a hundred flowers bloom together, let the hundred schools of thought contend." Mao had encouraged intellectuals to voice their criticism of the Party but he did not think that they would subject the Party to severe attack. The Anti–Rightist Campaign was a backlash and a vehicle for purification and political revenge. So began a pattern of using ideology campaigns to serve important Party purposes, a practice that continues in China to the present, as discussed further below.

One of Mao's earliest economic reforms, the Great Leap Forward (GLF), led directly to a famine that killed some 20 to 30 million people from 1958–1960. The GLF was a misguided and aborted attempt to leapfrog China into the modern age. In 1958, the nation began a mighty effort to build new roads, factories, dikes, dams, and lakes. One of the most quixotic feats of the GLF was the campaign begun in July 1958 to produce steel in backyard furnaces. By some accounts, by October 1958 some 1 million backyard furnaces were set up and 100 million people were busy melting their farming and household implements to make steel that proved largely unusable. The GLF demonstrated the capacity of the Chinese people to unite in a national effort of great magnitude and intensity as never before even if the results were ultimately devastating and catastrophic. The national mood of fervent self-sacrifice and devotion to the nation infused many cadres with the desire to continually break production records and led to the totally unrealistic and false reporting of agricultural production figures. The reports of miraculous increases in productivity led to increases in requisitions of crops from Beijing. At the same time, diversion of water for public works and poor weather led to decreases in crop production. The combination of increased requisitions at a time when productivity was going down led to a man-made disaster of mass starvation in China's villages. Several years of more rational economic policies in the 1960s were necessary to bring China back to pre-GLF production levels.

From 1966 until his death in 1976, Mao plunged China into the maelstrom of political terror and mindless destruction of the Cultural Revolution. It directly involved 100 million people, its victims number about 1 million, and it cost more than 400,000 lives. Many more people were physically crippled, suffered permanent psychological scars, and a great number committed suicide. The Cultural Revolution has led to an entire generation of persons now in their fifties who lack a basic education because schools were closed down during this period. Combined with the depredations caused by the Anti–Rightist Campaign and the Great Leap Forward, China staggered through a wasted twenty-year period in which the nation made no progress in economic, cultural, or spiritual development, but instead suffered needless setbacks and destruction in all of these vital areas.

Although the origins and purposes of the Cultural Revolution are still being debated, many observers believe that one of the purposes served by this movement was to consolidate Mao's power and to destroy his enemies. In one of the best known features of the movement, Mao mobilized millions of China's teenage student youth, the Red Guards, who inflicted cruel destruction on their victims by breaking into homes of intellectuals and Party officials, destroying books and manuscripts, beating, humiliating, and even killing its occupants all in the name of supporting the revolution. Encouraged by Beijing, Red Guards from all over China seized power by expelling officials from their offices, examining and destroying their files, and taking their place even though they lacked any administrative experience or knowledge. Universities were closed or regular classes suspended to study Mao Zedong thought. Professors were sent to farms to learn from the peasants.

Although the Cultural Revolution spun out of control, Mao Zedong did not appear to be disturbed by the many lives that were needlessly lost or ruined. To the contrary, he believed that killings were an important part of the continuing revolution. In a passage that Mao considered among his most important writings, he evoked stark images of violent death as a necessary part of the work of the revolution:

> [A] revolution is not a dinner party, or writing an essay, or painting a picture, or doing embroidery. It cannot be so refined, so gentle, so leisurely, so temperate, kind, courteous, restrained, and generous. A revolution is an insurrection, an act of violence by which one class overthrows another.... In a very short time ... several hundred million peasants will rise up like a mighty storm ... and will send the evil gentry to their graves.

Mao's death in 1976 marked the end of the Cultural Revolution. By 1978, Deng Xiaoping had emerged from political infighting as China's new leader. Deng soon launched a series of economic reforms that has propelled the nation on its present path towards modernization.

4.   LESSONS FROM THE CULTURAL REVOLUTION AND TIANANMEN SQUARE

Although much about the Cultural Revolution is still unknown, several aspects are now clear and provide some important lessons about China. The Cultural Revolution was ultimately not a movement in the pursuit of revolutionary ideals as much as it was a state-instigated campaign of persecution and violence. Underlying the movement was the fear by China's leaders of conspiracy by hidden enemies and traitors engaged in a secret plot to usurp their power and to subvert the state. This fear of conspiracy by China's rulers is not unique to the CPC. Conspiracy and palace intrigue was a hallmark of Imperial China. It can be said that Sun Yatsen was engaged in a conspiracy much of his life to overthrow the Qing dynasty. It can also be said that both the Nationalists and the Communists were secretly plotting for the inevitable final conflict with each other even as they maintained the appearance of cooperation during the war of resistance against Japan.

Part of the explanation for false appearances masking clandestine plots is that China has never been an open society where dissent was tolerated by a government in power. China has traditionally viewed all dissent and opposition as disloyal. Some of these attitudes are deeply embedded in Chinese culture by Confucianist values, which preached obedience to authority and the maintenance of social harmony as a cardinal duty of the populace. All those who failed to show obedience, such as through the voicing of criticism or opposition, risked being accused of offending a basic civic duty and being branded as a traitor. As a result, all dissenters had to maintain the appearance of loyalty and to work clandestinely or risk destruction. Deceit became a method of survival for dissenters and China's rulers, sensing artifice and deceit everywhere, adopted a habit of suspicion and distrust.

In this light, the pro-democracy demonstrators at Tiananmen Square in 1989 must have struck China's leaders as bold traitors and enemies of the state. They not only ridiculed the Communist Party but also brazenly called for democracy, which, in the view of Party elders, could only mean the overthrow of the Party and the state. This traitorous insult may have motivated Party elders to shock the world by ordering units of the People's Liberation Army to kill thousands of mostly unarmed civilians during the early hours of June 4, 1989 in Tiananmen Square. On June 6, the CPC launched a nationwide manhunt for other hidden enemies, arrested at least 20,000 people, and executed dozens during the month of June alone. The state had discovered a hidden conspiracy and had to root out and destroy its enemies. These attitudes may also help to explain China's reactions to the U.S. bombing of the Chinese Embassy in Belgrade in 1999.

When the United States claimed that the bombing was the result of a tragic error, China's leaders refused to believe the explanation. The bulk of China's general populace also sincerely believed that the United States intentionally sought to bomb the Embassy and then concocted the subterfuge of mistake. The habit of looking for conspiracy and deceit is deeply ingrained in China.

5.   CHINA'S ECONOMY, 1949–78

To understand the revival of China's modern legal system and its current importance in the PRC, it is necessary to examine China's economy and the reforms begun after the end of the Cultural Revolution. The legal system had been abolished during the Cultural Revolution and its resuscitation can be traced in part to its role in supporting Deng Xiaoping's new economic program. The remaining sections of this chapter will review China's economy since the establishment of the PRC in 1949.

Although never subject to the type of overwhelming central control exercised by such countries as the Soviet Union, the economy of the PRC for most of the period since its founding until economic reforms begun in 1978 was a command economy. Under this system, the state owned all property and all enterprises were essentially administrative units of the state. The state received all revenues from industrial and agricultural enterprises, redistributed revenues in accordance with state goals, and subsidized or absorbed all losses. Production targets for all enterprises were set in accordance with a five-year economic plan promulgated by the State Council, the executive arm of the PRC government. The plans set forth production quotas for commodities, set prices for products, and allocated products for distribution. Although economic reforms have relaxed state control over the economy and China no longer sets production quotas for as many sectors of the economy, China still continues to use state sponsored economic plans. China is now in the midst of its Eleventh Five–Year Plan covering 2006–2010.

a. The Collectivization of Agriculture

Early in its history, from 1953–54, the PRC implemented a system of collectivization of agriculture in which private ownership of farmland and crops was abolished. The state confiscated lands owned by landlords, many of who were killed in the process, and redistributed the lands to large collectives of workers who farmed the land communally. By the 1960s, the collectives were reorganized into massive communes with responsibility for meeting government quotas set forth in the state sponsored five-year economic plans.

All crops grown and harvested by agricultural communes were sold to the state at government fixed prices. Government units then distributed revenues to the individual workers of the communes in accordance with a set of guidelines that awarded workers a number of work points for their daily work. In many cases, workers would accumulate the same number of work points whether they worked industriously or not, creating little incentive for effective performance. Many of these communes were massive in size. For example, on the eve of reforms in 1978 that would dismantle the collective system of agriculture, Guangdong province's 9.2 million farm families were organized into approximately 2,000 communes, each containing 46,000 farm families.

b.   Industry and the State Enterprise System

In the industrial sector, the foundation of China's pre-reform economy was the state-owned enterprise system. A state-owned enterprise (SOE) is owned by the state as opposed to any private entity, individual, or group of individuals. An SOE was expected to meet state production targets, to turn over all of its revenues to the state, and to have all of its losses subsidized or absorbed by the state. The state also controlled all of the enterprise's business and management functions including matters that fell within the business scope of the firm. While many governments, including the United States, regulate enterprise matters that affect the public interest, pre-reform China went far beyond this limited scope of government regulation and exerted control over all matters of the firm, including business strategies, marketing, distribution, and sales. Because the state also owned the enterprise, the state served both as regulator and entrepreneur in many cases.

SOEs were subject to the control and supervision of government departments at all levels. For example, a local chemicals factory would report to the local bureau of light industry, which would have supervisory authority over all enterprises engaged in the light industry sectors. Because of a massive and complex bureaucracy, however, complicated lines of authority resulted in a number of government bureaus exerting some control over the enterprise. For example, the planning departments at all levels of government determined how much capital investment was required for enterprises. The economic and trade committees determined the use of technology by enterprises in their operations. Labor and financial departments determined wages of employees. No single government bureau was completely responsible for all facets of the operations of the enterprise, but rather many entities had uncoordinated input into the management of the enterprise. This chaotic supervisory structure resulted in enterprises that were inefficiently managed and performed poorly. For most of the history of the PRC, SOEs have operated with chronic losses even during the period since economic reforms began in 1978 and even though the overall economy of the PRC has grown consistently during this same period.

Throughout most of the period since 1949, the state sector has played a major role in the PRC industrial economy. Prior to economic reform, the percentage of China's industrial output from SOEs stood at 83%. Since reforms in 1978, the state sector has experienced a diminishing role. By 1994, SOEs accounted for 38% of industrial output. Although the state sector rebounded to account for

48.3% of industrial output in 2000, its share of the total output of the economy has continued to shrink. By 2004, SOEs accounted for only about 15.3%. Despite the diminishing output of the state sector, SOEs continue to play a critical role in China's economy. All vital sectors of the economy, such as banking, telecommunications, steel production, oil and gas exploration and refining, electricity and water supply, and train and air transport continue to be controlled by SOEs. An ongoing challenge for China's rulers is that SOEs, while vital to the economy, continue to suffer chronic losses despite many attempts at reform. The continuing reform of the state sector remains one of China's most significant challenges in the years ahead.

c. Social Welfare Functions of SOEs

A primary reason for the inefficiency of SOEs is their social welfare role. Prior to reform, workers in SOEs found their professional, personal, and family lives to be inseparable and that all revolved around the work unit. Social services that are provided by the private sector or government social welfare agencies in the United States were all provided by the work unit in pre-reform China. SOEs not only provided employment, but also housing, schooling, medical care, and pension benefits. In a typical case, an SOE worker would live in a dormitory or housing provided by the SOE, work in the adjacent SOE factory or plant, send his children to the nearby school operated by the SOE, shop at the nearby markets owned by the SOE, visit the doctor at the nearby SOE hospital, watch movies at a theater operated by the SOE, and receive pension benefits supplied by the SOE upon retirement. Workers' personal lives became inseparable from their professional lives. For example, a worker was expected to seek permission from supervisors for marriage and other personal decisions. Seeking permission from the work unit supervisors was required because marriage meant that the new spouse and any children would create additional demands for employment, housing, and other services. The SOE work unit came to be viewed as a social net that provided its employees with a basic level of guaranteed social services. Typically, an SOE would not discharge workers for unsatisfactory work, and all workers received a common salary regardless of performance.

The role of the SOE as a provider of social welfare services meant that there was constant pressure to absorb more workers and their families. Some SOEs are the size of the world's largest multinational enterprises. For example, the Capital Iron and Steel Corporation in western Beijing at one time employed approximately 150,000 workers, more than most of the largest private companies in the world. Some SOEs have compounds that resemble small towns. The Wuhan Iron & Steel Corporation was considered to be a "company run society" and was known as "Red Steel Town." As many as one-third or more of SOE workers were redundant.

Given the social welfare role of SOEs, the main goals of such enterprises were not profits, efficiency, and productivity. When an enterprise lost money or faced bankruptcy, the state would intervene and grant it another subsidy or exemption because failure of the SOE would result in significant social costs. While this system served important social welfare goals, the inefficient and poorly managed state sector resulted in the bulk of China's economy operating at a loss, a situation that needed to be remedied if China was to step into the modern industrial age.

6.   CHINA'S REFORMS, 1978

With Mao's death marking the end of the Cultural Revolution in 1976, the CPC turned its attention to rebuilding the nation's long neglected economy. Party elders were shocked and embarrassed by China's backwardness and poverty by comparison to some of its neighbors such as Hong Kong and Japan. In 1978, the CPC, under the leadership of Deng Xiaoping, announced that the focus of its work would shift from class struggle to economic development.

To implement this shift, the CPC endorsed the development of some free markets and a limited role for private enterprise within an overall framework of socialism, creating a mixed economic system. This shift represented a relaxation of the command economy approach of the PRC that had been in place for most of the period since 1949. Under China's reforms, the private sector is viewed as an adjunct or complement to the state sector, which remains prominent, despite its many problems.

Some free markets and some private ownership of wealth will be developed, but the vital areas of the economy will continue to be state-owned and controlled. Consistent with Marxist–Leninist principles, the state will continue to own all real property and the means of production.

China's policy is to create a socialist market economy as distinguished from a market economy based upon liberal capitalism, such as that of the United States, which contemplates private ownership of property and the means of production. As long as China's political commitment to socialism remains firm, there will be limits on the private ownership of wealth and the state sector will continue to be a vital portion of the economy. For example, complete privatization of most state-owned enterprises will not be an option under the present approach. The state continues to own SOEs—in principle at least. In the view of China's rulers, the nation is undergoing economic, not political, reform.

a. Reforms in the Agricultural Sector

The 1978 reforms met with immediate and dramatic success in the agricultural sector. While the collectivization of agriculture was trumpeted with great fanfare, the dismantling of the system was done quietly and unobtrusively. In addition to disbanding the communes, the reforms instituted a basic shift in responsibility within the production system. Under the new system, responsibility for meeting production quotas was shifted from the massive commune organizations down to the family household unit. Once households met the assigned government quotas, they were free to sell any excess product at market prices and to keep the proceeds. In another major shift, fixed government quotas were gradually replaced by contracts between the state and local collectives, composed of individual households. The collectives in turn contracted with household units. These seemingly minor changes created a basic change in incentives. Farming households now had incentive to maximize production because they were allowed to keep revenues above certain levels. Under the old system of assigning work points, hard work or indolence was rewarded in the same way. The new household responsibility system was immediately popular with farming households and agricultural production soared in the years after the reforms.

b. Reforms in the State Sector

By contrast with reforms in the agricultural sector, effective reform of the state sector has been difficult to achieve and continues to be one of China's most significant challenges. Reforms have reflected two policy goals. First, China enacted legislation early in the reform era that granted SOEs independent legal status and the right to make their own managerial decisions. Subsequent legislation provided greater details about the types of decision-making authority that state-owned enterprises would enjoy, including greater independence to import and export, make investment and production decisions, hire and manage workers, and set prices and wages. This shift represented an attempt to protect SOEs from government intrusion into their business operations that would hamper their efficient operation.

Second, these reforms also attempted to wean SOEs from dependence upon state subsidies. For example, one fundamental change of the reform movement is that government funds are no longer given as free capital grants or investment subsidies, but are now treated as low-interest bank loans. SOEs are required to pay charges on their fixed assets and working capital. Equally important, SOEs are no longer eligible in principle to be rescued by state subsidies in the event of losses. In theory, SOEs are now in principle fully responsible for their own profits and losses. To create further incentives for enterprises to improve their economic performance, the reformers also enacted the Enterprise Bankruptcy Law (1986, revised 2006), requiring chronically mismanaged and inefficient enterprises to be closed down.

One of the obstacles faced by reformers in the state sector is coping with the broader social and political consequences of reform. As previously discussed, state-owned enterprises create a system of integrated social welfare institutions. Any reform of the enterprise system will affect the delivery of essential social services to industrial workers. Under this system, China cannot simply announce that SOEs will now be governed by principles of profit and loss and that unprofitable enterprises will be closed under the Bankruptcy Law. Closing an unprofitable enterprise will not only result in the loss of employment for workers, many of who will be unable to find new jobs, but will also result in a family catastrophe. The family loses housing, medical care, and schooling upon separation from the SOE. The costs of unemployment can be so severe that desperate workers use threats, demonstrations, and even violence against managers to avoid losing their jobs. Effective reform of the state sector involves creating alternative means for providing social services for the employable industrial worker as well as benefits for the unemployable and redundant workers for whom the state-owned enterprise has traditionally served as a caretaker. These are fundamental long-term reforms.

Some of China's reforms in the state sector have been bold. One reform involves restructuring state enterprises using international capitalist models of the corporate form. Recent legislation now allows for the "corporatization" of state-owned enterprises, which involves the reorganization of the SOE as a stock corporation, with the stock of some companies trading on public stock exchanges. The state maintains a controlling interest by owning a majority of the shares once the enterprise has been reorganized into a stock corporation. Other reforms include reorganizing and merging state-owned enterprises into mega-enterprise conglomerates. Not long ago, the very notion of state enterprises as corporations with stock openly traded on public stock exchanges and available for private ownership would have been regarded by China's leaders as repugnant to socialism. These new directions indicate China's willingness to experiment and its receptivity to western corporate and business law concepts.

Other sweeping changes are underway. In recent years China has been able to create a substantial private housing market and has now largely removed cost-free housing as a benefit of the SOE. The booming construction of high-rise apartment buildings in the teeming cities of Shanghai and Guangzhou serve as a testament to the new private housing industry. Efforts are under way to establish an independent social welfare system in order to decrease the social welfare role of SOEs so that they can be further subjected to the pressures of the competitive marketplace. Re-employment centers have been established to help retrain and find new jobs for workers who have been terminated from SOEs undergoing reform. Basic pension programs and general health care programs are all in the process of being established outside of the SOE system.

Despite more than three decades of reforms, however, effective changes have been difficult to achieve because of the complex and interrelated issues involved in reforming this fundamental sector of the economy, which continues to operate with chronic losses. New and even greater challenges may await this sector with China's entry into the WTO, as China will need to open protected areas of industry to international competition.

7.   CHINA'S ECONOMY SINCE 1978

Since economic reforms began in 1978, China has achieved unprecedented economic growth for an economy of its size. From 1978–97, China experienced an average annual GDP growth rate of 9.8%. Despite the economic retrenchment in Asia in 1999, China reported an average annual growth rate of 7.5% for 1999–2001 and a 7.6% growth rate in 2002. In 2007, China had the fourth largest economy in the world measured by GDP with $3.01 trillion and was behind only the United States, Japan, and Germany. China's growing economic power stands as a remarkable achievement for a nation that was mired in poverty and backwardness and caught in upheaval and turmoil for the bulk of the twentieth century.

GDP OF TOP TEN COUNTRIES

Country	2003 US$m	rank	2004 US$m	rank	2005 US$m	rank	2006 US$m	rank	2007 US$m	rank
USA	10,8572	1	116675	1	12486624	1	14979169	1	139800	1
Japan	4,2907	2	46234	2	4663823	2	5083367	2	52900	2
Germany	2,3862	3	27144	3	2730109	3	2812558	3	32800	3
China	**1,3720**	**7**	**16493**	**7**	**1772724**	**6**	**2587999**	**4**	**30100**	**4**
U.K.	1,7750	4	21409	4	2227551	4	2292149	5	25700	5
France	1,7316	5	20026	5	2054880	5	2108307	6	25200	6
Italy	1,4554	6	16723	6	1709668	7	1728474	7	20900	7
Canada	8505	8	9798	9	1034532	8	1057291	9	13600	9
Spain	8271	9	9914	8	1019024	9	1069499	8	14100	8
Brazil	5070	15	4923	15	587784	15	6207.41	15	9340	12

In foreign trade, China has been able to become a world leader in the span of just three decades. China's foreign trade rose from twenty-seventh in the world with $20.6 billion in 1978 to third in the world in 2007 at $2.17 trillion, an increase of almost 103 fold. China now has the largest foreign currency reserves in the world, with reserves rocketing from $167 million in 1978 to $1.53 trillion in 2007.

a. The Role of Foreign Investment in China's Development

The pace of foreign investment in China has increased dramatically within the past two decades and has played a major role in the nation's rising economy. Ninety percent of China's foreign investment has occurred since 1992 when Deng Xiaoping's southern tour of China helped to propel his reform policies forward. Since 1992, China has been the world's second largest recipient of foreign capital behind the United States with foreign investment reaching $69 billion in 2005 up from an average of $11.7 billion during 1985–1995. Foreign direct investment in China accounted for one-fifth of all FDI in developing countries in 2005.

Foreign investment enterprises, such as joint ventures and wholly foreign-owned enterprises, have now assumed a major role in China's economy. According to China's most recent official statistics, foreign investment enterprises accounted for approximately one-half of all of China's industrial output and for 10.95% of all annual tax revenues in the industrial and commercial sector and are one of the fastest growing sources of tax revenue for the PRC. At present there are 56,378 foreign investment enterprises in operation employing 18.9 million people or approximately 10% of the entire nonrural labor population. There are now approximately 200 multinational enterprises with foreign investments in China, including seventeen of Japan's largest companies, and nine out of ten of Germany's largest companies. Some of the largest companies in the United States, such as Coca–Cola, General Motors, General Electric, McDonald's, Motorola, Boeing, and Procter & Gamble, all have sizeable business operations in China.

b.   Standard of Living

Economic reform has resulted in a significant improvement in the wealth and spending power of the average Chinese citizen and has lifted the overall standard of living for the nation. While still low by international standards, average income in China across all sectors is 8,030 Renminbi (literally "people's currency" and commonly abbreviated as RMB) or $1,172, an increase of two hundred fold over 1978 when the average income was just RMB 40. The average income figure may be somewhat misleading and may understate the spending power of the average Chinese consumer because many Chinese continue to receive government subsidies in the form of benefits through the workplace. There are also genuine millionaires in China's new economy, some of whom are celebrated in the many stories of the "bicycle to Benz" entrepreneur. Reflecting the rise of consumer wealth and the introduction of international brands into China's markets by multinational enterprises, China's consumer market retail sales grew at an annual rate of 17%

each year for the past two decades, from $15.3 billion in 1978 to $892 billion in 2007. The surge in consumer spending has allowed China to become the second largest consumer advertising market in Asia with a total annual market value of $5.3 billion in 1998, second only to Japan.

Just a generation ago, a young Chinese couple would dream of acquiring the "four bigs": a television, stereo, washing machine, and refrigerator and living out their lives in government housing and working for a state-owned enterprise. Today, the dreams of the young in China far surpass anything that previous generations could have imagined. Young Chinese today have dreams about the many opportunities for overseas travel, study, and work that were impossible just a generation ago. Whereas many Chinese dreamed of a job at a state-owned enterprise just a generation ago, this is the choice of last resort for today's ambitious Chinese many of who yearn to study abroad and work for a foreign investment enterprise.

8. MAJOR THEMES FROM CHINA'S JOURNEY TO MODERNITY

China's continuing journey to modernity has been a long and tortuous one, with periods of progress and retrenchment. As this chapter concludes, there are some major themes that should guide the reader in reviewing the materials that follow.

First, modern China is consumed by a drive for modernization and economic development. Achievement of this goal would represent, in many ways, the final step in overcoming the last lingering effects of the long period of decline in the nineteenth and early twentieth centuries that was characterized by foreign domination and internal weakness. Just a century ago, China was a nation in desperation seemingly about to perish under the onslaught of foreign imperialism. After China was able to regain control of its own sovereignty, the nation turned to rebuild its shattered economy and found itself mired in dire poverty and backwardness. At the end of the Second World War, much of China's daily life had scarcely progressed, if at all, from medieval times. In the space of three decades, China has managed to put itself firmly on the path to modernity. Just as the nation was consumed and united by a mighty paroxysm of effort during the disastrous Great Leap Forward, China is now also consumed by a drive to lift itself up to the level of advanced industrialized nations and to resume its place among the leading nations of the world. Law and legality need to be understood in the context of the nation's all-consuming goal. The legal system was rescued from desuetude at the end of the Cultural Revolution because Party elders believed that it could help to prevent the reoccurrence of chaos and be instrumental in supporting China's economic development.

Second, the CPC sees its role as the savior and unchallenged ruler of China and destined to finally lead the nation into the modern age. Although China's rulers have experimented with a number of bold economic reforms, it would be a mistake to believe, as some have in the past, that China's eagerness to experiment has somehow signaled a willingness to move beyond Communism and one party rule. It may be tempting to believe with so much change and innovation in the air that China is open to political reform. Even President Ronald Reagan, known as one of China's harshest critics, referred to China in 1984 as "a so-called Communist country" during a tour in Beijing. In the flush of China's economic development and the rapid pace of change, many observers might hope that political reform will inevitably follow economic reform. While this might occur, the events of June 4, 1989 in Tiananmen Square should serve as a stark reminder that China's rulers will accept no challenges to their authority.

This overview of the underpinnings of modern China and its legal system provides a context for understanding the role of law and legality in China. What is the role for law in the context of the major themes that animate modern China? Can the rule of law exist in modern China? What explains why law, morality, or any other mechanism of social control, did not protect the nation as it plunged into the mass self-delusion of the Great Leap Forward or the mass zealotry of the Cultural Revolution? The next chapter explores these topics.

CHAPTER TWO

THE HISTORY OF LAW
IN IMPERIAL AND
MODERN CHINA

An understanding of the role of law in modern China must start with a review of the relationship of law to dominant social and political theories in Imperial China (221 BC–1912 AD). Some of the concepts contained in these theories continue to be influential in China today.

MAJOR PERIODS IN CHINESE HISTORY

Eastern Zhou	771–256 BC
Warring States	403–221 BC
Qin	221–206 BC
Han	206 BC 220 AD
North–South Disunion	220–589
Northern Wei	385–535
Sui	589–618

Tang	618–907
Song	960–1279
Yuan	1279–1368
Ming	1358–1644
Qing	1644–1912
Republic of China	1912–1949
People's Republic of China	1949–present

A. SOCIETY, MORALITY, AND LAW IN IMPERIAL CHINA

Although the current PRC legal system is only about three decades old, law has a long tradition in China that stretches back over two thousand years to the earliest periods of Chinese history. Two of the most important schools of political, social, and legal thought in Chinese history, Confucianism and Legalism, arose during the Eastern Zhou period (771–256 BC).

Confucianism, founded by Confucius (551–479 BC), stressed the importance of government by education, persuasion, and moral example and laid less emphasis on government through the coercive use of law. Confucius, a contemporary of Plato (429–347 BC) and Aristotle (384–321 BC), viewed morality as the foundation of society. Citizens should be taught the difference between right and wrong and should be inculcated with the *li,* or a code of moral and social values. Once imbued with the correct Confucian values, citizens will behave according to conscience and will feel shame when they have violated the dictates of conscience. Citizens will become productive and law abiding members of society because of conscience and moral education, not because of the fear of legal sanctions in the case of disobedience. In contrasting the difference between a society based upon morality as opposed to one based upon law, Confucius stated:

> Lead the people with orders, keep them in line with penal laws, and they will avoid punishment but they will develop no sense of shame; lead them with virtue, keep them in line with propriety and they will not only have a sense of shame but will govern themselves.

Legalism, a school of thought contemporary with Confucianism, advocated government through the heavy use of law. The Legalists believed in *fa,* clear legal rules, applicable to all people regardless of rank, backed by strict sanctions in the case of disobedience. Legalism was adopted by the short-lived Qin dynasty (221–206 BC), which became known for the fearsome cruelty of its criminal laws. Confucianism became accepted as the state philosophy when the Han dynasty (206 BC) overthrew the Qin and remained the dominant state ideology of Imperial China until the fall of the Qing dynasty in the twentieth century. The ascendancy of Confucianism as the orthodox state philosophy, however, did not mean the abolition of all laws. Laws and legal institutions continued to be developed and to co-exist with *li* in Imperial China. The co-existence was explained by the need to resort to law to maintain social order when the higher dictates of conscience failed.

Although systematic criminal codes were developed in the Qin and Han dynasties, the earliest surviving code is the Tang Code promulgated in the seventh century AD. By pre-modern standards, the Chinese codes were monumental achievements for their time. The Tang Code subsequently became the basis for all later legal codes of the Song, Yuan, Ming, and Qing dynasties. Compiled in 1740, the 436 statutes and 1900 sub-statutes of the Great Qing Code was the last dynastic legal code of Imperial China and, like its predecessors, was chiefly a criminal code. A comprehensive legal system, although one based on criminal law, has existed in China for over 2,000 years, with significant continuity for over half of that period up to modern times.

Confucianism contained a moral and social vision based upon a hierarchical system in which the role of each individual was determined by his or her position in society and by familial and personal relationships. The vision integrated family and society as well as morality and politics. The same moral values and code of conduct prevailing in the family extended to society and the nation as a whole. The same moral conduct for the individual in his or her familial and personal relationships also became a code of political conduct in dealing with government and society. The nation was an extended family and both were governed by the same precepts. In Chinese, 'state' is *guo jia,* which is a combination of the two Chinese words for 'state' and 'family.'

Within family and society, all key relationships were those of superior to inferior with a general duty of obedience owed by the inferior to the superior and a reciprocal duty of caring, support, and guidance owed by the superior to the inferior. The basic relationships were those between father and son, brother and brother, and husband and wife. The moral obligations and duties owed in these relationships were created entirely by one's position. In the father and son relationship, the son was expected to exhibit filial piety and obedience. In return, the father was expected to nourish and care for the son and set a good moral example. The younger brother was expected to honor and respect the older brother and the wife was expected to be obedient to the husband. In none of these basic relationships does the notion of equality play a role. Only in the relationship of friend to friend does the notion of equality have any relevance, but this relationship, as it was outside of the family, was not considered fundamental. The concept of equality had little moral or political relevance in Imperial China.

The same concepts governing the family in Confucian society also governed society and the nation as a whole. Just as the duty of filial piety was the cardinal virtue within the family, the duty of absolute loyalty and obedience to the ruler was the paramount virtue within society. In the extended family of the nation, the emperor was the patriarch and was owed the same duty of filial piety by his family, which consisted of the entire nation. The status of the emperor was further exalted by the notion that he held his throne by the Mandate of Heaven or by a celestial right. This notion added a metaphysical or supernatural dimension to the status of the emperor, who as the Son of Heaven, answered only to Heaven alone and not to his people. The emperor was the ultimate superior being in the chain of superior-inferior relationships that characterized Chinese society and government. Although the emperor held this supreme status, his power was not absolute. The reciprocal duties in all superior-inferior relationships applied even to the emperor, and, because of his great responsibility, with greater force. In return for absolute obedience and loyalty owed to the emperor, Heaven required that the emperor, like any Confucian patriarch, had to exercise his powers benevolently and care for his people. If he failed to do so and descended into tyranny, then he became at risk of forfeiting the Mandate of Heaven. A successful rebellion would be proof that the emperor had lost the Mandate of Heaven and that Heaven had conferred a new Mandate upon another person, usually the leader of the successful rebellion.

After more than two thousand years of influence, Confucianism was displaced as the prevailing state philosophy at the beginning of the twentieth century with the demise of the Qing dynasty and the end of Imperial China. However, Confucianism continues to be reflected in many different aspects of modern China.

1. THE ROLE OF LAW IN IMPERIAL CHINA

Confucianism exerted a strong influence on the role of law in Imperial China. As further discussed below, some of these features of Imperial Chinese law continue to have an influence on the current legal system of modern China.

a. Law and Celestial Authority

In Imperial China, there was no notion of government limited by laws, which is a fundamental concept of Anglo–American jurisprudence. The authority and legitimacy of the emperor was based upon a celestial source, the Mandate of Heaven. By contrast, under a natural law theory, which was influential early in the history of the United States, law derived its legitimacy and binding authority from being found in nature similar to the laws of physics and biology. Whereas law derived its ultimate authority over human affairs from its supernatural origin under the natural law theory in the United States, the emperor derived the same ultimate authority from Heaven under Imperial Chinese ideology. This difference meant that whereas law was the ultimate arbiter of human affairs in the United States, the emperor was the ultimate arbiter in China.

The emperor's celestial authority meant that the emperor was above the law. The emperor had supreme legislative, judicial, and executive powers. He could enact laws, change or alter them at will, render judicial judgments, and alter the judgments of other judicial authorities. There was no concept of checks and balances. To the contrary, such limitations on the emperor's power would be considered to be treason. The emperor could enact laws binding on all subjects but these laws could not bind the emperor himself. Imperial China was governed by the rule of man not by the rule of law.

b. Individual Rights

The concept of individual and human rights did not exist in Imperial China. Confucian ideology emphasized social relationships that created duties not rights. The paramount virtues of a person and a citizen were the duties of filial piety in the family and the general duty of obedience to authority in society. There was no notion that the individual had rights that were sacred and could be protected by law. Rather, the law was concerned with enforcing duties in order to maintain social order.

The emphasis on duties rather than rights did not mean that individuals did not have legitimate interests. A son could expect the support and guidance of his father just as subjects had legitimate expectations in receiving the benevolence of the emperor. But the interests in care and support from a superior were viewed as a reciprocal benefit derived from the prior duty of obedience created by the relationship and not as based upon individual rights. Moreover, while individuals were recognized to have legitimate interests, Confucianism did not recognize a right in these individuals to insist that their interests be protected through the coercive power of a public social institution such as a court of law.

The concept of individual rights was also inconsistent with the Confucian emphasis on the priority of the family, society, and nation over the individual. Confucianism did not consider the individual to be a self-sufficient entity but as always defined by a position within a group. The group, not the individual, was the fundamental unit of society. Harmony within the group, established by the concepts of duty and obedience, was paramount over the interests of any individuals comprising the group.

c.   Equality Before the Law

Imperial China did not have a concept of treating all subjects equally before the law. To the contrary, how one was treated under the law depended upon one's status within society. One major aim of the Imperial legal system was to serve as a tool of social control to maintain the Confucian hierarchy of social relationships and the social order. The penalties for the same act depended upon the social status of the actor or kinship relationship within a family. The most heinous crimes were those that subverted the social hierarchy as in the case where an inferior in a relationship committed an offense against a superior. For example, a son who struck his parent could face death by decapitation whereas a parent who killed a child for disobedience might receive a light physical punishment only. A wife striking her husband would result in physical punishment to the wife whereas a husband striking his wife would receive punishment only if she was badly injured. Husbands could divorce their wives on any of seven grounds (including being disobedient to parents-in-law, inability to bear a son, physical disability, among others), but wives could not divorce husbands.

d.   Law as Distinguished from Morality

Imperial China did not mark a clear distinction between morality and law. This lack of clear boundaries between law and other disciplines should be contrasted with jurisprudential traditions in the United States and some other western countries. A basic notion of legal positivism, a dominant jurisprudential theory of the twentieth century in the United States, is that law is a discrete and self-contained set of rules, backed by the sanction of the state, and is distinct from morality and other social norms. Laws are distinguished from other norms by their pedigree. In the United States, all laws are enacted by legislatures or by bodies with delegated legislative authority. Courts interpret and apply laws, all within federal and state constitutional constraints. In the United States, issues of morality, social norms, and social policies are relevant considerations for legislatures in developing and drafting laws but, as a technical matter, these issues are viewed as extraneous to the law and should play no role in the application and enforcement of the law.

By contrast, in traditional China, there was a blurring of the distinction between morality and law with morality playing a dominant role. In Chinese society, the role of morality in governing society was viewed as paramount and law was considered to play a secondary and supplementary role only to be invoked when moral precepts could not sufficiently maintain social order. The Confucian system was viewed as the essence and spirit behind the legal system. As a result, morality was often relevant in legal decision-making, the application of law, and the administration of justice. In some cases in certain periods of Chinese history, officials even advocated the practice of deciding cases directly in accordance with the principles of the Confucian classics. As a practical matter, Confucian doctrines could be given priority or even supplant statutory laws in the course of deciding cases.

e. Separation of Powers and Judicial Independence

The lack of a clear distinction between law as a distinct and self-contained system of rules may also explain another salient feature of the Imperial Chinese legal system. There was no effort in China to create a clear separation of judicial powers from executive or legislative powers at any level of government. As previously discussed, all supreme executive, legislative, and judicial powers were concentrated in the emperor who exercised them all simultaneously, but the same was true at all levels of government below the emperor. The most important local official in Imperial China, the county magistrate, was both the chief administrator and judge of the local region. The county magistrate would simultaneously exercise administrative, police, and judicial powers over the locality and the same structure combining all these powers was true for magistrates at the higher levels of the prefecture, province, and the capital. The law was not an independent specialty but a part of the tools of state administration in general.

Since law was not deemed to be a separate system requiring a formal separation of functions, there was also no concept of judicial independence or conflicts of interest. Higher officials within the Imperial system not only had the power to supervise local magistrates but could also exert pressure on local officials to decide cases in certain ways. There was no concept that the exercise of judicial power should be separate from and independent of the larger state administrative apparatus. Rather, the legal system was considered to be, in many ways, a secondary and minor part of a larger administrative system.

f. Lack of a Developed Civil and Commercial Law

As Confucianism viewed law primarily as a mechanism to maintain social control, the Tang Code and its successors were chiefly criminal in nature, which contributed to a general perception among the populace that law was something to be feared. A number of features in the administration of the criminal law system in Imperial China helped to intensify the public's general apprehension. For example, officials could apply criminal statutes by analogy to punish conduct not expressly prohibited by existing law. This feature, once also a part of the legal system of the PRC, instilled the fear in the general population that no one was safe from criminal prosecution since any activity could potentially be deemed criminal. In addition, criminal laws in Imperial China imposed fearsome and cruel punishments on the guilty (death by decapitation was often viewed with welcomed relief by the accused), used torture to exact confessions from the accused, and imprisoned and tortured witnesses. Corruption among officials was also rampant, adding the burden of paying bribes and fees to the misery of subjects unlucky enough to find themselves in court. Most subjects sought to avoid the legal system if at all possible.

There were additional reasons why China never developed a system of commercial and business laws of a sophistication and complexity similar to those of the United States and some other western nations. Merchants in China were never able to establish themselves as an independent class. The many oppressive powers of government officials to supervise and tax kept the merchant class subordinate to the landed gentry and their representatives in the government bureaucracy. As a result, the merchant class was never able to break free of official domination and control and to establish themselves as a driving force within Chinese society. The agrarian nature of Chinese society also prevented the growth of capitalism. Instead of channeling capital investment into the support of industrial production, China's agrarian society channeled capital into the practice of usurious money lending to farmers. In addition, merchants also suffered from the traditional Confucian disdain for valuing profit over scholarship. In sum, the inability of capitalism and the merchant class to develop in China hindered the development of a sophisticated commercial and business law regime. Although some scholars have recently taken issue with the view that China never developed a civil and commercial law, the prevailing view among Chinese historians has been that law in traditional China was mainly penal in nature and was used chiefly as an instrument of social control.

Law in Imperial China also never developed as a tool for the resolution of private disputes between ordinary subjects. Citizens viewed law as being administered vertically, from the state upon the individual, as opposed to being used horizontally to resolve disputes between actors with one another. As discussed earlier, the use of law as a form of state administered power upon individuals also struck fear in most of the general population with good reason. Ordinary subjects who had disputes resolved them through informal means and mediation by various customary and unofficial channels such as through the use of craft or merchant guilds or through the intervention of village elders. The aversion to using the legal system among the general populace meant that China did not develop a civil law system useful in resolving civil disputes. Formal law only served the public interests of the state and was not viewed by ordinary Chinese as a tool to resolve private disputes.

g. The Legal Profession in Imperial China

The failure in Imperial China to recognize law as a separate and independent discipline and to separate the legal function from other government functions restricted the development of law as a profession. As law was not viewed as a specialty or as a discrete profession, law schools did not exist to train lawyers. As early as the Tang dynasty (618–907 AD), however, experts in litigation did begin to appear to help clients in litigation matters. These so-called experts learned their knowledge of law and judicial proceedings by observation, apprenticeship, or self-study and offered their services on matters such as the drafting of pleadings and petitions. These experts, however, were never officially recognized as a profession and they had no right to represent their clients in courts or legal proceedings. Government officials often viewed these experts as opportunists, shysters, and troublemakers engaged in an activity that was not entirely respectable.

B. LAW IN MODERN CHINA, 1912–1978

The discussion in the preceding sections traced the development of law during Imperial China, which ended with the eclipse of the Qing dynasty in 1912. Belated efforts during the final stages of the Qing dynasty were made to adopt various modern laws based upon the laws of western nations and the newly modernized Japanese legal system. Qing reformers realized that one of the reasons why foreign nations demanded that their citizens in China be exempted from Chinese law and subject to foreign law was because China did not have an adequate legal system. China's criminal laws were thought to be barbaric and no adequate commercial laws had been developed. Before legal reforms could be fully implemented, however, the Qing collapsed and a new provisional government headed by Dr. Sun Yatsen was installed. Both the northern warlords and the Nationalist government led by Chiang Kai-shek with its headquarters in Nanjing continued the process of legal reform. The Nationalist government, however, never fully established control over the whole of China and its reforms, an amalgamation of continental, Anglo–American, warlord and Qing legal traditions, were never fully implemented. The nascent Nationalist legal system was abolished when the PRC was established in 1949.

The period after 1949 marked the construction of a new formal legal system in the PRC, but only as a means to achieve larger Party policies. This period was marked by a number of mass movements initiated by the CPC to root out the old evils of feudal and Nationalist China. These movements were also intended to begin the transformation from feudal to socialist China. Some of the major movements, such as the Anti–Rightist Campaign and the Great Leap Forward, have already been discussed, but there were many other smaller movements designed to raise the political consciousness of the general populace. Among these were the mass trials held all over the country in which mobs of angry citizens meted out a rough revolutionary justice on class enemies of the old order. These so-called trials were held in public before frenzied crowds where the victims were bound, often made to kneel, and had to suffer verbal and physical attacks without any opportunity to defend themselves. By Mao Zedong's own account as many as 800,000 people met their deaths through these cruel and brutal methods. Other campaigns were instituted to attack classes of landlords and rich peasants, to cleanse corruption in the Communist Party, and to eradicate cheating, stealing of government property, and tax evasion, all considered to be widespread at the time among industrial and commercial enterprises.

These movements were guided at first by Party policies, but over time these policies became codified as laws. During this first stage of legal development in the PRC, the law was used as a tool to facilitate the fledgling nation's rejection of the old evils and its transformation into a new socialist republic. In 1954, an important milestone was reached when the new National People's Congress promulgated the first Constitution of the PRC. A great deal of progress in building a legal system was achieved during this period. Not only did the PRC implement a wide number of laws to assist in the socialist transformation, but the nation also began to build a number of legal institutions, to develop a legal profession, and to establish a system of law schools.

Some retrenchment in the development of the legal system occurred with the Anti–Rightist Campaign, which was a reaction to the short-lived and misconceived Hundred Flowers Movement, in which the Party invited criticism only to be stunned when some intellectuals took the invitation seriously and actually leveled stinging attacks on the Party. Once the Party felt itself under attack, it moved swiftly to punish its enemies, but the legal system and the very concept of law also suffered as a result. The Party saw the law as creating constraints upon its power and the administration of justice as a rival to Party control. After 1957, the prestige of the legal system fell sharply and major parts of the system were dismantled. This same inclination to attack the legal system would emerge with even greater ferocity during the Cultural Revolution, which, as further detailed in a subsequent section below, resulted in the abolition of the legal system altogether.

1.   THE LEGAL SYSTEM AFTER 1978

The end of the Cultural Revolution and the emergence of Deng Xiaoping as China's new leader also marked the beginning of a new era of economic reforms and a new role for law. In 1978, the watershed Third Plenum of the Eleventh Central Committee of the Communist Party of China, the central policy-making body of the Party and the nation, issued a communiqué containing a resounding endorsement of the role of law:

In order to safeguard people's democracy, it is imperative to strengthen the socialist legal system so that democracy is systematized and codified into law in such a way as to ensure the stability, continuity and full authority of this democratic system and these laws; there must be laws for people to follow, these laws must be obeyed, their enforcement must be strict and law breakers must be punished. From now on, legislative work should have an important place on the agenda of the National People's Congress and its Standing Committee. Procuratorial and judicial organs must maintain their independence as is appropriate; they must faithfully abide by the laws, rules and regulations, serve the people's interests, keep to the facts, guarantee the equality of all people before the people's laws, and permit no one to have the privilege of being above the law.

There are a number of features of the decision to resurrect the legal system that are helpful in understanding its role in China today. Understanding these reasons will also be useful in assessing the extent of China's political commitment to the legal system, and the extent to which the rule of law has taken root in China.

a. Law as a Lesson from the Cultural Revolution

Party elders believed that the nation's failure to fully accept the authority of law was a major reason why zealots during the Cultural Revolution were able to usurp power and seize control of social and governmental institutions and persecute millions of victims. In a nation such as the United States, law serves to control and protect its citizens against the blind and fanatical adherence to authority. Nothing approaching the Cultural Revolution could have ever transpired in the United States because of, among other reasons, a commitment to law and legal process. In China, however, at the point in time that law was most needed to protect the nation against the excesses of the Cultural Revolution, the law and the legal system were powerless to stem the mindless assault.

For the advocates of legal reform in 1978, it was telling that the abolition of the legal system during the Cultural Revolution was not an unintended by-product of the widespread attacks on the nation's social and political institutions. The zealots of the Cultural Revolution consciously targeted the legal system for destruction precisely because they felt that law operated as a constraint upon their ability to inflict destruction upon counterrevolutionaries. In the warped thinking of those times, angry zealots believed that the more they abused and mistreated class enemies, the more they showed their commitment to the Party and the revolution. Law operated as an unwanted restraint on the infliction of wanton cruelty and inhumane treatment on victims. As a result, the legal system itself was deliberately targeted for attack as counterrevolutionary and the very idea of law was rejected. Legal institutions, such as courts and procuratorates, were shut down or paralyzed, law schools closed, and members of the legal community were forced to shift professions or were sent down to farms to learn from peasants. Law itself was a bad element that had to be purged from Chinese society. Lawlessness and legal nihilism, which gave free reign to random and unpredictable political terror, descended upon China during the darkest days of the Cultural Revolution. The advocates of legal reform believed that the Cultural Revolution left the important, if painful, lesson that a strong commitment to law and a legal system was necessary to protect the nation from spinning out of control in the face of zealotry and hysteria.

b. Law and Economic Development

Party elders also believed that a viable legal system was necessary to support the new goal of economic development. The Third Plenum of the Eleventh Central Committee of the Party confirmed that the end of the Cultural Revolution meant that the emphasis of the nation would no longer be on class struggle, purging class enemies, and purification of the nation. Rather, the focus of the nation would shift to economic development and modernization. A legal system was necessary to support both internal changes brought on by reform and to create the conditions necessary to attract foreign investment. As the economic reforms required the relaxation of central controls and the use of market principles for certain sectors of the economy, there also arose a need to define and protect new property rights and interests. Enterprises and businesses needed both the protection and predictability created by a legal system for their new relationships created by contract rather than by the administrative fiat of the state.

Party elders also had in mind a crucial and decisive role for foreign investment in China's economic development. For most of the period since 1949, China had turned inward and shunned foreign trade and investment with the rest of the world with the notable exception of the Soviet Union. By 1978, Party elders realized that an isolationist policy had failed. They now believed that rapid modernization of the nation could be accomplished only by the capital and advanced technology that foreign investment would bring to China. Most of the foreign investors that China wanted to attract, however, were from advanced industrialized economies with sophisticated legal systems and would balk at investing in an environment without a legal system that was stable, predictable, and that would protect their rights and interests. China would need to develop a commercial and business law regime that would satisfy international standards if it wanted to do business with the rest of the world.

The years following 1978 were ones of great progress in the rebuilding of China's legal system. In the first decade of reform alone from 1979–89, over 3,000 laws and regulations were enacted, including over one hundred major legal codes. The PRC enacted its fourth Constitution, which expressly stated that all organizations, including the Communist

Party, must operate within the scope of the Constitution and laws. Law schools were reopened and lawyers were once again allowed to practice. The Ministry of Justice was re-established and the system of courts and procuratorates was restored and strengthened. As China moved into the second decade of reforms in the 1990s, the pace of change accelerated. Large increases in foreign investment were reflected in significant expansion of laws in the areas of foreign investment and intellectual property. Not only were these new laws designed to enhance China's business climate, but they were also enacted in anticipation of China's entry into the WTO. China's formal accession to the WTO on November 11, 2001 signaled a new era of legality as China now became a member of the world's largest and most respected commercial law regime.

c. The Role of Law at this Stage in China's History

This overview of China's legal and political traditions and of the background of its modern legal system sets the stage for an evaluation of the role of law in China at this point in its history and going forward. Any assessment of the current status of China's legal system, however, must be tempered by the realization that building a legal system is a process that cannot be completed in the span of three decades or even in a generation. China's current legal system, dating from reforms begun in 1978, is barely over three decades old. Such a fledgling system cannot realistically be compared with that of the United States, which is many times older. In addition, while the American legal system borrowed from and built upon several centuries of the common law tradition in England, China's current legal system represents in many ways a break with Confucianism, a dominant ideology that is many centuries old. However, while it is one matter to formally break with traditions, it is another matter to completely overcome the influence of traditions so deeply embedded in centuries of Chinese culture. What follows is an assessment of a still developing system and a work in progress that contains a number of conflicts and tensions.

First, neither Imperial China nor pre-reform modern China recognized or accepted the rule of law and some of its important corollaries such as the separation of powers, judicial independence, and the law as a discrete and independent discipline. The most important feature of the rule of law is the concept that law stands above the government, which itself derives its authority from law and is subject to the law. In Imperial China, the emperor derived his authority from the Mandate of Heaven. He was the supreme authority and was above the law. While China's line of Imperial rule ended in 1912, some of these concepts of the supremacy of the ruling government continue to hold sway in modern China. Whether it is because of the continuing influence of Confucianism or simply because of expediency, the Communist Party views itself as holding unchallenged authority. In modern China, the Communist Party is supreme.

Although a western concept of the rule of law failed to take root in China, China's rulers did use law as an instrument of social control. Even as an instrument of social control, however, law would be periodically viewed as an unwanted restraint on the state's ability to protect itself from its hidden enemies. As discussed in the previous chapter, the CPC, like its predecessors, is wary of conspiracy, hidden enemies, and traitors, a characteristic of authoritarian states that force all opposition to hide behind artifice in order to survive. For such a government, law can become an obstacle. Law requires evidence, establishing a case, and following a set of procedures. All of these requirements can be difficult to meet when dealing with clever protagonists who work clandestinely and who hide or destroy evidence. Legal requirements can also be burdensome in times of crisis when immediate action is essential. In times of turbulence, such as the Anti–Rightist Campaign and the Cultural Revolution, the availability of law as a defense against arbitrary power was viewed as an indictment of the law itself.

Second, the development of law in modern China has been directed to achieving the two goals of (1) safeguarding the nation against chaos through maintaining social control and (2) developing commerce, trade, and foreign investment. These goals can be traced to the basic shift in policy that occurred after the Cultural Revolution, as previously discussed above. China has made important progress in establishing rights of the individual as protection against the type of mindless persecution of innocent victims by mobs that reached its peak during the Cultural Revolution. China has also made particularly significant strides in enacting new laws in the areas of commercial and business law, intellectual property, administrative litigation, and reform of the judiciary. On the other hand, China has not made significant progress in the use of human rights as a safeguard against state power. China views law as a bureaucratic tool to govern and control society as opposed to a shield against arbitrary power. Imperial China did not have a concept of individual rights; to the contrary, traditional China emphasized the primacy of the group, not the individual. In modern China, human rights also pose a threat to the Communist Party's desire to maintain its vision of social order and harmony among the masses. Human rights serve as a limit upon the power of the state. Moreover, human rights and individual political freedoms are based upon the principle of the sovereignty of the people, which forms the basis and foundation of democracy, a political system that is antithetical to the present system in the PRC. Human rights and individual political freedoms create the basis for a fundamental challenge to the authority of the CPC and are in tension, if not direct conflict, with the present system of government.

Third, the modernization of China's legal system, like that of other developing countries around the world, has also been a process of westernization. Concepts such as the rule of law and individual rights are derived from western political traditions and have no equivalents in Chinese history. That China was forced to accept some westernization in the nineteenth and twentieth centuries at the point of a gun created great resentment during those early periods of reform. Some lingering effects of China's initial contacts with the west may still be felt today. At the same time, the westernization of legal systems, among other social institutions, is now a world trend. The growing importance of the World Trade Organization, dominated by western nations, has added to the growing influence of western legal systems. Most developing countries have now adopted as models for their legal systems either the Romano–Germanic or the common law tradition, both of which can be traced to eleventh century Europe. Recently, however, a growing cadre of developing nations has begun to challenge the dominance of western values in world trade and development. Some of these nations have formed blocks or coalitions in the WTO and have become a significant influence in the on-going development of world trade law. In Asia, a recent surge of nationalism has caused some countries to openly reject an unthinking adoption of western political and legal systems as appropriate for Asia. As we have seen, China has long viewed the west with a mixture of admiration and hostility and has long grappled with the extent to which it needs to adopt western traditions and the extent to which such traditions are appropriate for China. Along with the desire to modernize its legal system, China must also grapple with ambivalent attitudes toward westernization on the one hand and the conservative forces of tradition, perhaps stronger in China than in many other nations, on the other hand. These conflicting attitudes toward adopting western-based legal concepts continue to create tensions as China continues to modernize its legal system.

CHAPTER THREE

CONSTITUTION, STATE STRUCTURE, AND HUMAN RIGHTS

This chapter examines the basic structure of the state and fundamental rights as set forth in the PRC Constitution. The current Constitution, promulgated in 1982, is the fourth in China's history and has been hailed as the most complete of all China's constitutions. The 1982 Constitution consists of a preamble and three chapters. The preamble sets forth the basic ideology of the Constitution; Chapter 1 sets forth general principles; Chapter 2 concerns fundamental duties and rights of citizens; and Chapter 3 sets forth the basic structure of the state. The discussion below begins with a general review of the role of constitutions in China and their historic role in other communist states and then examines the major organs of state power, the legislative and executive branches of the state structure. A discussion of the judicial organs, also established in the Constitution, is deferred until Chapter 6 of this volume. This chapter then concludes with an examination of human rights in China, starting with the 1982 Constitution as a basis for the discussion.

A. THE ROLE OF THE CONSTITUTION IN NATION STATES

Constitutions serve different purposes in different types of states and it would be a mistake to transfer assumptions about constitutional law drawn from American jurisprudence to the case of China. Constitutions in China do not have the same significance as their counterparts in democratic governments, such as the United States. Moreover, unlike in the case of the United States, the structure and power of the Chinese state is not apparent from examining legal documents such as its Constitution. To the contrary, an examination of the PRC Constitution without an appreciation of the larger social and political context of which it is a part might give a misleading picture of the PRC. A cursory review of the plain language of the PRC Constitution suggests a political structure in the form of a pyramid in which power is transferred from the base upwards; lower levels in this structure, starting with the lowest level, the general population, grant authority upwards by electing representatives of government. At the higher levels, these local representatives in turn elect other representatives for national seats of power in a parliamentary form of government. At the highest level, representatives elect top government leaders, such as the president of the PRC and the premier of the State Council, the two top officials of the PRC. In this structure, authority and legitimacy of the government can be traced directly to the people.

In reality, however, the power structure of the PRC is actually almost the opposite, with a small group of leading individuals in the Communist Party of China exercising most of the power and control from the top of the pyramid down through the ranks. Moreover, the Communist Party is not a government organ, but a political party, and its role and power is not fully discernible from the PRC Constitution itself or in any written laws or documents. The real power structure is created through a set of behind-the-scenes practices and relationships that are embedded in the current political and legal culture of the PRC that are not entirely accessible to outsiders. This distinction between an apparent government and legal structure and a real behind-the-scenes power structure is a basic and pervasive feature of the PRC state. A discussion of why China maintains an apparent and a real power structure and how real power is exercised is deferred until the next chapter on the Communist Party.

The distinction between apparent and real power is also found in the area of human rights, a topic discussed at the end of this chapter. The PRC Constitution sets forth the basic principles governing human rights in China. Based upon the face of the constitutional text, it would appear that PRC citizens enjoy a set of rights consistent with international standards. In reality, however, as the discussion below indicates, the PRC imposes significant limitations on the exercise of those rights.

B. THE NATURE OF CONSTITUTIONS
IN THE PRC

Governments in democracies such as the United States are limited by law and derive their authority from law. In such states, the constitution is the most basic and highest law of the state and represents the highest degree of authority within the state. In the United States, the federal Constitution enjoys the highest level of respect and fidelity from the government, courts, and the people.

Constitutions in Communist and authoritarian states serve a different role. Law has never received the same level of respect in Communist nations as in democratic governments. Some of these reasons are linked to ideology. According to Marx, law, unlike economics, is not one of the major forces that can move history and change the course of nations. Marx also viewed law as a tool used by the bourgeois classes to dominate the working classes. In modern times, China has attempted to find a role for law by recasting law as part of a socialist legality in which law embodies the will of the people. Nevertheless, a basic conflict exists between the law and the authority of the Communist Party. In any political and legal system, there can be only one final authority. The Communist Party sees itself as the leader and savior of the Chinese people and the final guardian of its interests. In such a system, where there is a conflict between the law and the will of the Communist Party, the law may have to yield.

Under these circumstances, it may be useful to think of the Constitution of the PRC as an embodiment or expression of the current policies and thought of the Communist Party as opposed to a fundamental source of authority. As a policy document, it is doubtful, as further discussed below, whether the current PRC Constitution has direct legal effect in the absence of implementing legislation. PRC constitutions are not viewed as enduring and permanent monuments creating the basic conditions for society. In the short span of its existence since 1949, the PRC has had four different constitutions whereas the United States has had one constitution in its over 200–year history. As further discussed below, some of the PRC's constitutions are radically different from each other. The most recent constitution, the 1982 Constitution, stands as a repudiation of its two predecessors enacted in 1975 and 1978. In this context, studying the PRC Constitution can serve as a guide to understanding the direction of the CPC and the state, but it would be misleading to view the PRC Constitution as having legal supremacy.

C. A HISTORICAL SURVEY OF CONSTITUTIONS IN THE PRC

A brief historical review of the constitutions of the PRC may provide a useful guide on how constitutions are regarded and the purposes they serve in modern China. The CPC has always regarded constitutions as serving as a valuable tool in legitimizing its authority. Even before the establishment of the PRC in 1949, the Communist Party had used several constitutions to justify its rule of areas under its control. After 1949, the CPC convened the Chinese People's Political Consultative Conference to promulgate the Common Program, which served as a provisional constitution until the National People's Congress (NPC) enacted the first formal constitution in 1954. The purpose of the 1954 Constitution was to legitimize the transformation of China's economic and political structure to socialism. The 1954 Constitution, however, soon lost any legal authority that it might have had because many of its provisions were soon completely disregarded. As the nation began a series of political campaigns and mass movements that would last for the next twenty years, it appeared as if the 1954 Constitution did not exist so blatant and complete was the disregard for the authority of its provisions. For example, although the 1954 Constitution promised that capitalist ownership of property and the means of production would be protected by law, all ownership was nationalized by 1957. The 1954 Constitution also provided that the NPC was the highest authority of the state, was to be elected every four years, and was to meet once a year. As the highest organ of state power, the NPC, in theory, should have made the decision to launch such important national movements as the Anti–Rightist Campaign, the Great Leap Forward, and the Cultural Revolution. In reality, the NPC neither considered nor discussed any of these movements that would have major and devastating consequences for the nation. In fact, for the ten-year period from December 1964 to January 1975, the NPC did not even convene because the Cultural Revolution so disrupted the nation and paralyzed many of the organs of state power.

The NPC was convened in January 1975 to adopt a new constitution, the second for the PRC. Adopted during the Cultural Revolution, the 1975 Constitution reflected the extreme views and anarchy of that period. The basic premise of the 1975 Constitution was that the revolution was incomplete; that the nation still had to carry on the struggle between the "capitalist road" and the "socialist road"; and that class struggle and political purification was the overriding goal of the nation. In a further reflection of the times, the 1975 Constitution abolished various major provisions of the 1954 Constitution that were designed to create the basic conditions for the state. For example, the 1975 Constitution abolished provisions that required the equal treatment of citizens under the law and the independent exercise of judicial and prosecutorial powers. The office of the presidency was abolished and the NPC was made expressly subject to the leadership of the CPC. The 1975 Constitution was intended to explicitly increase the direct power of the CPC over the state and to abolish limitations on the CPC's power that might impair its ability to lead the continuing revolution. Many PRC scholars view the 1975 Constitution as a disastrous example of how a constitution can be twisted to support anarchy and to undermine the authority of law itself.

The 1975 Constitution was short-lived. The nation was plunged into political instability by the death of Mao Zedong in 1976 and the fall from power of Jiang Qing, Mao's wife, and her partners in the "Gang of Four," widely vilified as the instigators of many of the worst excesses of the Cultural Revolution. As a result, the Fourth NPC, convened in 1975, like its successor the Third NPC, convened in 1964, never met again in disregard of the plain language of the 1975 Constitution calling for a plenary meeting of the NPC once a year.

In 1978, the Fifth NPC was convened to adopt the 1978 Constitution, the third in the history of the PRC. Although the 1978 Constitution rolled back the radical and extremist views of the 1975 Constitution, it preserved the basic philosophy that the goal of the nation was to continue the revolution and to engage in class struggle. The 1978 Constitution also preserved the features of the 1975 Constitution that provided for explicit control of the state by the CPC.

Like its predecessor, the 1978 Constitution would also be short-lived. Its brief tenure can be ascribed to the rise to power of Deng Xiaoping and the fall of Hua Guofeng, Mao's chosen successor, and his line of Mao Zedong supporters who wanted to continue the revolutionary struggle. By the December 1978 Third Plenum of the Eleventh Central Committee of the CPC, Deng's victory was clear. The 1978

Third Plenum announced that the energies of the nation would shift from class struggle and political campaigns to economic development and modernization. The nation would need a new constitution to embody this fundamental shift in policy. In December 1982, the Fifth NPC adopted the 1982 Constitution, the fourth in the history of the PRC. Amended in 1988, 1993, 1999 and 2004, the 1982 Constitution continues to be in effect and will form the basis for the discussion that follows.

D. BASIC FEATURES OF THE 1982 CONSTITUTION

The 1982 Constitution is generally regarded as the best in the history of the PRC. Although it has many important new features, this section focuses on three features of the 1982 Constitution that will help provide a framework for understanding its significance. First, the 1982 Constitution rejected the extreme political nature of the 1978 and 1975 Constitutions that explicitly vested control of the state in the Communist Party. Rather, the 1982 Constitution restored the scheme of a government by state organs duly constituted through a set of lawful procedures set forth in the Constitution. The role of the CPC in this scheme is to provide leadership for the nation as set forth in the most important of the four basic principles contained in the preamble to the 1982 Constitution. The other three are following the socialist road, adherence to the principle of the people's democratic dictatorship, and following "Marxism–Leninism Mao Zedong–

Deng Xiaoping thought." *See* PRC Const., Prmbl. at ¶ 7 (as amended, 1999). While affirming the leadership of the CPC, the 1982 Constitution deleted the provisions of the 1978 and 1975 Constitutions creating explicit control of the state by the CPC. The deletion of these explicit control mechanisms from the Constitution did not in reality reduce the level of control that the CPC exercises over the state apparatus. To the contrary, as the next chapter will discuss, the CPC enjoys de facto control of the PRC state. But rejection of these explicit control provisions did signal a repudiation of the extreme overt political nature of the 1978 and 1975 Constitutions.

Second, the 1982 Constitution also formally incorporated the directives of the CPC stating that henceforth,

the basic task of the nation is to concentrate its efforts on socialist modernization along the road of building socialism with Chinese characteristics. [The] Chinese people ... will work hard and self-reliantly to modernize industry, agriculture, national defense, and science and technology step by step to turn China into a prosperous, strong, democratic, and culturally advanced socialist country.

PRC Const., Prmbl. at ¶ 7 (as amended, 1999). Amendments in 1988 to Article 11 explicitly recognize and protect "the private sector of the economy ... as a complement to the socialist public economy." The spirit of the 1993 Amendments is to introduce new changes to support the pace of economic development. Six of the eleven articles comprising the 1993 amendments are related to developing a market economy within a framework of socialism, two articles re-emphasize the leading role of the CPC, one is related to the overall direction of the state, one emphasizes the right of all citizens to work, and one concerns term limits of delegates to the people's congresses. The 1999 Amendments were designed to incorporate decisions made by the Fifteenth Congress of the CPC. The bulk of the six 1999 amendments were designed to enhance the status of the individual and private sectors of the economy subject to the limitation that the "state exercises guidance, supervision, and control over the individual and private sector of the economy." PRC Const., Art. 11 (as amended, 1999). Prior to their enactment, the substance of the 1988, 1993, and 1999 Amendments had already been implemented in practice in the PRC. The 2004 Amendments, which were adopted at the Second Session of the Tenth National People's Congress of the PRC on March 14, 2004, were designed to enhance the protection of the rights of citizens to own and inherit private property and to enhance the respect for and protection of human rights. The incorporation of these amendments into the Constitution was intended to legitimize existing practices. This legitimating function is consistent with the role that the Constitution serves in the PRC.

Third, in rejecting the extremist policies of the Cultural Revolution reflected in the 1978 and 1975 Constitutions, the 1982 Constitution placed a new emphasis on the authority of law. The Preamble states that the Constitution "is the fundamental law of the state and has supreme legal authority." PRC Const., Prmbl. at ¶ 12. Article 5 provides:

> All state organs, the armed forces, all political parties and public organizations and all enterprises and institutions must abide by the Constitution and the law. . . . No organization or individual is privileged to be beyond the Constitution or the law.

The 1999 Amendments incorporated for the first time an explicit reference to the rule of law: "The People's Republic of China shall be governed according to the law and shall be built into a socialist country based upon the rule of law." PRC Const., Art. 5 (as amended, 1999). Law appears to have reached a new pinnacle of respect and authority in China.

Despite these provisions, however, the supremacy of the Constitution and law over the CPC may be more theoretical than real for several reasons. Many scholars in the PRC view the Constitution as declaratory and as stating policy and doubt whether it has direct legal effect in the absence of implementing legislation. Courts in the PRC have not applied constitutional provisions directly in cases before them but apply the ordinary legislation that implements and embodies constitutional provisions. In addition, courts in the PRC do not have the power to determine whether a constitutional violation has occurred or to interpret the Constitution.

The power to supervise the enforcement of the Constitution resides in the National People's Congress, the national legislature, and its permanent Standing Committee. *See* PRC Const., Arts. 62 & 67. The power to interpret the Constitution, as distinguished from the power to supervise its enforcement, has been assigned to the Standing Committee of the NPC. *See* PRC Constitution at Art. 67 (1), (7) & (8). The new Law on Legislation, adopted in 2000, has clarified the division of authority between the NPC and its Standing Committee but has not otherwise changed this basic approach. As both the NPC and its Standing Committee are subject to the control of the Communist Party of China, it would appear that in practice the final arbiter of whether a law or act is constitutional may be the CPC.

Whether the CPC is subject to the law, as is stated in the Constitution, or is above the law because it has de facto control of the state's legal apparatus, which appears to be the case in reality, will continue to be debated. There is little doubt, however, that other state officials, enterprises, and citizens believe themselves to be subject to laws and have an increased awareness and respect for law. The 1982 Constitution's explicit recognition of the rule of law is a repudiation of the lawlessness that prevailed prior to the 1978 reforms and marks a new era of legality in the PRC. The full scope and significance of this new emphasis of law is still developing in the PRC and will be examined throughout the remainder of this volume.

1. THE STATE STRUCTURE

This chapter now turns to an examination of some of the major government institutions that comprise the state structure as set forth in the Constitution. The institutions that are the focus of the discussion below are the legislative and executive organs and their counterparts at lower levels of the state structure. A discussion of the judicial organs is deferred until Chapter 6 of this volume.

In China, there are seven major organs of state government. The National People's Congress and its permanent Standing Committee stand at the peak of state power; the other five organs are under the authority of the NPC. The five subordinate organs include the President of the PRC, a largely ceremonial office, the State Council, the administrative and executive organ of government, and the Central Military Commission, a powerful office that controls China's military forces. The two judicial organs, the Supreme People's Court and the Supreme People's Procuratorate, a supervisory and prosecutorial organ, also fall under the authority of the NPC.

While there are functional divisions between the various state organs, China does not have a separation of powers doctrine similar to that of the United States. There are a number of major areas in which PRC state organs have overlapping powers. For example, although the NPC and its Standing Committee have legislative powers, it is the State Council and its ministries and administrations that in practice initiate most legislation in the PRC. Other state organs, including the Supreme People's Court, also have legislative powers. The PRC also does not have a concept of separate but equal branches of government that create a checks and balances system. In the United States, the doctrines of co-equal branches of government and checks and balances help to prevent a concentration of power in one organ and the aggrandizement of power by one organ from others. In China, the NPC is, under the constitutional scheme, the supreme organ of government power, although in practice the State Council is more powerful.

Government Structure of the PRC

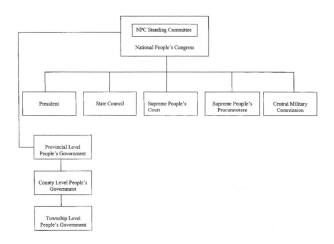

a. Levels of the State

The state structure, discussed below and in the next chapter on the judiciary, is organized in a hierarchical structure of four to five levels. At the highest level is the national or central level with its seat in Beijing. The next highest level consists of thirty-one provincial level authorities. This level not only includes the twenty-three provinces, but also four special municipalities, Beijing, Shanghai, Tianjin, and Chongqing, and five autonomous regions, Guanxi, Inner Mongolia, Ningxia, Xinjiang, Xizang (Tibet), and two special administrative regions, Hong Kong and Macau. The establishment of provinces, municipalities, and regions under the control of the central government follows, with some minor modifications, the administrative divisions historically adopted by Imperial China. The five autonomous regions were established to recognize the importance of ethnic minorities in China and their relationship to the Han majority. The five autonomous regions contain a larger concentration of ethnic minorities and a decision was made to allow ethnic minorities to enjoy greater autonomy with regard to certain aspects of local affairs.

(1) Local Levels

Provinces and their equivalents have a rank just below the central government in the political administrative hierarchy. Provinces have a rank that is analogous to the rank of a ministry in the central government in the government hierarchy. This high rank means that provinces are important political actors. Because all provincial level authorities are formally equal in rank to central government ministries, none of these units can issue binding orders to the other. Provinces are also major political actors because they can provide significant financial support to the central government and because all major central construction projects and enterprises require the active cooperation of the provincial level authorities in mobilizing and organizing resources and support services. While the central government can impose demands on the provinces, central level leaders understand that cooperation is a better long-term strategy than coercion in working with the provinces. The size of some provinces—Sichuan and Guangdong each has over 80 million people, both larger than some European countries—increases the importance of the cooperation of the provinces to Beijing. Central level leaders understand that it is not possible to govern a country the size of China without giving considerable authority to provincial level authorities and depending upon them to execute crucial tasks of developing and delivering goods and services at lower levels.

Below the provinces is the prefecture level, which exists only in some parts of the country. All told there are 143 prefectures and their equivalents in the autonomous regions and 185 cities of prefecture rank. Below the prefectures at the fourth level are the counties, which now include 1,919 counties. While adjustments are constantly being made to county boundaries, counties have been a basic administrative unit of the Chinese state for millennia. Some counties in China can trace back their continuous histories for over 2,000 years. Below the county level are the 910 cities or city districts; many cities, however, fall within a higher rank in the political administrative hierarchy because of their size or importance. As previously noted, Beijing, Shanghai, Tianjin, and Chongqing have provincial level status. Another 447 cities have the rank of county or higher and fall just below the provinces in the administrative hierarchy. At the fifth or lowest level are the townships of which there are more than 56,000. The organs of state government discussed below exist at all of these levels.

China also has two special administrative regions, Hong Kong and Macau, that contain a government structure that is quite different from those described in this chapter, due to historical reasons. Sovereignty over parts of Hong Kong and Macau was ceded in perpetuity by China to England and Portugal respectively as colonies. Hong Kong was under British rule for over 150 years and Macau was under Portuguese rule for over 500 years. Over time, both of these regions developed a culture and lifestyle vastly different from that on mainland China. In order to maintain the confidence of the residents of those two regions and of the international community, China decided to allow those two regions to enjoy far greater autonomy than any administrative divisions in China after Hong Kong and Macau were returned to Chinese sovereignty in 1997 and 1999 respectively.

Where the state apparatus and the lives of most individuals intersect is at the level of the "unit" or *danwei*. For most individuals, the *danwei* is the work unit in the factory, research institute, university, state-owned enterprise, or government bureau. For students, the *danwei* is the school or university and for unemployed urbanites, it is the residents' committee. The *danwei* is an extension of the state and is an integral part of the political administrative hierarchy; it is not a separate social organization. The state uses the *danwei* system as an extension of the government apparatus to control the behavior of individuals at the most basic social level. Prior to reforms, most urban enterprises consisted of *danweis* that provided employment, housing, schooling, and medical and pension benefits. The *danwei* also provided food coupons, administered the state family planning and birth control program, and mediated marriage disputes. Permission of the *danwei* was required for marriage, divorce, or changes in employment. Each of the higher-level political units had direct influence upon the *danwei*. For example, a large urban enterprise would have a cultural and education office subordinate to the local Party propaganda committee, a Party committee subordinate to the municipal Party committee, and a security committee subordinate to the local police organization. The state was able to extend its tentacles to reach the basic level of social life of the individual through the *danwei*.

Economic reforms have eroded the *danwei* system as a method of social control. Foreign investment enterprises such as joint ventures and wholly foreign-owned enterprises provide work units that are not merely extensions of the government apparatus but that are truly separate organizations from the government. Economic reforms have abolished the commune system, the *danwei* system for the massive agricultural sector. Reforms have also increased mobility in the countryside and in cities, creating a floating population of about 100 million people who are not tied to any urban work unit. The reforms have eroded the fundamental link between the state and the individual and one of the major tasks for China's leaders is to reestablish this link in the form of an alternative to the *danwei* system that has existed since the early history of the PRC.

With the exception of Hong Kong and Macau, the two special administrative regions, all of China's political and administrative units attempt to duplicate all government structures, described further below, with few exceptions, at every level of government from the highest central level to the lowest local level. Where this duplication may not be possible in detail at the *danwei* level, higher-level political and administrative units would extend their control to the *danwei* level by exerting influence over the *danwei* itself.

(2) Relationship of the Central and Local Level Authorities

A basic constitutional principle of the PRC is "democratic centrism" set forth in Article 3 of the 1982 Constitution. The basic tenets of democratic centrism, which apply to all facets of Chinese political life, including the Communist Party, are: the individual is subordinate to the group, the minority is subordinate to the majority, lower level authorities are subordinate to higher level authorities, and local authorities are subordinate to central level authorities. The application of democratic centrism to the state structure can be seen in the explanation in Article 3 of the relationship between the various levels of the state structure: the National People's Congress and the local people's congresses are elected by, responsible to, and subject to the supervision of the people; all administrative organs of the state are created by, responsible to, and subject to the supervision of the corresponding level of people's congresses; and local level authorities are subject to the unified leadership of central level authorities.

Under China's system, all sovereign state power resides in the central level authorities (as elected by the people) and the power that is enjoyed by provincial level authorities and below is delegated power from the central level authorities. This should be contrasted with the U.S. federal system in which the fifty states are sovereign entities and exercise all sovereign power except those delegated to the federal government by the U.S. Constitution. In the United States, the people, through the Constitution, have created a federal entity that is supreme over the states, but only in those areas where the federal government has been specifically delegated power by the Constitution. Other than in those areas where authority is delegated to the federal government, the states remain supreme in the U.S. system. By contrast to the U.S. federal system, which is a dual system of government, China is a unitary system that deposits all power in the central level authorities.

b. The National People's Congress

Article 2 of the PRC Constitution provides that "[a]ll power in the People's Republic of China belongs to the People. The National People's Congress and the local people's congresses at various levels are the organs through which the people exercise state power." The people's congress system exists in an ascending structure with congresses at the township, county, provincial, and national levels. The people's congresses at the county and township levels are directly elected by the people. The people's congresses at the provincial and national levels are elected by the congresses one level below. Although these elections are in theory democratic, they are in reality controlled by the CPC as further discussed below.

The National People's Congress is at the pinnacle of the system and is the "highest organ of state power." PRC Const., Art. 57. The NPC is elected for a term of five years and must meet in session once a year. Among other powers, the Constitution authorizes the NPC to amend the Constitution; supervise its enforcement; enact and amend basic laws; elect, appoint, and remove top officials, including the president of the PRC, the premier of the State Council, and the president of the Supreme People's Court; approve the state budget, plans for national economic and social development, and reports on the implementation of those plans; alter or annul decisions by the NPC Standing Committee; make decisions on questions of war and peace; organize inquiries into government organs and activities; and exercise other functions it deems appropriate for the highest organ of state power. *See* PRC Const., Art. 62. Apart from the Constitution, two other laws govern the structure of the NPC, the Organic Law of the NPC (1982) and the Procedural Rules of the NPC (1989). Both of these laws contain detailed rules on the structure and operation of the NPC.

The seats in the NPC are elected by thirty-four constituencies: the thirty-one provincial level constituencies discussed above, the People's Liberation Army (PLA), the Hong Kong Special Administrative Region, Taiwan (representatives are elected by the PRC for Taiwan), and since December 1999, the Macau Special Administrative Region. In 1998, 2,979 deputies were elected to the Ninth National People's Congress with 2,651 deputies elected from the thirty-one provincial level authorities and the second largest constituency of 268 elected from the PLA. The NPC's smallest membership was 1,226 in 1954 and its largest size was 3,497 in 1978, but otherwise it has consistently maintained a membership of approximately 3,000 members, with 2,978 members at the Sixth NPC (1983–1988), 2,970 at the Seventh NPC (1988–93), 2,977 at the Eighth NPC (1993–1998), 2,980 at the Ninth NPC (1998–2003), 2,985 at the Tenth NPC (2003–2008), and 2,987 at the Eleventh NPC (2008–2013). Not only does the large size of the NPC make it unwieldy as a working group, but also it meets only once a year at a session lasting several weeks. Most NPC deputies are not paid but have their major occupations outside the NPC. As a result, the NPC cannot be considered to be a professional deliberative body actively involved in its substantive work. In the past, the NPC has served mostly as a rubber-stamp approving decisions that have been made elsewhere by the state and Party apparatus. There are some indications, however, that the NPC has begun to take a more active role in law-making. This trend is discussed in more detail in Chapter 5 on the legislative process in the PRC.

The deputies in the NPC are formally elected by the people's congresses at the provincial level, except that special procedures are used in the case of Taiwan, Hong Kong, Macau, and the PLA. A list of the names of all of the candidates at all levels, including the county and township levels, however, is put forth by the Communist Party. The list of names generally corresponds exactly to the number of positions to be filled and the task of a particular constituency consists of approving the list. In the Ninth NPC, workers and farmers, who are supposed to be the leaders of the counties under Communist ideology, represented less than one-fifth of the deputies as compared with 26.6% in 1983. The military is over-represented with 9% of the seats for a population of just 3 million. The percentage of intellectuals has remained stable at 21% versus 23.4% in 1983 but the percentage of deputies holding an undergraduate degree has increased steadily from 44.5% in 1983 to 92% in 2008. One has to remain cautious about the quality of the education that the deputies claimed to have received, however, given that one can acquire a degree in China without actually fulfilling course requirements if one has the right position of power and influence. Perhaps the most noticeable trend in the NPC is the growing number of seats controlled by the CPC. Of the 2,087 delegates to the Eleventh NPC, about 73% of the seats are occupied by members of Communist Party, representing a noticeable increase from 68.4% in 1993 and the 62.5% in 1983.

The annual sessions of the NPC are convened by its Standing Committee, further discussed below. The session itself is managed by an elite group of the NPC, called the Presidium, elected at an informal meeting of the NPC held right before the formal session. The NPC Standing Committee prepares a list of persons to serve on the Presidium and as its executive chairmen. The executive chairmen conduct the meetings of the Presidium and the representatives take turns in chairing the plenary sessions of the NPC. The Presidium of the NPC nominates persons for many of the top government posts in the PRC, including the president of the PRC, the members of the NPC Standing Committee, the president of the Supreme People's Court, and the chairman of the Central Military Commission, among other top positions. The Presidium also decides which legislative bills will be included in the agenda for the NPC's plenary sessions. The Presidium, in effect, controls the NPC because it dictates the matters that are sent to the NPC for a vote of approval. Because the NPC Standing Committee nominates the persons who serve on the Presidium, the Standing Committee, in effect, controls the NPC.

c. The NPC Standing Committee

Under the Constitution, the NPC Standing Committee is the next highest organ of state power, although in practice the Standing Committee is far more powerful than the NPC as a whole, which only has marginal influence in the PRC. Much smaller, more professional, and meeting every two months usually for one week, the Standing Committee actually fulfills most of the functions of the NPC. The Standing Committee consists of a chairman, a number of vice-chairmen, and a secretary general. Under the Constitution, the chairman and vice-chairmen cannot serve more than two consecutive five-year terms. Most of the work of the Standing Committee occurs in the main areas of law-making, supervision of government organs (including the judiciary), and budgetary affairs. The members of the NPC Standing Committee are elected from among its members by the NPC from a list of names submitted and approved by the CPC.

By contrast to the approximately 3,000 members of the NPC who have other main occupations, the Standing Committee consists of 155 members who are supposed to work full-time for the NPC, although the prohibition against holding other employment applies only to other government jobs and does not include party, mass organization, teaching, or private jobs. In practice, about one-fifth of the Standing Committee works full-time only for the NPC. The 155 members are divided into three groups. There are 134 ordinary members of the Standing Committee, twenty-one members of the chairmanship, and a Standing Committee Party core group. The members of the Standing Committee are elected by the NPC in plenary session from among its general membership on the basis of a list submitted and approved by the Communist Party.

The twenty-one members of the chairmanship form the Standing Committee Council of Chairmen, which is the leading core of the NPC. The Council consists of the chairman (Wu Bangguo (2003–present)), nineteen vice-chairmen, and the secretary general of the NPC. Under the Constitution, this Council "directs the work of" and "handles the important day-to-day work of the Standing Committee." PRC Const., Art. 68. It is not known how often the Council of Chairmen meets, but it is likely that the Council meets at least once a month, with the most elite core meeting once a week. All of the members of the Council of Chairmen are elected by the NPC plenary session for a term of five years. Consistent with all other important elections, the list of candidates for the Standing Committee Council of Chairmen is submitted and approved by the CPC.

Directly under the NPC Standing Committee are nine specialized committees designed to focus on specific topics, such as the Law Committee, Nationalities Committee, Financial and Economic Affairs

Committee, Foreign Affairs Committee, and the Education, Science, Culture, and Public Health Committee. Six of the nine committees were restored by the 1982 Constitution and three additional committees, reflecting the increasing professionalization of the NPC, were created by the Seventh, Eighth, and Ninth NPCs respectively. Each committee consists of between twenty to thirty members, with five to six vice-chairmen among them. The committees consist of members who are considered specialists in the field and are generally scholars or administrators who have studied or served in the field for long periods. These committees conduct their work on a permanent basis under the supervision of the NPC Standing Committee or more directly under the Party core of the Standing Committee. The membership of the Standing Committee and the specialized committees overlap to a considerable extent. Of the 134 members of the Standing Committee (excluding the twenty-one chairmen of the 155 total Standing Committee members), 70% serve on the specialized committees. Of the total of 210 members of the specialized committees, two-thirds are members of the NPC Standing Committee. The overlapping membership means that there is little interaction between the specialized committees, the NPC Standing Committee, or the NPC as a whole. The specialized committees tend to conduct their work independent of the NPC, with supervision by the Party core.

Within the twenty-one members of the Council of Chairmen is the most elite subgroup, the Party core group, which consists of the NPC chairman, the NPC secretary general, and the NPC vice-chairman. The Party core group is an executive council that sets the agenda and organizes the meetings of the Standing Committee. The Party core group also supervises the larger NPC Party memberships group and through this organization can direct all party members how to vote in the case of legislative bills, nominations, or resolutions.

The organizational structure of the NPC, its specialized committees, and the Standing Committee and its subgroups illustrate how power is divided among a pyramid structure with a large base of about 3,000 deputies to an elite group of about twenty-one chairmen within the Standing Committee and the ultra elite Party core of three or so members. While in theory power and authority flows upward from the base of the pyramid towards the top, the reality is quite the opposite. Rather than flowing from the bottom to the top, power is controlled by a small elite professional group at the top that controls a much larger, less professional base constituency.

d. Powers of the NPC Standing Committee

Under Article 67 of the PRC Constitution, the powers of the NPC Standing Committee are nearly as broad as those granted to the NPC itself. Only revision of the Constitution, voting on major laws, and nomination of the highest state leaders are within the exclusive authority of the NPC plenary session. The Constitution also allows the NPC to delegate functions and powers to its Standing Committee. As the Constitution does not specify procedures for the delegation of powers and does not require that such delegations be public, there can be all types of behind-the-scenes delegations and transfers of power. For example, although the Constitution provides that the NPC has the authority to appoint the premier of the State Council, it was the NPC Standing Committee that appointed Li Peng interim premier in November 1987. Presumably this power of appointment was delegated by the NPC to its Standing Committee, but when and how the NPC delegated this power of appointment to the Standing Committee has never been made public.

The authority and influence of the NPC Standing Committee are further enhanced by stipulations in Article 67 that the Standing Committee enjoys some powers that the NPC as a whole does not. These powers include supervising the work of the State Council, the Central Military Commission, the Supreme People's Court, and the Supreme People's Procuratorate; annulling central and local regulations, decisions, and actions that violate the Constitution; appointing ambassadors; ratifying treaties; and making decisions on the granting of special pardons, general mobilization, or the imposition of martial law on the nation or in a particular province. Detailed regulations on the exercise of the powers of the Standing Committee are contained in Procedural Rules of the NPC Standing Committee enacted by the Standing Committee in 1987.

e. The State Council

Under the Constitution, the State Council is defined as the central people's government of the PRC, as the executive body of the NPC, and as "the highest organ of state administration." PRC Const., Art. 85. On internal matters, the State Council is the organ that operates the government, economy, and industry of the PRC. On external matters, the State Council represents the sovereignty of the state and handles the state's diplomatic matters. The State Council is under the direct authority of the NPC, although in practice the State Council is more powerful than either the NPC or its Standing Committee.

The State Council consists of a premier, several vice-premiers, state councilors (equivalent to vice-premiers), the ministers of the various ministries and commissions, the auditor general, the governor of the People's Bank, and the secretary general. Under the State Council are a set of national level ministries, commissions, and bureaus that are in charge of the numerous and varied sectors of the PRC economy and government affairs. Ministries are generally in charge of specialized administrative affairs whereas commissions are in charge of more comprehensive administrative affairs or in charge of issues that concern a number of different ministries. For example, the Ministry of Finance and the Ministry of Education are in charge of regulating financial and educational affairs whereas the State Economic and Trade Commission is in charge of regulating economics and trade nationwide that cross many ministerial lines and the State Development and Planning Commission is in charge of long-term and annual comprehensive economic development plans. Ministries are largely in charge of operating the urban economy whereas the rural sector has been under the more direct supervision of the Party bureaucracy. Ministries are divided into those that operate the major economic sectors of the urban economy and those that operate major government functions. For example, separate ministries have been put in charge of electronics, metallurgy, communications, railways, and water resources. Other ministries are in charge of important sectors of governance. The Ministry of Public Security is in charge of safeguarding the public against crime and other dangers, the Ministry of Justice oversees the legal system and the legal profession, and the Ministry of Commerce is in charge of domestic and foreign trade and investment. Over the years, the ministries have been reorganized, merged, and split apart in numerous permutations in order to achieve higher efficiencies and to resolve internecine disputes over jurisdiction and resources.

Also beneath the State Council are a number of administrations, bureaus in charge of specific industries, and various research institutes, banks, and news agencies. Several of the administrations are involved in the regulation of key industrial and economic affairs, such as the State Administration of Industry and Commerce, which is charged with both regulating and developing domestic industry and commercial activity, and the General Administration of Customs, which is in charge of tariffs and border control. A number of the bureaus are in charge of specific key industries, such as the State Light Industry Bureau in charge of chemicals and consumer products, and the State Tobacco Monopoly Bureau. As of this writing, there are a total of twenty-two ministries (at the peak there were over sixty ministries), twenty-four administrations and commissions, and a smaller number of offices, research institutes, banks, and news agencies. This bureaucratic structure is reproduced at the provincial and local levels with the lower level entities under the leadership of the corresponding central level authorities. The terminology changes somewhat as one goes down the bureaucratic structure, but the overall organizational structure remains the same at all levels. Virtually every ministry, commission, administration, bureau, and other central level entity heads its own national hierarchy that extends from Beijing down to the provinces, cities, counties, and townships. Some of these bureaucracies are highly centralized with most of the power at the top and lower level units accountable to higher level units but in other cases the lower level units are largely responsible to local Party and government units, giving rise to issues of local protectionism, a serious problem in many parts of China where local interests are served at the expense of national policies. The distribution of lines of authority, power, and accountability often vary and are constantly being changed, giving rise to individual problems. At the national level, these organizations are headed by ministers and directors all under the supervision of the premier of the State Council. In sum, the State Council and the various entities under its direct supervision and control form the massive administrative apparatus that operates the economic and governmental affairs of state, although, as previously noted, the lines of authority extending downward to the local levels can vary greatly depending upon the bureaucracy.

The premier of the State Council directs the work of the State Council. In effect, the premier is in charge of the administration and operation of all aspects of the state and is one of the most powerful positions in the PRC government. Under the Constitution, as in the case of the chairman and vice-chairmen of the NPC, the premier and vice-premiers of the State Council cannot serve more than two consecutive terms, with each of the terms corresponding with each of the five-year terms of the NPC. *See* PRC Const., Art. 87. The State Council has about fifty total members and meets either in plenary or executive session. As in the case of the NPC, the more powerful and effective group is the executive committee, which in turns leads the entire State Council. The executive committee consists of the premier, the vice-premiers, the state councilors, and the secretary general.

Among other powers granted by the Constitution, the State Council is authorized to direct its ministries and commissions; to supervise the work of local organs of state administration; to draw up and implement plans for economic and social development; to devise the state budget; to direct and administer economic affairs; to direct and administer matters pertaining to education, science, culture, public health, physical culture and family planning; to direct and administer civil affairs, police and security functions, and judicial affairs; to conduct foreign relations and conclude treaties with foreign nations; to direct and build national defense; and to exercise any other functions delegated to it by the NPC or its Standing Committee. *See* PRC Const., Art. 89. In addition, the State Council also has legislative powers; it can enact administrative measures that have the force of law. Indeed, although the NPC is regarded as China's legislature, in practice the State Council conducts the bulk of law-making in China. Some 70% of all law bills originate from the State Council and its organs, either drafted by a particular ministry under the State Council or by a special working group made up of the departments involved. Once the bill is submitted to the State Council, it is screened and approved by the State Council Legislative Affairs Office and the State Council executive committee; the bill is then sent to the Communist Party for approval and then forwarded to the NPC and put on its agenda.

f. President of the PRC

The official head of state of the PRC is its president, elected by the NPC. As with other top positions, the office of the president is limited to two terms to coincide with the terms of the NPC. *See*

PRC CONST., Art. 79. The position, first established under the 1954 Constitution but with substantially more powers, was left vacant during the anarchy of the Cultural Revolution. A telling indication of the levels of lawlessness that existed during the Cultural Revolution is that the first president of the PRC, Liu Shaoqi, was detained and tortured to death by Red Guards. The office of the presidency was abolished by the 1975 and 1978 Constitutions; it was reestablished by the 1982 Constitution.

The office of the presidency is largely a symbolic or ceremonial position. The president is to perform functions such as promulgating statutes, appointing or removing top government officials, conferring state medals of honor, and receiving foreign visitors all in pursuance of the decisions and directions of the NPC and its Standing Committee. *See* PRC Const., Arts. 80–81. As of this writing, Hu Jintao is the President of the PRC. An office of the vice-presidency of the PRC has also been created by the 1982 Constitution to assist the president in his work. Xi Jinping is the vice-president of the PRC as of this writing. Xi is expected to become president when Hu is required to step down in 2012.

While the office of the presidency is largely ceremonial, the power of any particular president can vary greatly depending upon his personal prestige and any other offices that he might hold concurrently. The case of Liu Shaoqi, discussed above, is an indication of how little power the office can represent. But two other presidents, Mao Zedong and the current officeholder, Hu Jintao, represent the opposite extreme. Like Mao, Hu also holds the position of secretary general of the CPC, the top position in the Party hierarchy, and the chairmanship of the Central Military Commission, which empowers him to control the military. The most important offices in the Party and state hierarchy are the secretary general of the CPC, the premier of the State Council, and the chairman of the Central Military Commission and Hu, like Jiang Zemin, his immediate predecessor as president, now holds two of these three positions. The third position, the premier of the State Council is currently held by Wen Jiabao. While the presidency is a ceremonial office, the two other positions held by Hu wield significant power. The combination of the presidency, the symbolic head of state, and his two other positions allows Hu to enjoy absolute authority in China and to be an actual, not merely a symbolic, head of state for China. While Hu's tenure as president is limited to two terms, he may be able to exert considerable influence and power if he maintains his two other positions, for which there are no term limits, after he steps down as president in 2012. Jiang Zemin, Hu's immediate predecessor, continued to hold the chairmanship of the Central Military Commission until Jiang finally relinquished it to Hu on March 13, 2005. Jiang's case is one example of how individuals can continue to maintain power and influence despite the existence of explicit term limits in the formal government structure. Another prominent example is Li Peng who was at one time the premier of the State Council.

After he left this position in March, 1998, he then became chairman of the NPC Standing Committee. After he stepped down as premier, Li also maintained his position as a member of the Politburo Standing Committee, the highest authority within the Communist Party. PRC leaders whose terms in one office expire are able to continue to exert power for some period afterwards by assuming another powerful office or by holding other offices for which there are no term limits.

g.   The Central Military Commission

Under Article 93 of the Constitution, the Central Military Commission (CMC) directs the armed forces of the PRC. The CMC is composed of a chairman, vice-chairman, and several members. The chairman assumes overall responsibility for the work of the CMC and the chairman, not the CMC, is under the authority of the NPC and its Standing Committee. Unlike most other top positions, the chairmanship of the CMC and its other seats are not subject to term restrictions.

Prior to the 1982 Constitution, the CMC was entirely an organ within the Communist Party and was not an organ of the government. The 1975 and 1978 Constitutions abolished all government organs in charge of the armed forces and explicitly provided that the armed forces were under the leadership of the CMC of the Communist Party. Consistent with its general approach of restoring government offices abolished by the 1975 and 1978 Constitutions, the 1982 Constitution established the CMC as an organ of government power, but it did not alter the existing structure of having a CMC within the Party. As a result, there are officially two CMCs, one that is an organ of government, and a second CMC, which is an organ of the Communist Party. The membership of the two CMCs is identical. The Communist Party nominates all of the members of its CMC, including the chairman, to fill the same positions on the CMC within the PRC government and expects the National People's Congress to endorse them. From the inception of the 1982 Constitution to the present, all candidates nominated by the Party for the CMC have been endorsed by the NPC and there is no indication that this pattern of rubber-stamping the Party's nominations will change in the near future. This present political structure ensures that the Party controls China's military forces and reinforces its status as the supreme authority.

The chairmanship of the CMC is an important position that can influence other organs of government. Deng Xiaoping, who never held the position of president of the PRC or secretary general of the Party, held the chairmanship of the CMC during the 1980s and 1990s. From this position, he engineered China's economic reforms that changed the course of its history. As chairman of the CMC and through the force of his personality, prestige, and loyalty from others, Deng was regarded as having absolute authority in China; it was not derived from the Constitution or any written laws.

2. HUMAN RIGHTS

Chapter 2 of the 1982 Constitution is entitled "The Fundamental Rights and Duties of Citizens." It comes before Chapter 3 on the state structure and is intended to emphasize the importance of human rights in modern China. China's incorporation of human rights into the 1982 Constitution has been influenced by developments in the international community and by the western approach towards human rights. China is a signatory to the two most important international treaties concerning human rights, the International Covenant on Civil and Political Rights and the International Covenant on Economic, Social, and Cultural Rights. These two covenants were designed to implement the influential Universal Declaration of Human Rights, a non-binding aspirational instrument adopted by the General Assembly of the United Nations in 1948. While the two covenants are binding international treaties and while China is a signatory to both, China has yet to ratify these covenants by obtaining the approval of the National People's Congress or its Standing Committee. As a result, the treaties have yet entered into force creating binding international legal obligations on China. (However, as China is a signatory to the 1969 Vienna Convention on the Law of Treaties, 115 U.N.T.S. 331, China is bound under Article 18 of the Vienna Convention to refrain from any acts that would defeat the object and purpose of treaties awaiting ratification.) Although both treaties continue to await ratification, China has adopted the language and general concepts contained in these treaties in its Constitution and domestic laws. China has also acceded to and ratified other international human rights treaties and is in theory bound by these treaties although it is unclear whether China considers itself to be bound by international laws that conflict with China's own domestic legislation. With the enactment of numerous recent laws, China now has a substantial and comprehensive legislative framework concerning human rights that appears to be consistent with international standards. But relying on the language alone of China's constitutional and legislative materials would present a misleading picture of human rights in China. While China has been influenced by international developments, China continues to view the subject of human rights in ways that are fundamentally different from certain western traditions. Before turning to a detailed examination of the contents of the Constitution, the discussion below sets forth some general observations about human rights in China.

China does not have a tradition of a natural rights theory, which continues to be influential in the United States and some other western countries. Under a natural rights theory, human rights are inherent in all persons and are inseparable from persons and at least some rights are absolute and inviolable. These rights serve to protect individuals against the improper use of state power. The law recognizes and enforces such rights, but these rights precede and transcend the law. By contrast, as previously discussed, traditional China did not have a concept of human rights at all. While the 1982 Constitution creates a new emphasis on human rights, it proceeds upon the assumption that these rights are created and recognized by the state and conferred upon individuals through law. Human rights are not inherent and inviolable and do not exist outside the law; they are created and conferred upon individuals by the state. As the creator of these rights, the state can, in theory, also limit or even abolish them. The rights created by the 1982 Constitution were intended to prevent the type of social chaos and anarchy created by the Cultural Revolution but they were not intended to create safeguards for individuals against the power of the state.

In contrast to western traditions emphasizing the rights of the individual, the emphasis in both traditional and modern China has been on the interests of the group or collective over the interests of the individual. Order and harmony, not individual freedoms, are the highest values of society and the rights of the individual must yield when in conflict with the interests of the collective. This concept is explicitly incorporated into the Constitution in Article 51:

> Citizens of the People's Republic of China, in exercising their freedoms and rights, may not infringe upon the interests of the state, of society or of the collective, or upon the lawful freedoms and rights of other citizens.

A number of other provisions in the Constitution also limit the exercise of rights if they conflict with state interests. For example, Article 36 begins with the broad principle that "[c]itizens ... enjoy freedom of religious belief" but then adds the caveat that "[n]o one may make use of religion to engage in activities that disrupt public order, impair the health of citizens or interfere with the educational system of the state." PRC Const., Art. 36. Many other examples exist in the 1982 Constitution. In addition, the PRC has also repeatedly emphasized that any exercise of constitutional rights is unlawful if it violates any of the four basic principles set forth in the preamble to the Constitution: the leadership of the CPC, adherence to Marxism–Leninism–Mao Zedong Thought–Deng Xiaoping Theory, upholding the people's democratic dictatorship, and keeping to the socialist road.

Consistent with a priority on collective interests and a national agenda and direction provided by the government, the rights created by the PRC Constitution emphasize social, economic, and cultural rights, such as the rights to work and to an education, as opposed to civil and political rights. This emphasis is consistent not only with the practice of socialist countries but with developing countries as well. The Constitution also introduces the notion of duties as well as rights and connects the enjoyment of rights to the fulfillment of duties. All nations impose some duties on their citizens but China appears to be unique in setting forth these duties in its Constitution. Among the duties are safeguarding

the security, honor, and interests of the motherland; preserving the nation's unity; observing the
law and social ethics; performing military service;
and paying taxes as required by law. *See* PRC
Const., Arts. 52–56. The explicit incorporation of
duties into the Constitution reinforces the less than
absolute nature of human rights by emphasizing
their reciprocal dependence on the fulfillment of
civic duties. The linking of rights to duties also
indicates that duties are more fundamental than
rights, that the enjoyment of rights is based upon
the prior fulfillment of duties, and that the failure
to fulfill duties will result in the forfeiture of rights.

In March 2004, Article 33 of the PRC Constitution was amended to provide that "[t]he state respects and protects human rights." This is the first
explicit recognition of the importance of human
rights in the history of PRC Constitutions. However, this amendment does not portend a fundamental
change in the PRC. As previously noted, the PRC
Constitution should be viewed as an embodiment of
the current policies of the Communist Party and
does not have any direct legal effect in the absence
of implementing legislation. The inclusion of an
explicit reference to human rights in the Constitution does not offer any new protections to individuals within the PRC and no one in China views this
new amendment as a source of new protections. Nor
does the amendment signal a policy change within
the Communist Party. The CPC has made it clear
in the past that it will severely punish any one who
challenges its authority or who subverts the inter-

ests of the state. Despite the reference to human rights in the 2004 amendment, there is no indication that the position of the CPC in these matters has changed.

What then is the purpose or effect of the 2004 amendment on human rights? First, the amendment allows China to claim legitimacy and to answer its critics. The Communist Party can now assert that China explicitly protects human rights. Even if the 2004 amendment serves a largely symbolic purpose only, the amendment does remedy omissions in the previous Constitutions, which never mentioned the state's recognition of human rights. Second, the amendment is a reflection of current world trends and recent developments. The recognition of human rights has gained increasing importance in recent world history and human rights are increasingly the subject of recent multilateral treaties and other international instruments. A prominent example of an influential multilateral instrument is the Charter of the Fundamental Social Rights of Workers promulgated in 1989 by the European Union in the form of a non-binding declaration. The explicit reference to human rights within the PRC Constitution is an acknowledgement of these world trends. Third, the 2004 amendment on human rights might embolden reformers within China as well as international groups to seek further concrete progress in the area of human rights. The existence of the reference to human rights in the Constitution, even though without legal effect, may serve as the basis for arguments by reformers that China must respond with real, not merely symbolic, changes in the area of human rights. From the Party's perspective, this may be an unintended consequence of the 2004 amendment.

3. CONSTITUTIONAL RIGHTS

The rights enumerated under the 1982 Constitution are (1) equality before the law; (2) political rights and freedoms, such as the right to freedom of speech, publication, assembly, association, procession, and demonstration, the right to criticize government entities and officials, and the right to compensation for the violation of citizens' rights by government entities and officials; (3) religious freedom; (4) personal freedom; (5) social and economic rights, such as the right to social welfare and the right to work; (6) rights of equality for women and rights relating to the family; (7) rights of overseas and returning Chinese; and (8) cultural and educational rights, such as the right to receive an education. See PRC Const., Arts. 33–49.

The inclusion of the right to equality before the law is a significant development. As previously noted, traditional China did not have a notion of equal treatment regardless of status before the law but discriminated on the basis of one's place in the Confucian social hierarchy. In the early history of the PRC, the Anti–Rightist Campaign rejected the notion of equality and a system of institutionalized discrimination was implemented against millions of people on the basis of their class origins. Persons with 'bad class origins' included landlords, rich peasants, and counterrevolutionaries and anyone else who might have oppressed peasants and workers. Anyone with such origins was stigmatized, viewed as potential criminals, and suffered discrimination in employment and educational opportunities. Anyone with a bad class origin who committed an offense was treated more harshly than someone with 'a good class origin' such as a peasant, worker, or revolutionary. During the many mass campaigns, persons with questionable backgrounds were the prime targets of the hunt for class enemies, were the first victims of struggle sessions, and were the most likely to be found guilty of some crime against the state. The mindless persecution and ruin of many such persons during the Cultural Revolution was one reason for the rejection of this discriminatory approach and the institution of the principle of equality before the law. Other improvements include provisions in the Constitution that prohibit unlawful intrusions into homes and the false accusations against others, which were common terror tactics during the Cultural Revolution. *See* PRC Const., Arts. 38–39. These steps, designed to prevent mass anarchy and social disorder, represent a significant improvement of the human rights environment in modern China.

The March 2004 amendments, discussed in the previous section, also amplified the rights of citizens to own and inherit property. Article 10 of the Constitution was amended to provide that in the event that the state expropriates property for public purposes, the state must pay compensation. The 2004 amendment added the requirement of compensation, which had been missing in the prior version of Article 10. The 2004 amendment to Article 13 emphasizes that the lawful private property of citizens may not be encroached upon and replaces earlier language that the state protects private property. This new language strengthens the rights of citizens to own and inherit private property free from the interference of the state. As in the case of the 2004 amendment concerning the state recognition of human rights, however, these amendments relating to private property do not provide any new concrete rights to citizens because the PRC Constitution has no direct legal force and creates no new legal protections. The amendments do create greater confidence on the part of PRC citizens in their ownership of private property and may be intended to assuage China's growing middle class that their private holdings and personal wealth are safe. The amendments may also be intended to provide greater confidence to multinational companies and foreign investors that the business climate in China is stable and that profits earned will be protected.

In the area of civil and political rights, there has been less progress if measured by international and western standards. While China recognizes a number of civil and political rights in theory in the Constitution, these rights are not recognized in practice because of an absence of implementing legislation. As previously noted, the Constitution is not self-implementing and in the absence of legislation, PRC citizens find that they have no way to exercise their constitutional rights. For example, while the Constitution recognizes the freedom of association, there is no valid legal procedure to register a new political party. Recently, two individuals attempted to set up a political party called the "Chinese Democratic Party" as part of their right of association as set forth in the Constitution. They were arrested and sentenced to jail for the crime of attempting to subvert the state.

In the view of the Communist Party and some scholars, China is not yet at the stage of economic development that justifies a widespread recognition of civil and political rights. According to the CPC, the state sector continues to play a significant role in the economy and there is not yet a sufficiently large and independent middle class in China that would be the base for exercising political and civil rights. Until a large middle class emerges, it is not yet appropriate to create the political reform that would be the result of granting civil and political rights. The lack of implementing legislation in the area of civil and political rights, the lack of more detailed definitions of broad terms describing human rights in the Constitution, and the lack of interest on the part of the CPC to recognize and enforce civil and political rights have combined to create an environment in which such rights are not widely available to PRC citizens.

A recent example of the clash between civil and political rights and the interests of the state is the crackdown on the Falun Gong movement, which mixes Buddhist beliefs with slow motion martial arts exercises. By the PRC's own count, at its peak the movement attracted between 3 and 6 million followers of an ideology that in many ways clashed with the ideology of the Communist Party. Party leaders became alarmed in April 1999 when 10,000 Falun Gong followers surrounded the leadership compound in Beijing in silent protest. This protest, although peaceful, was considered by the Communist Party to be a bold and insulting challenge to its power and incensed Party leaders. With its millions of members, Falun Gong represented for the Party the most serious challenge to its monopoly on power since the democracy movement of the late 1980s that culminated in the use of military force in Tiananmen Square in 1989. Since the crackdown on the movement began, there have been reports of sudden disappearances of Falun Gong followers, torture, brainwashing, and up to 250 deaths of followers in custody. Some of the tactics used to hunt down Falun Gong members are similar to those used during the mass terror campaign movements conducted by the Party under the leadership of Mao Zedong.

E. THE CONSTITUTION AND THE STATE

The 1982 Constitution and its amendments set forth the basic ideology of the state, the state power structure, and the rights and duties of citizens in China. The Constitution embodies the fundamental national goals of economic development and modernization. It also represents significant progress in the area of human rights by comparison with the

policies of the Cultural Revolution as embodied in
the 1975 and 1978 Constitutions. China fares less
well in the area of human rights if measured by
some international and western standards. A reading of the Constitution alone, however, would create
an incomplete and misleading picture of state power
and human rights in modern China. Indeed, although the Constitution sets forth the basic out-
lines of state power, the real power structure in
China is not to be found anywhere in the Constitution. Real power lies in the hands of the Communist
Party, the subject of the next chapter.

CHAPTER FOUR

THE COMMUNIST PARTY OF CHINA

Given the pervasive role of the Communist Party of China in all facets of the Chinese state and society, any treatment of China's legal system would be wholly inadequate without an examination of the CPC. This chapter examines the role of the Communist Party in the Chinese state and society, its structure, and how it maintains and exercises its power.

At the outset, it may be useful to set forth the relationship of this chapter to the prior chapter on the PRC Constitution and state structure as well as the relationship between the Communist Party and the PRC government. As discussed in the previous chapter, the PRC Constitution vests power and authority in the political and administrative structures that form the lawful government of China; the exercise of power through these structures is the legitimate exercise of power. This chapter focuses on the CPC, which is a political party and not a governmental entity. A political party is a body of voters formed for the purpose of influencing or controlling the policies and conduct of government through the nomination and election of its candidates for office. By installing its top leaders in leading government positions and its members throughout the PRC government apparatus, the CPC is able to influence and control the PRC government. At certain points, the organs of the PRC government and the CPC appeared to be fused or merged together with the CPC exercising effective power through its control of the government organs. When the CPC exercises power through the government apparatus of the PRC as set forth in the Constitution, it exercises legitimate power. If the CPC were to exercise powers directly and not through the filter of government organs, as appeared to be provided for under the 1975 and 1978 Constitutions, there might arise concerns about the legitimacy of its rule as it is not a government entity. Under the present political system in the PRC, the government structure serves the important purpose of legitimizing the power exercised by the CPC. These themes will be developed throughout this chapter.

A. THE ROLE OF THE CPC IN CHINESE SOCIETY

The CPC views itself as the leader of the Chinese people because of reasons traced to history and destiny, much in the same way that ruling governments have always viewed their legitimacy in traditional China. The official state ideology, expressed in the four principles in the preamble of the Constitution, is that twentieth century history has shown that only the Communist Party can save the Chinese people and lead them to happy lives. In many ways, the CPC sees its legitimacy as based upon its rightful insurrection and overthrow of an existing ruling government that had forfeited its right to rule the people much in the same way that a successful insurrection in Imperial China demonstrated that an existing emperor had forfeited the Mandate of Heaven. The success of the Chinese revolution has affirmed that the CPC is the legitimate ruler of China and has been chosen by the Chinese people much in the same way that the Mandate of Heaven passed to the leader of a successful insurrection in Imperial China. Besieged and near extinction at various points at the beginning of its existence in the 1920s and 1930s, the Communists were able to surmount seemingly overwhelming odds to vanquish the Nationalist government after the defeat of Japan in the Second World War. The Communists were able to triumph even though the Nationalists had the backing of the United States and had numerical superiority in fighting men, superior weapons, and equipment. If the lessons of Chinese history are an accurate guide, the CPC, once having overcome seemingly overwhelming odds and paid the costly price of obtaining power, is not likely to relinquish it voluntarily. In the more than 2,000 years of Chinese history dating back to the earliest Imperial Dynasty, the Eastern Zhou (771–256 BC), no ruling government of mainland China has ever voluntarily relinquished or transferred power to a succeeding government. No succeeding government has ever assumed power without destroying the presiding government.

1. HISTORY OF THE CPC

The CPC was formed in 1921 at a time of turmoil and great political uncertainty in China. The last Qing emperor had abdicated the throne but early attempts to form a stable republican government were unsuccessful as a succession of warlords competed for power through the use of their private armies. A tenuous consolidation of power was accomplished by Chiang Kai-shek in the Northern Expedition of 1927 when he defeated or absorbed the warlords in his Nationalist government, but in 1921 when the Communist Party was formed, China's future course and its political fortunes were far from settled. The goals of the CPC were to overthrow the ruling gentry class through revolution and to install a dictatorship of the proletariat, but this bold scheme seemed scarcely possible when the CPC held its first meeting in Shanghai in 1921 attended by only fifty members. Several times in the next decade, the CPC teetered on the brink of extinction at the hands of Chiang's Nationalist government, which launched a ruthless campaign of extermination against the CPC beginning in 1927 and hunted Party members as outlaws and bandits, executing many suspected Communists by beheadings on the spot in the streets. The famous Long March from 1934–35 allowed the battered and beleaguered CPC to regroup and gather strength in the remote mountains of Yenan. It was also during the arduous Long March that Mao Zedong achieved primacy within the CPC. The "Long March cadres" were to enjoy a prestige that would set them apart from within the Party itself and would lead the Communist Party movement from the time of the March to the 1990s when the last of the cadres passed from the political scene.

When Japan launched an all out invasion of China in 1937, Chiang was forced to agree to form a united front with the Communists in a war of resistance against Japan, although neither Chiang nor Mao ever trusted each other. The united front allowed the Party to gain strength in numbers and the support of the peasants in the countryside. By contrast with the Nationalist soldiers who were notoriously corrupt and who abused the peasantry through rape, killings, and pillaging, Communist soldiers were polite and respectful to the general populace. This represented quite a change to the long-suffering peasants for whom soldiers and bandits appeared to be one and the same. Whereas Chiang seemed indifferent to the plight of the peasants and workers, the Communists made the welfare of the peasants and workers the centerpiece of their political program. By the time Japan was defeated and the nation was on the verge of civil war in 1945, the CPC had grown to over 1 million members. Currently, the CPC has over 73.36 million members and is the largest political party in the world. Approximately one out of every eighteen persons in China is a member of the Party and virtually all of China's government and business elites are Party members. Membership in the Party is required for professional advancement in government, academia, business, and most other professions.

2.   OTHER POLITICAL PARTIES

Given the dominance of the CPC over Chinese society and its own view of its leadership role, it may be surprising that China officially endorses a multi-party system of political parties under the leadership of the CPC. A multi-party system does not mean that anyone can organize a political party. There are eight officially recognized democratic parties; they are also known as the united front parties because they joined the united patriotic front in the 1940s during the civil war between the Nationalists and the Communists. During the turbulent era of the 1960s and most of the 1970s, these democratic parties came under criticism and vanished from the political scene, holding no party congresses until October 1979 when the party congresses were resurrected during the new era of reform and the democratic parties were encouraged to play a limited role in the political system.

There are now over 720,000 members of the eight democratic parties. The CPC exercises firm financial and supervisory control over these parties and has allocated special responsibility for them to the United Front Work Department of the CPC Central Committee. Many members of the democratic parties are also members of the CPC. The budgets of the democratic parties are incorporated into the state budget and employees of these parties are registered as official state employees with regular government salaries.

Apart from the democratic parties, the Chinese People's Political Consultative Conference (CPPCC) is the most important institution of the system of multi-party cooperation and political consultation. The CPPCC is comprised of representatives of the CPC, the eight democratic parties, non-party personages, social organizations, ethnic minorities, Taiwan, Hong Kong, Macau, and returned overseas Chinese. The CPPCC has a national committee; local committees are established at the provincial level and can also be established at the county level. Like the National People's Congress, the CPPCC National Committee meets once a year usually at the same time as the yearly meeting of the NPC to allow members to sit in on the NPC meetings. Also like the NPC, the CPPCC has a five-year term and is led by a standing committee. The main function of the CPPCC is to offer views on political matters and to give advice on government matters to the CPC. The CPPCC is also encouraged to exercise supervision over government and CPC work by putting forth criticism and suggestions.

The major political purpose served by the CPPCC and the multi-party system structure is a legitimating function for the CPC, which can claim that it has consulted with representatives from all walks of life in the PRC before going forward with its program. As the ruling party, the CPC hears all points of view and criticism and makes an informed decision after consultation with the various representatives in the CPPCC.

The Structure of the Communist Party of China

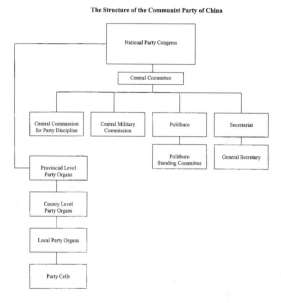

3. THE STRUCTURE OF THE CPC

The structure of the CPC is set forth in its 1982 Constitution (as opposed to the 1982 Constitution of the PRC), which was most recently amended in 1997 to adopt Deng Xiaoping Thought as the guiding principle of the CPC. The formal organizational structure of the CPC is similar to the structures of the National People's Congress examined in the previous chapter. Both institutions use a pyramid structure in which, in theory, power is granted by the lower levels to representatives at higher levels. As in the case of the NPC, the reality is also quite the opposite in the CPC. A small elite group actually makes most of the decisions for the CPC.

The leading organs of the CPC are its National Party Congress and its Central Committee. The National Party Congress is held once in every five years with the number of delegates and the method of their selection to be determined by the Central Committee. The Party Congress is generally held at the same time as the National People's Congress to allow Party members to sit in on both sessions. The term of office of the members of the Central Committee is five years. The Central Committee is required by the Party Constitution to hold a plenary session or a plenum at least once a year. The Seventeenth National Party Congress was held from October 10 to 21, 2007 and was attended by 2,217 delegates. When it was elected, the Seventeenth Central Committee had 9 full members and 16 alternate members. The Central Committee has a number of departments at the national level that assume responsibility over a number of areas. Those units that have existed continuously since 1949 include departments for the following areas: organization (in charge of personnel appointments); propaganda (in charge of media, education, political study, and political health); united front (in charge of relations with other political parties and non-partisan comrades); and international liaison (in charge of foreign affairs and relations with communist parties from other countries). There is also a general office that coordinates many of the administrative details of the central level Party apparatus, a subordinate organs committee to do Party work in organs directly under the Central Committee, and a state organs committee, which is responsible for delivering Party documents and other materials to the appropriate Party groups in the central government of the PRC. At times, the Central Committee has also operated a policy research office.

The leadership of the Central Committee is exercised by its Political Bureau or Politburo consisting of between fourteen to twenty-four members. Each member of the Politburo is one of the power elite in China, although most members of the Politburo, like the Central Committee and the National Party Congress, have other major occupations. Usually some members of the Politburo head distant provinces, such as Guangdong province in the southeast, and presumably miss most meetings.

The inner circle of the Politburo, the Politburo Standing Committee, is the truly powerful core of the Party. This core group consists of from four to six members and meets frequently at least on a weekly basis, although their exact schedule is not known as their meetings are not announced publicly. One of the members of the Politburo Standing Committee is the general secretary of the Central Committee, considered to be the top post in the Party since 1982. Prior to 1982, the top post was the chairman of the Communist Party who headed the Politburo Standing Committee. Mao Zedong held this post from 1945 until his death in 1976. This post was abolished in 1982 to prevent others from using this post to create a personality cult and rise above the Party as Mao had done during his tenure. The general secretary is responsible for convening the meetings of the Politburo and its Standing Committee. The general secretary is also in charge of the secretariat, which serves as support for the Politburo and the Central Committee. The secretariat is in charge of producing documents for Politburo consideration and in conveying Politburo instructions to lower level bureaucracies to put into operation. The current general secretary is Hu Jintao (as of 2009) who is also the chairman of the powerful Central Military Commission and holds the ceremonial position of president of the PRC.

Also at the national level is the Central Military Commission (CMC) of the Party, which has been identical in membership to that of the Central Military Commission of the PRC since 1982. The CMC controls China's military forces and is one of the most powerful government organs in the PRC. The complete identity between the CMC of the Party and the CMC of the PRC government allows the Party to control the military. Members of the CMC are appointed by the Party Central Committee. Another national level Party organ is the Central Committee for Discipline Inspection, which is charged with enforcing party discipline and is elected by the National Party Congress.

Although the power structure appears to indicate that members at lower levels elect members at higher levels and that power is delegated or transferred by members at lower levels to higher levels, the reality is actually quite the reverse. As with the National People's Congress, power is actually concentrated in the small elite groups at the top of the pyramid structure. In the CPC structure, as with government institutions, the smaller the group, the more professional, elite and powerful it tends to be. At the level of the National Party Congress, the largest body in the CPC, meetings are held only once every five years and are used mainly for announcements and rubber-stamping decisions made by Party elites. Delegates at the National Party Congress have little control over the meeting agenda, which is determined by the Politburo or its Standing Committee. Even the Central Committee meetings are used to ratify major decisions made at the highest echelons of the Party. Although the Central Committee is smaller than the National Party Congress, its membership in recent years has been close to two hundred members who meet only once or twice a year. While individual members of the Central Committee representing particular sectors of government or industry may be consulted, the Central Committee as a whole is not a deliberative body that plays a major role in Party decisions. While the membership of the Central Committee is in theory chosen by the National Party Congress, the list of candidates is prepared by the Politburo or its Standing Committee. Until 1987, the number of candidates and the number of positions to be filled were identical (the 1987 list included five more people than positions). The Central Committee then elects the Politburo and its Standing Committee, but the list of persons for these positions is also prepared and submitted for approval by a core of Party elites at the highest level.

4. LOWER LEVEL CPC ORGANIZATIONS

The Party seeks to duplicate as fully as possible both the organization and actual distribution of power of the central level Party organs at the provincial and local levels although the terminology is a bit different. At the provincial level, the equivalents of the central Party organs are the provincial Party congresses, which meet once every five years and the provincial Party committees, which meet once a year. The provincial level equivalent of the Politburo is the standing committee of the provincial Party committee. The first secretary of the provincial Party committee also heads its standing committee and is considered the top Party official at the provincial level. At the county level the basic structure is the same except that the county level congresses meet every three years instead of five.

The Party Constitution also provides for Party core groups that exist in every branch of government administration, including the ministries, commissions, bureaus, and other offices of state administration, in leading government and political institutions such as standing committees of the people's congresses and of the Chinese People's Political Consultative Conference and its committees at all levels, and in leading social institutions such as trade unions, women's federations, universities, and research institutions. Each of these core groups is appointed by the Party committee at the appropriate level and occupies leading positions in these institutions. From these positions, these Party members can ensure that the institution follows Party policies and implements Party decisions.

At the basic level unit of society or the *danwei*, the Party forms primary Party organizations or cells that link the Party to the lives of the general populace at its most basic social level. Most of these basic units are the workplace for those in the workforce and schools and neighbor committees for others. All *danwei* organizations such as schools, factories, shops, city neighborhoods, farms, townships, villages, and business enterprises must form a primary Party organization whenever there are three or more Party members in the organization. Each primary Party organization is answerable to a higher-level Party organ called a primary committee established whenever there are one hundred or more Party members, a general branch committee established whenever there are fifty to one hundred Party members, or the branch committee established whenever there are fewer than fifty members. These basic level Party organizations carry out tasks such as membership recruitment, promotion of Party ideology, and keeping the Party in touch with China's general populace at the grassroots level. These basic level organizations also allow the Party to penetrate to reach every level of Chinese society down to the most basic level of daily existence.

5. PARTY CONTROL AND THE NOMENKLATURA SYSTEM

The basic mechanism used by the Party to exert control over the Party system, the government, and all other social and economic institutions is what some political scientists have referred to as the "nomenklatura system." The nomenklatura system refers to a list of Party or government positions kept by Party leaders that can be filled only by certain persons whose names appear on a list of candidates or nominees for those positions. Party organs decide on both the posts and the list of names available to fill those posts. In general, the posts are the leading positions for all Party and government organs. Party organs at different levels will keep different nomenklatura lists. In general, the nomenklatura list of a Party organ will cover all government and Party positions at or below the level of the Party organ. At the national level, the Central Committee will have a list for all ministries, commissions, bureaus, the Supreme People's Court, the Supreme People's Procuratorate, and the Standing Committee of the National People's Congress.

By the use of the nomenklatura system, the CPC is able to ensure that persons approved by the Party fill all leading positions at all levels of the state from the highest to the most basic level. This control extends even to positions that are in theory to be elected by the electorate, such as Party congresses at lower levels. Before any elections occur, there is a screening process whereby a list of candidates or nominees will be presented to the electorate.

Through the nomenklatura system, Party organs can determine the list of names on the candidate list, which often corresponds exactly with the number of positions available. This system is not apparent from the election laws or the Constitution of the PRC.

The nomenklatura system allows the CPC to create a system of interlocking directorates that control both the Party and the state. Hu Jintao, the president of the PRC, is also general secretary of the CPC Central Committee and in charge of convening the Politburo and its Standing Committee. Xi Jinping is the vice president of the PRC and a member of the Politburo Standing Committee. Wu Bangguo is chairman of the Standing Committee of the National People's Congress. By installing its leading members in the top posts in the PRC government, the CPC is able to merge the Party and the state at crucial points in the political administrative apparatus and to allow the Party to rule the state. Perhaps the clearest example of the act of fusing government and Party organs at the national level is the Central Military Commission, which first existed as a Party organ and now exists also as a state organ and has exactly the same membership. At local levels of government, it has also been the practice to establish simultaneously a department of the Party committee and a department of government dealing with the same subject matter at the same level. Occasionally, major policy documents have been issued jointly by both government and

Party organs. The budget for Party organs has been included in a single unified state and Party budget. In this and many other ways, the Party and the state are fused together with the Party exercising power through the organs of the state.

6. PARTY CONTROL AND THE QUESTION OF LEGITIMACY

While the CPC has absolute authority in China, the Party is careful to give the appearance of operating within a legal framework and careful not to give the appearance, as was the case during the Cultural Revolution, of acting above the law. Provisions in the 1982 Constitution explicitly subject all political parties to the rule of law and make clear that no organization or individual is above the law. *See* PRC Const., Art. 5. In the 1987 Report of the Thirteenth Plenary Session of the National Party Congress, the CPC made clear that its leadership should be political leadership, rather than direct control of the PRC. The 1987 Report also acknowledged the need to separate Party and state organs so that the Party will not usurp the legitimate powers of state organs. This approach is quite a departure from the lawlessness of the Cultural Revolution when the legal system itself was under attack for creating restraints on the work of the CPC in hunting down its enemies and in carrying out the revolution. The 1975 and 1978 Constitutions expressly subjected the PRC government to the direct control of the CPC and also abolished various major provisions of the 1954 Constitution that established the basic principles of a legal system such as the equality of citizens under the law, the independent exercise of adjudicative and procuratorial powers, and the legal protection of succession rights to people's private property. The general approach of the 1975 and 1978 Constitutions was that the legal system needed to be abolished because it created unwanted restraints on the Party and its disciples in destroying their enemies. The 1982 Constitution rejected the legal nihilism of this approach and created an approach based, in theory at least, upon the rule of law.

The problem for the CPC under the approach of the 1975 and 1978 Constitutions is that if the Party is perceived to be above the law then it may appear to be exercising arbitrary power. Operating within the legal constraints of a government system that appears to be representative and in which power is transferred from the people through popular elections to a parliamentary system in which lower level delegates elect higher level delegates allows the CPC to claim that its leadership is supported and affirmed by the will of the people. The process of political consultation created by the multi-party political system and the Chinese People's Political Consultative Conference discussed above further allows the CPC to claim that it has consulted with and has been advised by PRC persons from all walks of life and that its policies are representative of the people's will. The CPC can claim that it is acting in the interests of the state and the Chinese people under a system of representative government with legal constraints against the exercise of arbitrary power. In other words, the present legal and political framework allows the CPC to claim that it is exercising legitimate power on behalf of the state and the people.

As the earlier discussion has indicated, however, the political system actually operates quite in reverse of appearances. Decisions are actually made by a small group of Party leaders and then are ratified and rubber-stamped by Party and government organs under the control of a core of Party elites. The outcome of elections for all important government positions is controlled by the CPC through the nomenklatura system in which the CPC is able to place its approved candidates into those positions. The government of the PRC, under the control of the CPC, does not really exercise the independent powers of government. Rather, the CPC uses its control of the government apparatus to justify or legitimate the CPC's own actions, decisions, and policies. This may seem to be unnecessary given that the CPC has absolute authority, but the legitimating function of the current system is quite crucial to the CPC. If the CPC is exercising legitimate power ratified by the state then any challenge to the CPC is a challenge against the state itself and qualifies as a crime of treason against the state. Such a serious offense may justify the use of extreme measures to maintain power in the face of serious challenges, such as the use of force against the democracy movement in Tiananmen Square in 1989 and more recently against the Falun Gong movement. Much in the same way that past rulers of China were imperiled if they lost the Mandate of Heaven by neglecting their obligations to the people, the CPC is cognizant that it must stake a claim to legitimately represent the interests of the Chinese people if it is to continue to maintain its power. For this reason, it is important that the organs of government continue to confer legitimacy upon the actions, decisions, and policies of the CPC.

One other important feature of the present political and legal system of the PRC is that there is a separation between the apparent apparatus of government and the real locus of power, which operates behind-the-scenes and away from public scrutiny. Only the workings of the government and some Party organs are conducted in public and most of these public meetings involve matters on which decisions have already been made and where little of consequence is accomplished. Little is known about the inner workings of the core group of elites, the Standing Committee of the Politburo, and how decisions are made. This separation of apparent and real power contributes to a certain lack of transparency in the PRC system. Only the ceremonial and non-essential workings of the major PRC government organs are somewhat accessible to public scrutiny, although these are the organs charged by the Constitution with the exercise of legitimate power. The secrecy surrounding the higher levels of decision-making and which individuals or organs within the government and the Party are influential and on the rise or out of favor and on the decline create a barrier to those observers who seek an in-depth understanding of the PRC. A barrier against public scrutiny can be an advantage to an authoritarian government that is interested in implementing its own vision for the nation free from the constraints of dissent and public accountability. In addition, control of knowledge and information about its inner workings creates an important advantage for the Party that seeks to maintain its power. A lack of information about the Party helps to shield the Party against its critics and opponents.

7.   IDEOLOGY CAMPAIGNS

The prior discussion has examined how the CPC is able to exercise control over PRC government organs. A second major part of the CPC's ability to maintain power is through its exercise of control over society and those elements in society that may mount a challenge to its authority. As discussed previously, the Party is able to exercise control over society on a daily basis through the use of Party organizations that exist in government and social institutions that extend down to the basic level of society. Beyond these organizations, the Party engages in periodic political movements or ideological campaigns designed to reinforce its authority and to quell any restless elements in society.

Prior discussion of political movements indicated that these were often fanatical movements using terror tactics to hunt down and root out hidden enemies during the chaotic and lost twenty-year period from the late 1950s to Mao's death in 1976. The most extreme of all of these political movements, the Cultural Revolution (1966–76), spun out of control. Although it is generally acknowledged in China that the Cultural Revolution was excessive, the CPC continues to use some of the same tactics from that period today in controlling the general population and in rooting out subversives. The CPC continues to periodically launch ideology campaigns in which all Party members and persons in leadership positions, usually Party members, must participate. The publicly stated goals of these campaigns are the goals of purification, strengthening the ideals of the Party, and identifying those within the Party and in leadership positions who fail to maintain Party ideals and loyalty. Each leadership group within a university, government organ, or state-owned enterprise is to hold sessions at which participants engage in criticism of themselves and their colleagues. In the past, the Party has required that each bureaucracy, unit, or identifiable group identify a mandatory minimum number of persons as "bad elements" who have failed the test of ideology. Anyone labeled as a "bad element" could suffer personal disgrace, professional ruin in the form of expulsion from the Party, and a loss of employment.

Today, the Party no longer requires that each group identify a minimum number of "bad elements." However, these campaigns can still create anxiety for all those involved. The standards—a test of ideology—are so vague that anyone can fail. In theory, no one is safe from the prospect of immediate personal and professional ruin if one is identified as being a bad element. Moreover, these campaigns involve sessions in which close associates are required to criticize each other, a process that can easily lead to unfounded accusations, long-lasting rifts, and personal animosities. Even when no one is identified as disloyal, few find sessions of self-criticism and criticism of others to be a pleasant experience. Like the Cultural Revolution, all other ideology campaigns, including more recent ones, display the same fundamental dynamics of self-criticism, criticism of others, reprimands for those falling short of Party ideals, and in serious cases, the purging of bad elements.

Ideology campaigns should be distinguished from the many social and legal campaigns that are frequently launched at the behest of the Party. In recent years, the PRC has launched numerous "strike hard" campaigns against corruption, smuggling, narcotics, and counterfeit and inferior quality products. These campaigns are targeted against persons who have committed concrete offenses in violation of existing laws. Those who have violated no laws generally have nothing to fear. Moreover, government organs conduct these campaigns against third parties and strangers whereas ideology campaigns require a self-examination by each unit and the critical examination of the actions, ideology, and loyalty of colleagues. There are also many other social campaigns, such as campaigns to raise the quality of adjudication in court proceedings and to raise the effectiveness of enforcement of court judgments, but all of these are directed at social institutions, have specific social goals, and do not target particular individuals for rectification.

a. Purposes Served by Ideology Campaigns

Ideology campaigns serve to reinforce the Party's power, bolster its influence, and disrupt the formation of rival ideologies. The criticism sessions that require individuals to criticize close associates are designed to prevent the formation of close associations that can lead to larger groups that can challenge the Party's authority. These campaigns also serve to identify hidden enemies and traitors, a persistent fear of China's rulers that long pre-dates the CPC. Whenever the Party finds the general population to be restless—Mao called for a political campaign every seven or eight years—the Party will launch an ideological campaign to quell restlessness and to disperse any potentially disruptive elements. The Party's practice of periodically launching ideology campaigns continues unabated to the present.

b. Ideology and the Party's Authority

The Party's use of ideology campaigns should not be taken to suggest that the Party's authority rests on the belief of the general populace in its ideology. To the contrary, many Party leaders today bemoan that the majority of the younger generations in China lack belief in any ideology but is simply consumed by a race for material wealth and personal advancement. Moreover, the use of ideology campaigns should not be understood as demonstrating even that most Party members believe in Party ideology. Rather as suggested above, these campaigns serve an important role in maintaining social control. While at one time early in the PRC's history, the mass of China's population might have believed in Party ideals, most people in China today harbor a certain cynicism about the Communist Party. Many Chinese believe that there is widespread corruption among all ranks of Party and government officials.

Rather than being based upon an accepted ideology, the Party's authority seems to rest upon an acceptance of its entrenched power by the general populace and upon a genuine belief in the Party's continuing ability to lead China to higher levels of economic development and higher standards of living. So long as they do not challenge the Party's authority, many Chinese find that they can now lead more prosperous lives and have opportunities for professional advancement that were not possible a generation ago. Many in China, especially its younger generations, enjoy the personal freedom to dress how they wish and lead lifestyles that would have been unimaginable a generation ago. The Party seems to have offered citizens an agreement that if they do not challenge the Party's authority or its core values and stay within certain proscribed limits, they can live as they wish and the Party will not sanction or punish them. This represents a significant improvement over the practice of unpredictable and random terror that marked much of the twenty-year period that ended in the 1970s with

Mao's death and the advent of economic reforms. But there are limits to the Party's tolerance of social behaviors. Those who live in China understand that the CPC draws a fundamental distinction between economic and political reform and between personal and political freedom. While the CPC will tolerate greater personal freedom among China's general populace than a generation ago, the CPC will not accept political dissent. Sudden personal and professional ruin, so prevalent in the early days of the PRC, continues to be the price of political opposition. Like their predecessors in Republican and Imperial China, China's current rulers do not accept the notion of loyal or patriotic opposition. By its nature, all opposition qualifies as a crime against the state. Also like its predecessors, the CPC is wary of hidden enemies, traitors, and conspiracies and will move swiftly to destroy them. For all of its recent changes, China continues to be a one party authoritarian state.

8.   DE JURE AND DE FACTO GOVERNMENT

The PRC has both an apparent and a real behind-the-scenes power structure and both a de jure and a de facto government. The apparent power structure and the de jure government are established by the Constitution as the legitimate organs of state power in the PRC. The real locus of power, however, is in the CPC, which operates behind-the-scenes away from public scrutiny, and views itself for reasons of history and destiny as the de facto ruler of the PRC. The PRC Constitution only hints at this role for the

CPC and the real division of power and exercise of power. No public documents set forth this power structure but it is established through the behind-the-scenes practices of the Party. A great deal of the inner workings of the Party remains inaccessible to outside observers, which only increases the Party's influence and protects it from critics. The PRC government is under the control of the CPC through a nomenklatura system in which the CPC controls the election and appointment of all important seats in government. The CPC and the PRC government are run by a series of interlocking directorates in which the same persons simultaneously hold key positions on both the Party and the government. At certain crucial points, the Party and the state are fused or merged together, with the Party exercising significant control over the state.

CHAPTER FIVE

LEGISLATIVE AUTHORITY AND LEGAL INTERPRETATION

This chapter exams the allocation of legislative authority among PRC central level organs and between central and local levels of government. This chapter will examine the legislative process, the hierarchy of law-making institutions and legal norms, and the method for resolving conflicts between legal norms. Next, China's system of legal interpretation will be examined. The discussion then turns to the role of the Communist Party in the legislative process. Finally, this chapter will discuss a number of unresolved issues and problems in the present law-making system and system of legal interpretation.

A. LEGISLATIVE AUTHORITY IN THE PRC LEGAL SYSTEM

China's concept of legislative authority differs in fundamental respects from those of some western legal systems. The United States adheres to a principle of separation of judicial, legislative, and administrative powers. Under the US system, all legislative powers are allocated to the legislative branch, which is supreme over the other branches of government in this area. Only the US Congress has intrinsic power to enact national legislation, which may be defined for present purposes as laws of general applicability. Congress has delegated limited and carefully circumscribed powers to many federal agencies to enact administrative laws and regulations, but only Congress at the national level and state legislatures at local levels have intrinsic legislative authority. In China, the situation is quite different. China has a single, unified political-legal system (*zhengfa xitong*), as opposed to separate co-equal branches of government. While China's government organs can generally be divided into legislative, administrative, and judicial organs, all three are part of one system that does not maintain a strict separation of powers. Rather, China's system includes legislative bodies, administrative and regulatory organs, courts, prosecutors, and police with overlapping legislative, judicial, and administrative powers within one system. In addition, China's massive state bureaucracy is marked by a proprietary system where government organs that compete for power and resources are deemed to be owners of their respective domains of authority. As a result, China's legislative, administrative, and judicial organs all have the authority to enact legal norms within their respective domains. For example, although China has a main legislative body, the National People's Congress, many other entities throughout the PRC government system also have intrinsic law-making authority. At the national level, the NPC, the NPC Standing Committee, and the State Council all have intrinsic legislative power.

Beneath the State Council are a large number of ministries, commissions, administrations, bureaus, departments, and offices. Each of these many entities also has legislative power to enact administrative legal norms within their respective domains. Judicial authorities such as the Supreme People's Court and the Supreme People's Procuratorates also have power to enact legal norms governing their sphere of work. A similar division of lawmaking powers exists at the local levels, although these authorities are limited by the constitutional constraints that local legislation cannot conflict with national laws or the Constitution.

In another important respect, however, the system in the PRC is consistent with many western legal systems in establishing criteria that distinguish legal from non-legal norms. In western legal systems, such as the United States, the jurisprudential theory of legal positivism holds that legal norms can be distinguished from non-legal norms by tracing the pedigree of the norms. The PRC Constitution sets forth the government organs that can exercise legislative power and the procedures that are to be followed in enacting legislation. The new Legislation Law, enacted in 2000, adds significant detail and clarity to the division of legislative powers, legislative procedures, and the hierarchy of legal norms. The significance of these basic documents is that they establish a concrete system whereby legal norms can be distinguished from non-legal norms, such as policy documents, by tracing the source of the norms back to a recognized legislative source. This is a significant development because China did not historically draw a sharp distinction between law and non-legal norms such as morality and politics. To the contrary, China has a long tradition of recognizing non-legal norms as having binding force. In some periods of Imperial China, courts directly applied Confucian morality in place of law. In China today, only those norms that have been enacted in accordance with the provisions of the Constitution and Legislation Law qualify as legal norms that are to be accorded binding legal effect. Moreover, by having their origin traced back to their source, legal norms in the PRC can be classified in a hierarchy of norms and can claim legitimacy as being based upon the Constitution.

B. LEGISLATIVE ORGANS

The division of legislative power is set forth in the 1982 Constitution and in the Legislation Law (2000). There are three national organs with intrinsic legislative power. First, the NPC is the supreme legislative organ in the PRC. The NPC has the power to enact and amend all basic laws (*jiben fa*), such as laws relating to criminal offenses, civil affairs, and the organization of state organs. *See* PRC Const., Art. 62; Legislation Law, Art. 7. The term "basic" is not further defined by the Constitution or laws; most Chinese scholars believe that the term refers to laws that fundamentally affect the whole of society, including laws concerning civil and political rights, personal freedoms, and organization and structure of the state and society. The NPC also has the power to amend the Constitution under a special procedure requiring a two-thirds majority vote (ordinary legislation requires a majority vote of the NPC for adoption). *See* PRC Const., Art. 64.

Second, the NPC Standing Committee has authority to enact and amend all other laws (*qita falu*) except for those enacted by the NPC itself. *See* PRC Const., Art. 67(2); Legislation Law, Art. 7. Chinese scholars argue that ordinary national laws, as opposed to basic laws, affect only a particular aspect of society. While the distinction between ordinary and basic laws can be maintained in theory, it is often difficult in practice to discern how these distinctions are made and to draw precise boundaries between the legislative jurisdiction of the NPC and the NPC Standing Committee. Moreover, when the NPC is not in session, the NPC Standing Committee has authority to amend and supplement basic laws enacted by the NPC in a manner consistent with the fundamental principles of those laws. *See* PRC Const., Art. 67(3); Legislation Law, Art. 7. The power of the Standing Committee to amend basic laws would appear to further cloud the boundaries of legislative power between the NPC and the NPC Standing Committee. These problems are further discussed in later sections of this chapter.

Third, the State Council exercises legislative power in at least five different ways:

(1) Under the Constitution, the State Council has intrinsic power to enact administrative regulations (*xingzhen fagui)* for subject matters within

its sphere of authority, which are enacted
through the use of the State Council's own legislative procedures and do not involve either the
NPC or the NPC Standing Committee. *See* PRC
Const., Art. 89; Legislation Law, Art. 56. Because
the State Council and its subordinate organs are
in charge of the administration of the Chinese
state and because its legislative powers extend to
the full scope of its administrative domain, its
legislative domain is vast and comprehensive.

(2) The State Council also has power to enact
administrative regulations when such regulations
are required to facilitate the enforcement or implementation of laws enacted by the NPC and its
Standing Committee. *See* PRC Const., Art. 89;
Legislation Law, Art. 56. When such regulations
are "required" to supplement existing laws is not
further clarified in any written laws. In many
cases, the administrative regulations passed by
the State Council are more comprehensive and
important than the law itself. As an example, the
Sino–Foreign Equity Joint Venture Law was originally enacted by the NPC in 1979 and subsequently revised in 1990, 1991, and 2000. The Law
consists of only sixteen articles. The State Council
enacted the Sino–Foreign Equity Joint Venture
Law Implementing Regulations in 1983, which
were subsequently amended and revised in 1986
and 1987. The Regulations are comprehensive
and consist of 118 articles.

(3) The State Council is the sponsoring or originating entity of the bulk of legislation that is

ultimately enacted by the NPC or its Standing Committee. Although the subject matter of a particular piece of legislation may fall within the scope of authority of the State Council or one of its subordinate organs, the importance and scope of the legislation may require the enactment of a law or a basic law, which can be enacted only by the NPC Standing Committee or the NPC respectively. For example, the Sino–Foreign Joint Venture Law is within the subject matter competence of the State Council as the law relates to one of the State Council's main areas of authority, foreign investment and trade within the PRC. The law was deemed to be of fundamental importance, however, and a basic law. As a result, the Sino–Foreign Joint Venture Law was enacted and subsequently revised and amended by the NPC. While the NPC formally adopted the Sino–Foreign Joint Venture Law, the State Council and its subordinate organs were the principal drafters of the law. The role of the State Council in sponsoring legislation is significant; since 1979, about 70% of the laws adopted by the NPC and the NPC Standing Committee were drafted and submitted by the State Council. Moreover, the State Council has played a major role in legislation directly sponsored by the NPC and its Standing Committee. For example, when the Criminal Law underwent a major revision and overhaul in 1997, the State Council and its relevant departments submitted a large number of amendments, most of which were adopted into the new Criminal Law, even though the Criminal Law is a basic law and is formally within the exclusive jurisdiction of the NPC.

(4) The State Council may be authorized by the NPC or the NPC Standing Committee directly or through a law to enact administrative regulations in an area that would otherwise first require the enactment of basic laws by the NPC or laws by the NPC Standing Committee. Unlike the legislative power described in (2) above that allows the State Council to supplement existing laws with administrative regulations, the authority described here would allow the State Council to enact administrative regulations in an area with no existing laws. For example, Article 8 of the new Legislation Law requires the enactment of laws by the NPC or its Standing Committees on a number of important areas, including national sovereignty, crime and punishment, and civil and political rights. The NPC or its Standing Committee is allowed to delegate authority to the State Council to enact administrative regulations on those matters on which no laws have been enacted (with the exception of crime and punishment, civil rights, and the judicial system). In the past, at least three open-ended delegations of power were made by the NPC or its Standing Committee to the State Council concerning the subjects of old and sick cadres in 1983, industrial-commercial tax in 1984, and economic reform in 1985. These delegations of power were made without time limits, defined limits on the scope of delegation,

and supervisory procedures or methods for identifying which laws were enacted based upon these powers. A major reason for these delegations of power is that certain areas are undergoing rapid reform and constant changes and the time and conditions are not appropriate for congressional law-making although there is an urgent need for regulation. The enactment of administrative regulations by the State Council will also allow the NPC and its Standing Committee to study the effectiveness of the regulations in ultimately formulating and enacting laws.

(5) The ministries, commissions, and agencies under the State Council may issue departmental rules, including instructions, provisions, measures, orders, implementing rules, and rules (collectively *guizhang*) in accordance with laws enacted by the NPC or its Standing Committee and with the administrative regulations, decisions, and orders of the State Council. In general, departmental rules are detailed and technical rules issued by ministries, commissions, and agencies when the subject matter of the enabling laws or regulations falls within the scope of authority and expertise of the entity involved. The enabling law is often too general to be useful in specific enforcement and application. The entity issuing the departmental rules is the entity that will be primarily involved in applying the particular law. Often the enabling law will stipulate that a particular entity will issue departmental rules. For example, Article 110 of the Negotiable Instru-

ment Law provides that specific rules on negotiable instruments will be issued by the People's Bank of China, one of the constituent entities of the State Council. The People's Bank has specific regulatory authority and expertise over banking and financial instruments and is in the best position to issue specific and detailed rules over negotiable instruments. In addition to serving to specifically implement legislation passed by the NPC and the State Council, departmental rules can also serve as explanations or interpretations of existing laws or administrative regulations. In other instances, the State Council will delegate the authority to issue temporary departmental rules where no laws or administrative regulations currently exist. Due to inexperience or lack of expertise, the NPC and State Council may be ill-prepared to issue legislation for a specific area where urgent regulation is needed. For example, before the Company Law was promulgated in 1993 and in the absence of a stock exchange law, the State Council conferred on several ministries the power to draw up departmental rules to establish an urgently needed system of regulation for China's nascent stock exchanges. Temporary rules are intended to be gradually replaced by formally enacted laws or administrative regulations.

Departmental rules are issued directly by the ministries and commissions without the use of the legislative processes in the State Council itself. Unlike administrative regulations that can in some cases be issued by the State Council as part of its intrinsic legislative power, all departmental rules must be enacted pursuant to an enabling law, administrative regulation, or through a direct delegation of law-making authority from the State Council. For example, the Wholly Foreign–Owned Enterprise Law was enacted by the NPC in 1986 and revised in 2000. The Wholly Foreign–Owned Enterprise Law Implementing Rules were issued by the Ministry of Foreign Economic Relations and Trade, one of the subordinate organs of the State Council, in 1990 and revised in 2001. There is no legal requirement that all departmental rules be published and some of them are regarded as internal and not published. In practice, departmental rules form the bulk of the legislation enacted by the State Council. For example, in the area of industrial and commercial administration, there are some 180 laws, regulations, and departmental rules. Of these, 130 are some form of departmental rules.

The State Council or its constituent entities have issued thousands of rules and regulations that affect all aspects of the political, economic, and social life of the PRC. In addition, leaders in the State Council have traditionally held higher leading positions in the Communist Party than leaders in the NPC or its Standing Committee. As a result, many Chinese and foreign legal scholars consider the State Council to be effectively the most powerful and influential legislative organ in the PRC.

Fourth, aside from these organs of national legislative power, there are also entities with local legislative power. Central level legislation contains broad language that may not be sufficiently detailed or suited to a local situation. As a result, local legislation plays a significant role in supplementing national legislation and has significant impact upon the daily social and economic life in the PRC. As previously discussed, central level authorities have supreme sovereign power in China's unitary government system, but will delegate authority to local level authorities to act within their appropriate spheres of competence. Local level legislation is subject to the constraint that it cannot violate any higher-level legal norms, such as the Constitution, basic laws, other laws, or administrative regulations enacted by the State Council. *See* PRC Const., Art. 100; Legislation Law, Art. 63. Subject to these constraints, people's congresses at the provincial level and municipalities directly under the central government are empowered to enact local regulations (*difangxing fagui*), which correspond to basic laws and laws at the national level. (In Chinese, local level legislation is referred to as regulations because "laws" are reserved for legislation enacted by the NPC and its Standing Committee). Autonomous regions are empowered to enact regulations in light of their particular political, economic, and cultural circumstances, but such legislation must be submitted to the NPC Standing Committee for approval. *See* PRC Const., Art. 116; Legislation Law, Art. 63. The people's congresses and their standing committees in capital cities of provinces and autonomous regions, cities in special economic zones, and other large cities that have been approved by the State Council also have the power to enact local regulations, which are subject to the approval of their respective provincial congresses. *See* Legislation Law, Art. 63. Local level people's governments of provinces, autonomous regions, capital cities, cities in special economic zones, and other large cities approved by the State Council are also empowered to enact local departmental rules (*guizhang*), which are the local equivalent of administrative regulations enacted at the national level by the State Council. *See* Legislation Law, Art. 73.

Hierarchy of Legislative Organs and Legal Norms

National People's Congress	Constitutional law (*xian fa*)
	Basic laws (*jiben falu*)
NPC Standing Committee	Other laws (*qita falu*)
	Amendments and supplements to basic laws when NPC is not in session
State Council	Administrative regulations (*xingzheng fagui*)
People's congresses and their standing commit-	Local regulations (*difangxing fagui*)

tees of provinces, autonomous regions, cities directly under central government, capital cities of provinces and autonomous regions, cities in special economic zones, and cities approved by the State Council	
People's governments of provinces, autonomous regions, cities directly under central government, capital cities of provinces and autonomous regions, cities in special economic zones, and cities approved by the State Council	Local departmental rules (*guizhang*)

The new Legislation Law also clarifies which entity has the power to resolve conflicts between various legal norms. In general the higher-level authority in the hierarchy of legislative organs has the power to invalidate or repeal legislation enacted by the entities directly beneath it in the chain of power. The NPC has the power to amend or repeal laws enacted or approved by the NPC Standing Committee. The NPC Standing Committee has the power to repeal administrative regulations enacted by the State Council and local regulations enacted by provinces, autonomous regions, and cities directly under the central government that violate higher-level legal norms. The State Council has the authority to amend or repeal departmental rules enacted by its ministries and commissions and local departmental rules. A similar allocation of power exists at the local level: provincial level people's congresses can repeal regulations enacted by their standing committees; provincial level standing committees can repeal departmental rules enacted by people's governments at the same level; and provincial level people's governments can amend or repeal departmental rules enacted by lower level people's governments. *See* Legislation Law, Art. 88. Courts play no role in this system of legislative review.

Note that departmental rules enacted by the ministries, commissions, agencies, and offices of the State Council are not included in the hierarchy of legal norms above, which are based upon the provisions of the new Legislation Law. *See* Legislation Law, Arts. 78–80. Departmental rules fall below the Constitution, laws, and administrative regulations, but the status of departmental rules in relation to local level regulations and local level departmental rules continues to be an unresolved issue. The Legislation Law appears to indicate that the State Council has authority to resolve conflicts between departmental rules enacted by State Council ministries and commissions and regulations and rules enacted by local congresses and local governments. *See* Legislation Law, Art. 85.

1. LEGISLATIVE PROCESS OF THE NATIONAL PEOPLE'S CONGRESS

As formalized in the recently enacted Legislation Law, the legislative process of the NPC falls into three stages: the submission of draft legislation in the form of a bill, the consideration of the bill by the relevant NPC committee, and the placement of the bill on the NPC agenda for a vote. Much of the legislation that is enacted by the NPC is done in accordance with a five-year legislative plan, approved by the Politburo of the CPC, which is designed to support the five-year economic and social plans that China continues to use.

There are three types or groups of entities qualified to submit a legislative bill to the NPC. First is the Presidium of the NPC, which also decides whether to place the bill on the agenda of the NPC for a vote. *See* Legislation Law, Art. 12. This is a crucial power delegated to the NPC Presidium, which can effectively derail any proposed legislation by refusing to allow its consideration for a vote by the NPC. There is no mechanism to overturn decisions by the Presidium not to proceed with a bill. The second group entitled to submit bills are the NPC Standing Committee, the State Council, the Central Military Commission, the Supreme People's Court, the Supreme People's Procuratorate, and the special committees of the NPC. *See id.* Each of these organs is entitled to submit a bill on matters that fall within the scope of its functions and powers. Note that in addition to being able to sponsor legislation before the NPC, all of these entities may have some legislative powers of their own. For example, the State Council has the inherent power to promulgate administrative regulations that do not need the approval of the NPC. Where the State Council finds that a particular area requires the enactment of a basic law and cannot be the subject of administrative regulations, the State Council will sponsor legislation for approval and enactment by the NPC. The third group entitled to submit a bill is a delegation of thirty or more NPC deputies on matters that fall within their expertise.

In practice, once a bill is submitted for consideration by the NPC, the Presidium decides whether to proceed further with the bill or to scuttle it. *See* Legislation Law, Art. 12. The Presidium can decide to place the bill on the agenda of the NPC. Before making this decision, the Presidium can refer the bill for consideration by the NPC special committees. Among the NPC special committees is the Law Committee, which is charged with oversight of the investigation by the special committees of all draft laws that are to be considered by the NPC or its Standing Committee. The Law Committee acts as a contact point for the other seven special committees and will assign draft laws for consideration by those committees most closely associated with a specific law. After deliberations by the special committees and the Law Committee, the Presidium will then put the bill on the agenda of a plenary session of the NPC and distribute the opinions of the special committees to the delegates to facilitate their deliberations. At the NPC session, a representative of the body presenting the bill will explain the bill to the delegates. *See* Legislation Law, Art. 16. Next, on the basis of the opinions expressed by the various NPC delegates and the special committees, the Law Committee will prepare a report on the bill and a revised draft of the bill for the Presidium. *See* Legislation Law, Art. 18. If the Presidium decides to approve the bill in its amended form, the bill will be presented to the plenary meeting of the NPC, which may approve the bill by a majority vote. After approval by the NPC, the bill is signed and promulgated by the president of the PRC.

Where there are major issues concerning a bill placed on the agenda of the NPC, the Presidium will not put the bill to a vote immediately but will attempt to build a stronger consensus before actual voting. The chairman of the Presidium can convene a meeting of the chairmen of the delegations to hold discussions and report back to the Presidium. *See* Legislation Law, Art. 19. If there are still further issues that need research and consideration, the NPC can entrust the NPC Standing Committee with the authority to engage in further deliberations and to enact the law after its deliberations and report to the NPC at its next session the following year or to put forth amendments to the bill for the NPC to consider at its next session. *See* Legislation Law, Art. 21. Note that so long as the NPC grants its authorization, the NPC Standing Committee will be able to enact a basic law on its own and simply report back to the NPC at its next session. The advantage of this approach is that it permits the NPC Standing Committee to enact a basic law without having to wait for an entire year for the next annual plenary session of the NPC for renewed consideration of the draft legislation.

2.   LEGISLATIVE PROCESS OF THE NPC STANDING COMMITTEE

The entities that are allowed to submit a bill to the NPC Standing Committee are the same as those entitled to submit bills to the full NPC, except that a group of ten or more members of the Standing Committee are allowed to submit bills before the Standing Committee rather than the group of thirty or more delegates in the NPC. *See* Legislation Law, Art. 25. The gatekeeper role at the Standing Committee level is assumed by the Council of Chairmen, which decides whether to put bills on the agenda of the Standing Committee or to assign the bills to the NPC special committees for a preliminary deliberation and report before deciding whether to put a bill on the agenda. *See* Legislation Law, Art. 24. As in the case of the Presidium in the NPC, the Council of Chairmen can effectively derail a bill by refusing to place it on the agenda. There is no mechanism to overturn a decision by the Council to refuse to proceed with a bill.

After the Council of Chairmen decides to put a bill on the agenda of the Standing Committee, the bill undergoes a three-part consultation and examination process before the Standing Committee before it is submitted to a vote. At the first meeting of the Standing Committee, the representatives of the bill's sponsors are to explain the bill before the Standing Committee breaks into sub-groups to consider the bill. At the second meeting of the Standing Committee, the Law Committee provides its first report on any amendments to the draft bill and major issues that need further consideration before the Standing Committee once again breaks into sub-groups to further examine the bill. At the third meeting, the Law Committee reports the results of its examination of the bill. *See* Legislation Law, Art. 27. The bill is then ready for a vote by the Standing Committee. If a majority of the Standing Committee approves the bill, it passes into law and is signed and promulgated by the president of the PRC. *See* Legislation Law, Art. 41. Where there is substantial agreement on the bill after two meetings of the Standing Committee, the bill can be put to a vote without a third examination. Where there are only minor changes suggested to a draft bill in the form of partial amendments and there is also substantial agreement on the bill, the bill can be put to a vote after one examination by the Standing Committee. *See* Legislation Law, Art. 28.

The Legislation Law contains no provisions for public consideration of bills before the NPC, although the NPC has in the past made available for public consultation those bills that it has considered to be of particular importance. The Legislation Law does provide for wide dissemination of draft legislation before the NPC Standing Committee. All bills on the Standing Committee agenda elicit opinions from the sponsoring entity and from all sectors of society through public seminars and meetings. All bills that are deemed "important" are further made available to the general public and public opinion is sought and considered by the Standing Committee and the special committees responsible for the bill. *See* Legislation Law, Arts. 34 & 35.

3.   LEGISLATIVE PROCESS OF THE STATE COUNCIL

Like the NPC, the State Council will prepare an annual legislative work plan based upon a five-year legislative plan designed to support the national five-year economic and social plan. In general about fifty items are included in each annual plan of the State Council, although additional items can be included depending upon the needs of reform and development. A preliminary legislative draft is usually prepared by a specific subordinate organ of the State Council on the theory that the legislation falls within the expertise of the department or organ in question. For example, the Ministry of Public Security completed the first draft of the Law on Fire Control because the subject matter of the law was within its peculiar expertise and scope of authority. The draft is then reviewed by the Legislative Affairs Office (LAO) of the State Council, which plays a central role in all legislation approved by the State Council. The LAO plays a role similar to that of the Law Committee in the legislative process of the NPC. In some cases, draft legislation is prepared directly by the LAO. These cases usually involve legislation that affect more than one department or subordinate organ of the State Council.

After the LAO reviews the draft, it will prepare an explanation of the draft along with any proposed amendments and revisions. The original draft and the explanation and report of the LAO are then submitted to an executive session of the State Council for review and discussion. Overall, about 80% of all executive sessions are used to consider draft legislation. Apart from the official members of the executive session such as the premier, the vice-premiers, the state councilors and the secretary general, the session also includes the leading officials from the relevant departments sponsoring the legislation. As the session proceeds with its deliberation, officials from the LAO and the relevant departments make presentations on the draft, explain major issues, and address concerns raised by State Council members. The LAO together with the relevant departments then further revise the draft based upon the views expressed at the executive session. The final legislative draft is then submitted to the executive session for its approval.

At this point, the next steps in the legislative process will depend upon the type of legislation that is involved. If the legislation involves a law, then once the executive session approves the draft, the draft is prepared in the form of a law bill proposal, is signed by the premier, and is submitted to the NPC or the NPC Standing Committee for review and approval. The Law on Fire Control drafted by the Ministry of Public Security, discussed above, was first approved in draft form by the State Council and then submitted as a bill to the NPC Standing Committee for approval and promulgation by the president. Where a basic law is involved, the State Council would forward an approved law bill to the NPC for approval and enactment. In the case of administrative regulations, which are within the intrinsic legislative power of the State Council, once the executive session approves the drafts, the premier signs a decree promulgating the new legislation.

Departmental rules issued by the ministries, commissions, and other departments follow a similar procedure to that used by the State Council itself, although on the whole the process is less formal and more flexible. Most ministries and commissions have established a legal affairs division that will coordinate and spearhead the drafting of departmental rules. The particular division of the ministry or commission that has authority over the subject matter involved will draft the departmental rules working together with its legal affairs division. The final draft of the departmental rules is submitted to a general meeting of the ministry, commission or other department of the State Council involved for consideration. Officials of the division in charge of drafting the rules will make presentations before the general meeting and address specific concerns. Officials from the legal affairs division and other divisions concerned will also give their views of the draft under discussion. The deliberation process in the general meeting will not culminate in a vote.

Ministers have full authority to decide whether to adopt, reject, or refer departmental rules for further work and consideration. After adoption, the minister must sign the departmental rule before it passes into law. The minister then promulgates the rules through publication in government gazettes, newspapers, journals, and through radio and television broadcasts. After promulgation, the rules must be filed with the State Council for the record. All departmental and local rules must be filed for the record by the ministries, commissions, and local governments within thirty days of their enactment; the Legislative Affairs Office of the State Council then checks their consistency with higher-level legislation.

4.   LEGISLATION AT LOCAL LEVELS

Legislative procedures at local levels are similar to those at the central level. At the local level, legislation is also divided into two categories: (1) local regulations, which correspond to basic laws or laws at the national level, which are enacted by local level people's congresses and their standing committees; and (2) local departmental rules (*guizhang*), which correspond to administrative regulations at the national level, which are enacted by local level people's governments (corresponding to the State Council at the national level). These legislative powers are enjoyed by people's congresses and people's governments of provinces, municipalities directly under the central government, national autonomous regions, capital cities of provinces and autonomous regions, cities in special economic zones, and other large cities approved by the State Council. Many local people's congresses have established a legal system committee or political-legal committee (corresponding to the Law Committee of the NPC) and many local governments have established legal departments (corresponding to the Legislative Affairs Office of the State Council) to help draft and move law bills through the legislative process, which involve the same type of review and deliberation process of draft legislation in the people's congresses and governments at local levels as described at the national level. It should be noted that there is less formality at the local levels as there are in many cases no provisions on legislative procedures, although a number of provinces and cities have now enacted procedures that detail the legislative process. All regulations enacted at the local level must be reported to the NPC Standing Committee and the State Council within thirty days of enactment. All local departmental rules shall be reported to the State Council and to the standing committee of the people's congress of the same level within thirty days of enactment. *See* Legislation Law, Art. 89.

In the twenty-year period since economic reforms were launched in 1978, the NPC and its Standing Committee have enacted more than 300 laws and the State Council has enacted some 770 administrative regulations. By contrast, in the five-year period from 1993 to 1997, local authorities enacted some 4,200 local regulations. In the twenty years since

1978, local authorities have enacted a total of over 6,800 local regulations. The sheer volume of local legislation and its recent dramatic increase indicate the growing importance of local legislation in the PRC legal system. The sharp increase in legislative activity over the past two decades stands in contrast to the paucity of legislation during the Mao era. Corresponding to this increase in law-making is a dramatic increase in personnel, expertise, resources, and organization in all of the PRC's major legislative organs.

5. INTERNATIONAL LAW AS A SOURCE OF LAW

As this chapter concerns sources of law in the PRC, a brief mention of international law is appropriate. Although there is no mention of international law as a source of law in the PRC Constitution, scholars in the PRC point out that under the prevailing theory of international law and recent legislative practice in the PRC, international law is part of the domestic law of the PRC and where there is a conflict between a rule of international law contained in a treaty or in customary international law and PRC local law, the rule of international law should prevail. There are also express provisions in the General Principles of Civil Law (Article 142), the Law of Civil Procedure (Article 238), and the Administrative Litigation Law (Article 72) providing that in the case of conflict a treaty provision prevails over an inconsistent rule of Chinese civil law, civil procedure, and administrative procedure.

All of these fundamental laws are further discussed in subsequent chapters.

It should be noted, however, that an international treaty signed by China does not become legally effective until it is ratified by the National People's Congress or the NPC Standing Committee. As discussed earlier, China has acceded to several international human rights treaties that have not yet been ratified so the treaties are not yet legally binding upon China. In addition, China, like other countries, maintains a distinction between self-executing and non-self-executing treaties. In the case of a non-self-executing treaty that has already been ratified by the NPC or its Standing Committee, China must undertake the additional step of enacting implementing domestic legislation before the treaty has binding legal effect within China.

C. LEGAL INTERPRETATION

No discussion of the PRC legislative system would be complete without an examination of how it handles legislative interpretation. A persistent problem in dealing with all types of legislation is that the drafters cannot anticipate all the contingencies that may arise in the application of any particular laws and include sufficiently detailed and comprehensive provisions in all legislation at the drafting stage. Furthermore, the inherent ambiguity of language and inevitable oversights in the drafting stage will almost certainly result in some gaps and unresolved issues in the final legislation that will require interpretation. Any system of legislation, including that of the PRC, will also need to have a system of legislative interpretation. This is the topic of this last section of this chapter.

At the outset, it should be noted that a major distinction between China and many western legal systems in the area of legislative interpretation relates to the role of courts. In a number of western legal systems, the general assumption is that law consists of a set of rules that are recognized and applied by courts in deciding cases. In these systems, courts play a central role in the administration of justice by determining the context and meaning of the law. Both by tradition and legal precedent, courts in the United States are entrusted with ultimate authority to interpret the law. Under the US system, judicial interpretations of ordinary laws are binding even upon the legislature that enacted the law. The legislature can only overturn the judicial interpretation by enacting a new law overturning the court's decision. In the case of constitutional interpretation by the US Supreme Court, only a constitutional amendment can overturn the High Court's decision. In China, courts do not play such a central role in the legal system and, with the notable exception of the Supreme People's Court, have only a limited role in the interpretation of laws. Rather, in general, the government organ that issued the particular set of legal norms is treated in effect as the owner of the norms and as the principal and appropriate authority to interpret what the norms mean. This division of interpretive authority is consistent with the allocation of legislative power under China's political-legal system in which a particular entity is generally treated as the owner of its proprietary sphere of competence with the power to enact legal norms within its domain of authority.

Against this background, Chinese jurisprudence generally divides legal interpretation into three categories: legislative, administrative, and judicial. In general, legislative interpretation refers to interpretations given by legislative authorities on laws and regulations issued by themselves; administrative interpretation refers to interpretations issued by administrative authorities on regulations and departmental rules issued by themselves; and judicial interpretations are those issued by the Supreme People's Court and the Supreme People's Procuratorates in their judicial and procuratorial work.

1.   CHINA'S SYSTEM OF LEGAL INTERPRETATION

The basics of the system of interpretation are set forth in the NPC Standing Committee's Resolution on Strengthening the Work of Interpretation of Laws (1981), still considered an authoritative source on interpretation, and the Legislation Law:

(1) The NPC Standing Committee has the authority to interpret the Constitution and supervise its enforcement and also has the authority to interpret laws that need to be further clarified or supplemented. The NPC Standing Committee has the authority to repeal administrative regulations

and local level regulations that contravene the Constitution and laws. *See* Legislation Law, Art. 88. This is an important clarification added by the Legislation Law; prior State Council directives vested exclusive power in interpreting administrative regulations in the State Council and its departments. In interpreting laws, the Standing Committee has the power to adopt decrees containing interpretations of laws, which are tantamount to legislative amendments.

(2) The Supreme People's Court and the Supreme People's Procuratorate have the authority to interpret questions of law arising out of specific applications of law in the adjudicative work of the courts and the work of the procuratorates respectively. Where the two bodies differ fundamentally in their interpretations, the matter is referred to the NPC Standing Committee for resolution.

(3) The State Council and its departments have the authority to interpret questions of law arising out of specific applications of law in areas other than adjudicative and procuratorial work.

(4) The standing committees of local level people's congresses may enact interpretations of regulations enacted by themselves or local people's congresses that need to be further clarified or supplemented. The local level people's governments may interpret questions of law arising out of the concrete application of local departmental rules.

Note that neither the Resolution nor the Legislation Law deals with the interpretation of administrative regulations and departmental rules. Under the Constitution, both the NPC and its Standing Committee are legislative bodies that have no jurisdiction over administration, which is within the authority of the State Council, and both therefore lack authority to issue laws governing the interpretation of administrative regulations and departmental rules, which are enacted by the State Council or its departments for the purpose of administration of the state. Under current practice, only the State Council and its departments have the power to interpret administrative regulations and rules to the exclusion of all other government organs, including the Supreme People's Court. While the Supreme People's Court has asserted wide powers to interpret laws, as further discussed below, it does not have the power to interpret administrative regulations and departmental rules.

With regard to (1) above, the Legislation Law now sets forth clear procedures through which entities can request constitutional or legal interpretation from the NPC Standing Committee. *See* Legislation Law, Arts. 43–47. The State Council, the Central Military Commission, the Supreme People's Court, the Supreme People's Procuratorate, and certain local level authorities can ask the NPC Standing Committee for legislative interpretation. In addition to these entities, any other government organs, organizations, and citizens can submit a request to the NPC Standing Committee to examine the consistency between (1) the Constitution and laws and (2) administrative regulations; and between (3) the Constitution, laws, and administrative regulations and (4) local regulations. *See* Legislation Law, Art. 88. When a request for legislative interpretation is put forward, the working organ of the NPC Standing Committee, the Legislative Affairs Office, will be responsible for preparing the draft interpretation. After the Council of Chairmen places the item on the agenda of the Standing Committee, the item is debated and then referred to the Law Committee, one of the special committees of the NPC itself, for preparation of the final version of the legislative interpretation, which is then put to a vote before a general meeting of the Standing Committee where a simple majority vote is required. Once the legislative interpretation is passed, it has the status of law. This process is tantamount to enacting legislative amendments in most legal systems.

While the NPC Standing Committee is entrusted by law with the exclusive power to interpret national laws, it has rarely exercised this power in practice, preferring to enact many supplements to national laws instead. It may be too burdensome to expect the NPC Standing Committee to undertake the task of issuing interpretations in addition to its heavy legislative responsibilities. In practice, all requests for legislative interpretation are referred by the Standing Committee to the Legislative Affairs Office, which offers an opinion directly on the matter rather than following the procedures contained in the Legislation Law of preparing drafts for review. The LAO is an organ of the Standing Committee and is not a legislative authority or vested with the power of legislative interpretation. The LAO's opinions do not have the force of law though they are often used as guidance in practice.

In practice, judicial interpretation by the Supreme People's Court (SPC) has emerged as the most frequent and important form of legal interpretation in the PRC, although such activity raises a host of constitutional and practical questions. Under existing guidelines, the SPC is empowered only to issue interpretations of questions of law arising out of concrete applications; general questions about ambiguities and gaps in laws are within the exclusive authority of the NPC Standing Committee. An example of concrete judicial interpretation is where a lower court submits a specific question of law arising out of a case that the court is in the process of deciding. The SPC (sometimes together with the Supreme People's Procuratorate) will issue a short reply that may refer to the specific facts of the case or merely state an abstract proposition of law. The SPC has also used other longer formats in answering questions from lower courts through combining several queries and using a question and answer format. So far these types of judicial interpretation can be said to fall within the legitimate interpretive power of the SPC. However, the SPC has often issued an interpretation of a specific law soon after it is enacted for the purpose of further elaborating on the law.

In some cases, the interpretation is much longer than the law itself and assumes an article-by-article format that clearly resembles a type of supplemental legislation. For example, after the Law of Civil Procedure, consisting of 270 articles, was enacted by the NPC in 1991, the SPC issued an interpretation consisting of 320 articles in 1992. Similarly, after the General Principles of Civil Law, consisting of 156 articles, came into effect in 1987, the SPC issued its 200–article interpretation in 1988. These interpretations, and many others, can hardly be considered judicial interpretations of questions arising in specific applications of law. To the contrary, they are often issued after the SPC has engaged in extensive consultations with legislative and administrative organs.

The SPC has also issued alone or in conjunction with the Supreme People's Procuratorate and other ministries interpretive documents relating to the administrative functions of various government organs. One of the SPC's constitutional duties is to supervise the administration of justice by the people's courts and documents issued by the SPC relating to the work of the courts may be viewed as administrative regulations or departmental rules for other government organs. When the SPC joins with other ministries and the Supreme People's Procuratorate in issuing interpretations, however, these administrative documents clearly surpass judicial administration as they become administrative directives for executive organs.

A review of the types of documents issued by the SPC discussed above indicates that it serves a role in the PRC legal system that is quite different from its counterparts in many other legal systems. The SPC is at once a judicial, legislative, and administrative organ. The SPC acts as a judicial organ when it decides cases (as discussed in the next chapter) or engages in judicial interpretation through addressing specific questions that arise in the application of laws by the lower courts. The SPC acts as a legislative body when it issues legislative interpretations that supplement and elaborate on existing laws issued by the NPC and the NPC Standing Committee and when it joins other ministries in issuing documents of a legislative nature. The SPC also issues what amount to administrative regulations or departmental rules when it promulgates documents relating to the work of the lower courts. Perhaps the authority to issue administrative regulations relating to the work of the courts can be inferred from the constitutional duty of the SPC to supervise the administration of the court system, but it is difficult to identify the source of the SPC's other legislative powers, which are clearly beyond the scope of the Resolution of the NPC Standing Committee set forth above. The SPC's judicial activism in the area of legislative interpretation may perhaps be attributable to its desire to carve out a more important role for itself and increase its stature and that of the court system as a whole in the PRC, but it is controversial and leads to a number of problems. Not only is the fundamental question of the legitimacy of the SPC's exercise of legislative powers raised because there is no apparent constitutional or legal basis for these powers, but there are also a number of knotty practical problems. For example, the SPC can apparently choose to issue comprehensive interpretations on any legislation that it wishes as the SPC does not consider itself to be bound by a requirement that interpretive issues are raised in a specific case that is being decided by the courts. In addition, there is also no mechanism to review the legislative interpretations issued by the SPC even where there is an apparent conflict between the SPC interpretation and the laws that are being interpreted.

To avoid being seen as exceeding its lawful powers, the SPC has made some efforts to restrain the exercise of judicial interpretation of legislation, although with some mixed results. In 1997, the SPC issued the Several Provisions on Judicial Interpretation, which provided that judicial interpretation is to be made by the SPC only and that lower courts are without power to issue interpretations. The provisions also reverse the prior practice by the SPC of requiring lower courts to cite judicial interpretations used in deciding cases. On the other hand, Article 4 of the Provisions declares that judicial interpretations of legislation by the SPC have the force of law and must be followed by lower courts. This assertion of what amounts to legislative power seems to be in violation of China's Constitution.

D.   THE ROLE OF THE COMMUNIST PARTY IN LAW–MAKING

Before turning to a discussion of some current issues with the PRC legislative system, this section turns to an examination of the role of the Communist Party in the legislative process. The previous chapter discussed the dominant role of the CPC in China's governance. The discussion below examines the role of the CPC in the legislative process, with a primary focus on the influence of the CPC on the NPC and its Standing Committee, as both are the highest legislative organs in the PRC.

For several reasons, the NPC and its Standing Committee have generally been viewed as docile, rubber-stamp bodies that routinely approve by unanimous or near unanimous vote legislation already approved by the CPC. The nomenklatura list of NPC appointments that must be approved by Party leaders includes all members of the NPC Standing Committee Party group, plus all of the approximately 155 members of the NPC Standing Committee as well as the top officials of the NPC special committees. The NPC Standing Committee Party group is the Party organization, consisting of the leading core of the Standing Committee, which serves as a conduit to the Central Committee of the CPC and ensures that the Standing Committee follows Party policy. Before each annual plenary session of the NPC, the CPC leadership convenes a meeting of all NPC delegates who are also Party members to discuss the NPC agenda as well as the suggestions and aspirations of Party leaders for the upcoming NPC session. Given that Party membership among delegates for the current Eleventh NPC is at 73%, these meetings determine most outcomes of the plenary NPC sessions. Moreover, until recently and perhaps still, the CPC had veto power over all draft legislation, which needed prior approval in principle by the Politburo and other central Party organs before being placed on the agenda of the NPC or its Standing Committee.

Recent changes in the voting patterns of the NPC and NPC Standing Committee indicate that these bodies have become less docile and subservient to Party instructions. In his book, *The Politics of Lawmaking in China*, Professor Murray Tanner indicates that when voting on work reports, economic plans and personnel appointments, the average dissenting vote in the NPC has risen from 5.1% in 1988 to about 12% in 1988 and was nearly 15% by 1995. When voting on draft laws, the NPC has averaged annual dissenting votes in a recent four-year period at 33%, 8%, 22% and 29%, far from the once almost automatic unanimous votes characteristic of the NPC. The NPC Standing Committee, a much smaller group, has averaged only a 4% dissent on any given vote. One of the most extraordinary instances of dissent was the negative vote by the NPC Standing Committee on the hotly contested Enterprise Bankruptcy Law, which was sent back for extensive revisions in August 1986 and eventually passed by the NPC Standing Committee in December 1986. The other remarkable instance occurred just several months after the crackdown at

Tiananmen Square when the Standing Committee voted down the draconian draft of the Law on Public Demonstrations submitted and sponsored by the Ministry of Public Security. Note that all of the draft legislation had been approved in principle by central Party organs so a dissenting vote represents an apparent disregard of Party directives.

The increased assertiveness of the NPC and its Standing Committee is attributed by Tanner to several factors. First, the attitudes of delegates have been changing as the penalties for speaking out and disobedience of Party suggestions has diminished; second, the NPC and its Standing Committee in particular have become stocked with retired Party elders who are persons of great ability and influence who sincerely want to increase the institutional capabilities of the Standing Committee; third, the substantial growth and development of the NPC's law-making departments, including its specialized committees, has led to the development of a powerful and influential professional law-making bureaucracy. Although these may be described as three separate developments, they can all be traced to the sincere desire by the Party to develop a stronger and more professional legislature and a more predictable and formal legislative process. It should not be surprising that one of the consequences of a stronger and more professional legislature is the rise of more independent minded legislators. Some dissent and increased assertiveness is the price of having more competent legislators, and the Party appears willing to tolerate some disobedience.

This desire for a stronger legislative system is motivated by some of the lessons that the Party learned from the Cultural Revolution, which had concentrated most policy decisions in the Party's own hands, leading to an excessive burden of responsibility for an unmanageable number of decisions without sufficient resources or expertise. The Party also sincerely wanted to establish a stronger legal system in order to prevent the excesses of the Cultural Revolution from reoccurring and a professional legislature was a vital part of such a system. In addition, Party elders such as Deng Xiaoping wanted the legislature to build laws to support new economic reforms and wanted to promote the instrumental goal of using the legislature to build consensus and support for bold new directions undertaken as a result of economic reforms. All of these reasons were involved in making the decision to decentralize decision-making. One of the most remarkable documents demonstrating the desire to decentralize is the CPC's Central Committee Document No. 8, "Several Opinions of the Central Committee on Strengthening Leadership over Lawmaking Work." The document's name is somewhat misleading as it advocates the relaxation of Party control over law-making. One key passage grants an unprecedented degree of autonomy to the NPC and its Standing Committee:

> Except for Constitutional revisions, political laws, and significant economic and administrative laws, the NPC and its Standing Committee undertake the organization, drafting, and review of

other laws, and normally do not report to the Party core. As for those few laws that need to be reported to the Party core for discussion, if the Party core has already expressed clear views or regulations, then these also need not be reported to the Party core again.

The most significant issues raised by some of these changes discussed above is whether they signal a fundamental shift in Party attitudes and the emergence in the future of a truly independent and deliberative legislature in the PRC. For a number of reasons, it is difficult to draw any conclusions on these questions as the record is unclear on how far reaching these changes really are. First, despite the language of the Central Committee Document No. 8, it is unclear that the Party has voluntarily relinquished its control over all legislation submitted to the NPC and its Standing Committee. Much of the inner-workings of the PRC government and Party work are secretive and unknown; the language in Document No. 8 alone cannot be considered to be a definitive indicator of a fundamental change in Party policy and its actual practice. As with many documents in the PRC, Document No. 8 may be a policy statement that is aspirational in nature and not reflective of current practices.

Second, although it is clear that the NPC and, to a lesser extent, the NPC Standing Committee, are no longer the docile rubber-stamp of the Party core, the levels of dissent registered in these bodies is far below comparable levels in democratic countries. While dissent levels have reached as high as 40% in the case of the Shenzhen Special Legislative Authority Law in 1989, only a majority vote is needed to pass any legislation and the dissent levels are only symbolic until they cross the 50% threshold. Moreover, without more research and information, it is difficult to draw conclusions about the significance of the dissents. The Party itself is not monolithic and it is known that there have been factions and disagreements within the Party elite. Dissent within the NPC, where the bulk of the delegates are Party members, may signal a genuine disagreement on policy issues among factions of the Party and its elites, but such dissent may not express disloyalty to the Party itself. Such disagreements may be more likely as legislation becomes more sophisticated and technical. In addition, the Enterprise Bankruptcy Law and the Public Demonstrations Law are still the only two known examples of draft bills voted down after approval by the Party and both of these laws may be special cases. Both were voted down by the Standing Committee, which is stocked with influential Party members and is under tighter Party control than the full NPC. The Politburo's approval of both laws was in principle and it may have been left to the Party cadres with more professional expertise to make the final decisions over both laws, which were passed overwhelming in the case of the Bankruptcy Law and unanimously in the case of the Public Demonstrations Law when they came up for a second vote before the NPC Standing Committee several months later after revision. In any event, the negative votes on the first drafts of these two laws do not indicate a growing trend in China.

Third, the real test of how tolerant the Party has become of dissent and independence in the NPC and its Standing Committee is when a draft bill that is of vital importance to a united Party leadership is rejected by one of these bodies. This would be a direct challenge to the Party's authority as opposed to registering some mild disagreement within Party ranks while ultimately agreeing with the Party elite's directives. At present, an outright challenge does not appear to have occurred. To be sure, important changes have occurred in the PRC's major legislative bodies, which have become more professional and competent, but it is premature to suggest that a fundamental shift in the Party's control over the legislative process has occurred.

E. ISSUES WITH THE CURRENT LEGISLATIVE SYSTEM

This section of this chapter now turns to an examination of some of the problems with the current legislative system in the PRC, some of which were alluded to or discussed briefly in the preceding discussion. Many of these problems can be traced to the structure of the current proprietary system in which different government organs are considered to be owners of their domains with intrinsic legislative powers and the authority to interpret their own legislation. This system gives rise to multiple legislative sources, each competing to protect its own domain of power. Adding to the complexity of the system is that its growth was more by accident than by design as China engaged in aggressive expansion of its legislative capabilities after 1978 in order to support its drive for economic reform and modernization. While the new Legislation Law has helped to clarify some of the issues plaguing the legislative system, a number of major issues remain. The discussion below briefly considers several of these issues.

1.   UNCLEAR BOUNDARIES OF AUTHORITY

No one has been able to satisfactorily distinguish in theory or practice between the authority of the NPC to enact basic laws and the authority of the NPC Standing Committee to enact other national laws. The distinction that some scholars have tried to make between basic laws that affect the whole of society and other laws that affect only a particular aspect seems to be little more than a tautology and, in any event, does not seem to reflect actual practices. The Trade Union Law was enacted by the NPC, although few in the PRC would consider the law to be basic or fundamental. Chinese scholars regard the Company Law to be a basic law, which falls within the jurisdiction of the NPC, but the law was actually enacted by the NPC Standing Committee. While the NPC enacted the Criminal Procedure Law, the NPC Standing Committee enacted the Law of Civil Procedure, although it appears difficult to make a distinction between the two. The boundaries between the NPC and its Standing Committee are further clouded by the Standing Committee's authority to amend or supplement basic laws when the NPC is not in session so long as the basic purpose of the original legislation is not contravened. There are no existing legal standards on what constitutes an amendment or when the amendment contravenes the basic purpose of the original statute. This lack of standards means that the NPC Standing Committee can, in effect, enact basic laws by making fundamental changes to existing NPC legislation. For example, after the Criminal Law was enacted in 1979, it was supplemented and amended more than twenty times by 1997 when a major new Criminal Law was enacted by the NPC. Most PRC scholars agree that some of the amendments by the NPC Standing Committee expanded and changed the basic principles of the original law.

It is also difficult to delimit the legislative boundaries between central and local level authorities. The Constitution and the Legislation Law seem to provide little guidance on this issue other than stipulating that local legislation is valid so long as it does not contravene the Constitution and central level legislation, applies within a local region, and is within the competence of the enacting body. Under this principle, any local legislation on any subject matter is valid unless one can point to a direct conflict with a higher-level legal norm. This would appear to create few controls over local legislation. In Fujian province, one local regulation prescribed criminal liability and penalties when dealing with the issues of compulsory education even though criminal matters are a subject matter of basic laws that are within the exclusive domain of the full NPC. While the new Legislation Law provides that the NPC Standing Committee has the power to repeal local legislation that conflicts with higher-level legal norms, the Standing Committee also had this power directly under the Constitution prior to the enactment of the Legislation Law, but it has never been exercised.

2. ACTING WITHOUT A CLEAR BASIS OF AUTHORITY

An earlier section has already discussed the questionable authority of the Supreme People's Court in issuing article-by-article legislative interpretations that are more comprehensive than the original laws. In addition, while the SPC and other ministries often work together to issue interpretive documents, there is nothing in the Constitution or laws that authorizes this type of cooperative effort among different government organs.

The SPC is not the most spectacular example of a legislative organ exercising power without a clear basis of authority. Prior to the enactment of the Legislation Law in 2000, there was no legal or constitutional authority for the Central Military Commission to exercise legislative powers. Yet, the CMC (sometimes jointly with the State Council) had issued 99 separate rules and regulations by 2005 and the number of legislative items issued by its subordinate organs had reach almost 900. In 1990, the chairman of the CMC showed little concern for this issue when he issued the Provisional Regulations of the People's Liberation Army on Legislative Procedures. Although the Legislation Law now recognizes the authority of the CMC to issue military regulations and the authority of its subordinate entities to issue rules, the new Law merely codified what had been a long time exercise of power without any apparent legal basis. Moreover, although Article 93 of the Legislation Law recognizes this authority in the CMC, this provision may be of questionable legality because the Legislation Law itself must abide by the Constitution, which does not recognize any such powers in the CMC.

The CMC's lack of concern about a legal basis for its exercise of legislative power may be traceable to its views that it had the inherent power to issue administrative regulations as it had complete dominion over its subject matter. For instance, in its 1993 suggestion to amend the Constitution, the CMC took the view that it can issue military rules for internal use in the army and that therefore the Constitution did not need to be amended. This assumption appears to be prevalent among China's many different government organs, most of which have some domain over which they assert ownership. This assumption may account for the thousands of rules, decisions, orders, notices, instructions, resolutions and other types of legal or quasi-legal items that are constantly being issued by China's many central and local level government entities. The hierarchy of legal norms set forth in this chapter based upon the Legislation Law does not encompass the bewildering multitude of items with different titles that are constantly being issued. Moreover, many of these items are far more pertinent to the daily conduct of social and business activities than national laws, which are usually too general for specific implementation. Many of these items are given some legal effect, although the basis of authority for these items is unclear and their status is ambiguous.

3. COMPETING AND CONFLICTING NORMS

The many different sources and types of legislation and the sharp rise in the amount of enacted legislation has led to a system in which there can be many conflicts and inconsistencies among various legal norms. For example, administrative regulations enacted by the State Council to implement the enforcement of a basic law enacted by the NPC may change, expand, or be inconsistent with the original law. Departmental rules issued by different ministries and commissions may be inconsistent with or compete with each other. The previous discussion of the Supreme People's Court indicated that its judicial interpretations of laws proceed in an article-by-article fashion and are often more comprehensive than the original laws. While the new Legislation Law provides further clarification on the power of various authorities, such as the NPC, its Standing Committee, and the State Council, to repeal inconsistent norms, the power to invalidate legal norms had already existed under the Constitution and, as previously noted, had rarely, if ever, been exercised by these authorities. In keeping with the practice existing prior to the enactment of the Legislation Law, while these authorities have the power to repeal inconsistent norms and to interpret legislation, they are not required to exercise it. Moreover, all of these bodies are busy with an active legislative agenda and it would appear to be unrealistic to expect them to engage in formal consideration of the myriad issues of inconsistencies between various legal norms, which would require placing these items on a formal agenda and assigning them to various work committees for a report and recommendation. Rather, based upon the author's own experience in the PRC, it is far more likely that issues concerning legal inconsistencies will be dealt with by an informal advisory opinion from a department or division of the concerned government organ and the opinion may be delivered orally in a meeting with no written records. Even where the opinion is written, it has no binding legal effect and can serve as guidance only.

4. LEGAL NORMS AND PARTY DOCUMENTS

Returning to the issue of distinguishing legal from non-legal norms raised in the beginning of this chapter, the PRC continues to give non-legal policy norms issued by the CPC some binding legal effect. Judicial organs in the early history of the PRC were encouraged to directly apply the policies of the Party in the absence of an applicable law. In times of turmoil, laws and legal institutions were completely disregarded in favor of directly applying Party policies and directives. This practice was justified based upon the theory that the policies of the CPC are the foundation of the state and are then subsequently concretized or embodied in laws through the legislative processes of the PRC. Laws are a formal and mature form of Party policies, which are fundamental. In the absence of a law, courts should then apply Party policies or directives. Under the modern PRC Constitution, however, the practice of directly applying Party policies can no longer be justified. The modern Constitution accepts the rule of law and subjects the Party itself to law. The Constitution and the Legislation Law also detail the division of legislative power among government organs and the legislative process. Policy documents issued by the Party do not fall within the category of law as they do not satisfy the criteria set forth in the Constitution. In theory then, PRC authorities should follow formal law and not CPC policies, but in practice, Party policies, directives, and orders continue to be treated as having binding force in the PRC. The CPC and government organs sometimes also issue policy documents together. Moreover, the Party continues to exert behind-the-scenes influence on the administration of law; both the courts and the procuratorates continue to be guided by Party policies and directives in controversial or important cases. Overall, while the continuing reform and development of the legal system has led to a sharper distinction between law and policy, Party policies, which are considered non-legal norms, continue to have some binding force in China and to exert a direct influence on the administration of law.

CHAPTER SIX

COURTS AND
PROCURATORATES

While the previous chapter examined the PRC's legislative organs, which are responsible for drafting and enacting laws, this chapter examines the courts and procuratorates, the basic institutions involved in the application and enforcement of the law. In the PRC, courts, procuratorates, and the public security organs are considered to be the judicial organs (*sifa jiguan*), i.e. those organs responsible for the administration of the law enacted by the legislative organs. The legislative and judicial organs of the PRC constitute the basic institutions involved in the creation, application, and enforcement of laws. Aside from the legislative and judicial organs, there is also the system of lawyers, legal education, mediation committees and other forms of alternative dispute resolution, which is the subject of the next chapter. All of these institutions together form the legal system of the PRC.

Of the legislative and judicial organs, the NPC, the NPC Standing Committee, the Supreme People's Court, the Supreme People's Procuratorate, and the organs of judicial administration and their counterparts at local levels may be considered to be the major legal organs. As the previous chapter noted, the State Council and its departments are more actively involved than the NPC and its Standing Committee in law and rule-making, but the primary concern of the State Council and its subordinate entities is the administration of the Chinese state; their legislative powers are viewed as supplementary or necessary adjuncts to their basic administrative powers. On the other hand, the law and policy-making duties of the NPC and its Standing Committee are viewed as their primary function. (That the State Council appears to surpass the NPC and its Standing Committee in importance as a legislative organ even though the State Council's exercise of legislative power is an adjunct to its administrative duties may be an indication of the relative importance of administrative organs as compared with legal organs in the PRC, but the State Council itself is not primarily a legal organ.) Similarly, the application, interpretation, and enforcement of the law are the primary functions of the judicial organs. Of the judicial organs, courts, which adjudicate cases, and procuratorates, which prosecute them, are the most closely involved in the type of legal work traditionally associated in western legal systems with the application and interpretation of laws. The primary role of the public security organs is the use of coercive means to uphold the law as opposed to the use of legal reasoning in the interpretation, application, and enforcement of the law, which are the basic duties of the courts and procuratorates. In addition, the Ministry of Public Security, which has overall responsibility for public security, is a department of the State Council and is primarily concerned with maintaining public order and safety as part of the State Council's overall responsibility for state administration. By contrast, the people's courts and procuratorates are given independent status under the PRC Constitution and are directly under the people's congresses at various levels. For these reasons, although the public security organs are considered to be judicial organs by the PRC, the discussion in this chapter will focus on the courts and procuratorates and devote less time to the public security organs. On the other hand, because the public security organs play a major role in PRC criminal prosecutions, the discussion of criminal justice in Chapter 8 will return to a more extended examination of the role of public security organs in the criminal process of the PRC.

One distinction between the PRC judicial organs and their counterparts in many western countries is that all of these organs are deemed to be an integral part of a single, coordinated mechanism designed to correctly implement the law. The public security organs are to investigate cases of illegal activity, the procuratorate is to prosecute cases, and the courts are to adjudicate cases. The system was designed with criminal prosecutions in mind and the public security organs and procuratorates are not usually involved in civil or economic cases. In the area of criminal prosecutions, however, the three organs and the three segments of the process are viewed as part of one larger, unified structure and coordination and cooperation among these entities has been expressly provided for in the laws. Unlike the case of the United States, the PRC legal system does not contemplate a system of mutual checks and balances with the courts and the law playing a major role in reviewing police and prosecutorial behavior in the criminal process. In the PRC system, the procuratorate serves as the organ of supervision, but it exists within a unitary system in which there is a single organ that checks upon the work of other organs.

A. THE ROLE OF THE COURTS

Article 123 of the PRC Constitution provides that the people's courts are the judicial organs of the state and are vested with the state's adjudicative powers. Unlike the US legal system in which the judicial branch is a co-equal branch of government, the people's courts are subordinate to the people's congresses at each level. At the national level, the National People's Congress is at the top of the hierarchy of government organs with three administrative organs created underneath the NPC: the State Council, the Supreme People's Court, and the Supreme People's Procuratorate. Further, although in theory each of the three organs under the NPC are ranked equally, the premier of the State Council is ranked one level above the president of the Supreme People's Court, who is bureaucratically ranked equivalent to a vice premier. Although this may seem like a minor technical distinction only, in China's rigid bureaucratic system the distinction indicates that the State Council is a more powerful organ than either the Supreme People's Court or the Supreme People's Procuratorate.

Article 126 of the Constitution provides that the "people's courts exercise judicial power independently, in accordance with the provisions of the law, and are not subject to interference by any administrative organ, public organization or individual." The ability of the courts to operate independently must be evaluated against a number of other provisions of the law and realities of the PRC government power structure. Article 128 of the Constitution provides that the SPC is responsible to and shall report on its work to the NPC and its Standing Committee and that lower level courts are responsible to the organs of state power that created them. Article 67(6) of the Constitution further provides that the Standing Committee shall supervise the work of the SPC. Neither the Constitution nor any written laws, however, further define the supervisory authority of the NPC or its Standing Committee over the SPC. The Constitution and the Organic Law of the People's Courts (1979, amended 1983) also provide that the NPC appoints or removes the president of the SPC and that the NPC Standing Committee appoints or removes its vice presidents and its judicial officers following the recommendations of the president of the SPC. Lower level people's congresses and their standing committees have a similar power to appoint or dismiss judges. At all levels of the court system, there is no security of tenure for judges and their terms of service are similar to that of other state functionaries. (In practice, many persons may be transferred back and forth from the courts to the procuratorates and other government organs several times in the course of a few years.) The NPC controls the funding and staffing of the SPC, duties which the NPC has delegated to the State Council and its Ministry of Finance. Similar structures also exist at lower levels where people's congresses also control key appointments and funding for courts. Specialty courts are generally funded by their organizational heads: the military, railway, and maritime courts are funded by the People's Liberation Army, Ministry of Railways, and Ministry of Transportation respectively. In sum, judges are beholden to the people's congresses or governments for funding, staffing, and appointments and have no security of tenure. The prescription to exercise judicial powers independently must be understood against the political and practical realities of the government system in which the people's courts operate.

1.   PARTY INFLUENCE AND THE COURTS

Aside from the influence of other government organs, there is also the issue of influence by the Communist Party. At the national level of Party organs, the CPC Central Committee has established a central political-legal committee, usually headed by a member of the elite Politburo. At each lower level, there is someone within the Party committee that is in charge of political legal work and works with the political-legal committee of the Party at the corresponding level, i.e. a provincial level political-legal committee. The political-legal committee is established to ensure Party leadership in the political legal organs at all levels; the heads of all important government organs involved in political legal work are members of the committee. The typical political-legal committee consists of the head of the public security organ, the president of the people's court, the president of the people's procuratorate, the head of the judicial administrative organs, and the head of the administrative organ for civil affairs at the provincial or local level. The political-legal committee in turn reports to the Party committee at the particular level.

The degree of involvement by the political-legal committee in the work of the courts has varied over the years. During the early years of the PRC, the courts would ask for instructions on how to decide cases from the political-legal committee. The recent practice has been for the Party to set overall policy guidelines and to avoid direct involvement in the review of individual cases. In interviews with the author, judges in the PRC have often denied that the political-legal committee will exercise heavy-handed control over court decisions; most judges indicate that the political-legal committee takes very little interest in routine cases and exercises no influence at all in concrete decision-making by the courts. In most cases involving ordinary business disputes, it is likely that the Party would find little reason to intervene unless there were unusual circumstances involving very large sums or political corruption. A few judges have indicated to the author, however, that in politically sensitive or controversial cases, courts may seek advice from the Party, but that this is the exceptional instance. As with many aspects of the PRC legal system, it is not possible to determine with any certainty the extent of the Party's influence on the courts. Judges naturally wish to present their institutions in the best light and it is understandable that they would indicate that as judges they act independently. Whether or not the Party continues to intervene in individual cases, however, there can be little doubt that the Party continues to influence the policy orientation and general direction of the courts. All of the leading officers of the court, including the president, are Party members and serve on the political-legal committee that reports directly to the Party committee. These leading judicial officers influence the court by serving on the collegiate panels that decide cases and on the adjudication committee that reviews decisions by the panels or individual judges (discussed further below). The Party also exercises continuing influence through the appointment of particular judges and judicial personnel and by the issuance of certain normative documents that become part of the internal handbook for judges. Whether the influence of the Party and other entities undermines the independence of the people's courts is a topic that will be further examined below.

2.   THE STRUCTURE OF THE COURT SYSTEM

The structure of the court system in the PRC is based upon four levels of courts with at most two trials to complete a case. The first trial is the case of first instance and the second trial occurs on appeal. Depending upon the gravity of the offense, the trial of first instance can occur at any level in the system with a final appeal to a court at the next higher level. Cases of first instance decided by the Supreme People's Court are final.

At the lowest level are the more than 3,000 basic people's courts at the county level. In order to provide additional access to the court system, the basic people's courts have established over 30,000 subordinate divisions known as people's tribunals in towns and villages below the county level. People's tribunals are considered to be a component part of the basic people's courts and the judgments of people's tribunals are considered to be judgments and orders of the basic people's courts. Above the county level are approximately 390 intermediate people's courts in cities and prefectures within provinces, thirty-one high level people's courts at provincial levels (including autonomous regions and cities directly under the central government) and the Supreme People's Court in Beijing. There is a three-tier court system (basic, intermediate, and high people's courts) in every province, autonomous region, and in the four cities directly under the central government, Beijing, Tianjin, Shanghai, and Chongqing. There are also specialty courts such as the approximately fifty-five military courts, seventy-five railway transport courts, and eight maritime courts. The jurisdiction of each level of the people's courts will be further discussed below.

The people's courts are normally divided into four divisions (*shenpan fating*): criminal, civil, economic, and administrative. Each division hears the corresponding type of cases. In some courts some of these divisions are further divided. In the SPC, the high and intermediate courts and some basic level people's courts, there is a second criminal division, which deals with petitions against criminal judgments that have become legally effective and for cases falling under adjudication supervision by the procuratorate (further discussed below). The high people's courts of Beijing, Guangdong, Fujian, and Hainan have established an additional division for intellectual property cases, which would otherwise be heard in the civil division. Other high people's courts, such as the court in Jiangsu Province, have established a second civil division dealing with intellectual property. The distinction between economic and civil cases is that the latter mainly involve individuals and their property, e.g. housing, business and labor disputes, inheritance, tort, and defamation. Economic cases are deemed to involve a sector of the economy such as transportation, machinery, consumer products, and mainly involve enterprises as opposed to individuals. Prior to economic reforms begun in 1978, such economic cases were handled administratively by government organs involved in economic management. The growing role of the courts since 1978 in resolving economic disputes attests to their increasing influence in the PRC. The administrative divisions of the courts were established even more recently beginning only in 1986. These divisions are designed to handle the growing number of cases brought by individuals against government entities that challenge the legality of administrative actions.

A review of the decade of the 1990s shows that the work of the PRC courts has been increasing steadily. In 1990, the courts dealt with a total of 2.9 million cases. By 1995, the workload of the courts increased to 4.5 million cases. In 2007, the courts dealt with a total of 8,108,675 cases, including 4,383,080 civil cases (54% of the total), 701,784 criminal cases (8.7%), and 95,370 administrative cases (1.2%).

3. COURT PERSONNEL

The personnel that staff a court include the court's president (*yuanzhang*) and vice-presidents. Each division will also have a chief judge (*tingzhang*), deputy chief judges, and assistant judges. The Organic Law of the People's Courts also provides for people's assessors, lay judges who participate as members of the court divisions and enjoy equal rights with judges during the period of their service. The people's assessors system was first established in 1951 to promote the ideal of popular participation in the administration of justice, although it has proven difficult in practice to find assessors with legal knowledge. As noted earlier, the leading members of the people's courts, including the president, vice president, chief judges of divisions, and deputy chief judges are appointed or removed by the people's congresses at the corresponding levels. The people's courts directly appoint assistant judges, who assist judges in their work and who are similar to apprentices or law clerks for judges in the United States. Prior to 1983, the only qualification for being a judge at any level was that the person must have reached the age of twenty-three, must be eligible to vote, must be able to stand for election to public office, and must not have been previously deprived of any political rights. There was no requirement of any legal education or background. The 1983 amendment to the Organic Law of the People's Courts added the requirement that judges must have professional legal knowledge. The Judges Law (2001) provides that qualification as a judge requires an advanced degree specializing in law or work for one or more years when combined with a college degree. Judges employed prior to the implementation of the Judges Law must undergo further training to attain these requirements within a specific period of time. These requirements were put in place because in the early history of the PRC, many judges did not have any legal training.

With the exception of the president of a court, which is an appointed position under the authority of the people's congresses, all other judges serve as civil servants. Most judges enter judicial service directly from law school or from college after working for one or two years. Judges who enter the judiciary do so at the lower levels by passing qualifying exams, but some judges are able to immediately enter higher courts, including the Supreme People's Court, as junior colleagues or as assistant judges. In general, judges are viewed as administrators within a system of legislative supremacy in which the NPC and its Standing Committee have the authority not only to enact laws but also have the authority to interpret them. Within such a system, judges have a role limited to the straightforward and mechanical application of the law to identify the correct solution without much need for judicial discretion or legal reasoning of the type that is identified with judges in the United States. Like other civil servants, judges undergo a continuing annual regimen of exams and evaluations. According to Article 20 of the Judges Law, judges are evaluated based upon a list of enumerated criteria, including results reached, moral character and ideology, work attitude, and judicial style. The annual examination is the basis for wage increases, adjustments in bureaucratic rank, need for further training, and dismissals. The typical salaries for judges, including those on the SPC, are now about RMB 5000 ($730) per month, which is on par with other mid-level bureaucrats and civil servants.

In addition to judges, courts have other personnel, including court clerks who keep records, marshals who execute judgments, forensic physicians, and judicial police who maintain security as required. The large number of personnel reflects the administrative functions of PRC courts, which have a number of administrative responsibilities in addition to their role in adjudicating cases. The Supreme People's Court has nearly 600 employees, including 1 president, 8 vice presidents, 80 judges, 120 assistant judges, and 50 judicial police. In addition to these personnel, the SPC also has a large number of personnel assisting in the general administration of the court system. In addition to the court and its divisions, the SPC includes a judicial administrative office, a foreign affairs bureau, a research department, a division for complaints and petitions, a general office, and a personnel department. Courts below the SPC have a similar though smaller administrative bureaucracy. In 2007, the PRC had a total of approximately 180,000 judges for all of its four levels of courts.

4. JURISDICTION OF THE PEOPLE'S COURTS

The Organic Law of the People's Courts (OLPC) and other laws set forth the jurisdiction of the courts based upon the importance of the case. (The jurisdiction of specialty courts is set forth in other laws.) The lines of jurisdiction between courts are not delineated with precision and, as a result, a number of courts can potentially exercise jurisdiction over any given case. With the exception of the basic people's courts, all other courts, including the Supreme People's Court, can act either as courts of original jurisdiction handling cases of the first instance or as courts of appellate jurisdiction handling cases of second instance.

a. Basic People's Courts

Article 21 of the OLPC provides that basic people's courts adjudicate ordinary criminal and civil cases of the first instance. Criminal cases involving the death penalty or life in prison and important foreign-related civil cases are excluded from the jurisdiction of basic people's courts. Under Article 21 of the OLPC, basic people's courts can decide to request transfer of cases of "major importance" to a higher people's court. Basic people's courts are also authorized to settle criminal and civil cases that do not require trials and to direct the work of the people's mediation committees.

b. Intermediate People's Courts

Article 25 of the OLPC provides that intermediate people's courts have jurisdiction over cases of first instance as provided by law, cases of first instance transferred from the basic people's courts, and cases of appeal or protest. As in the case of basic people's courts, intermediate people's courts can request that a case of major importance be transferred to a higher court. Article 19 of the Law of Civil Procedure (1991) further provides that intermediate courts have jurisdiction over major cases involving a foreign element, cases with significant impact, and cases determined to be under their jurisdiction by the Supreme People's Court. Article 14 of the Administrative Litigation Law grants intermediate courts jurisdiction over:

(1) cases confirming patent rights of invention and cases handled by Customs; (2) suits against specific administrative acts undertaken by departments under the State Council or by the people's governments of provinces, autonomous regions,

or municipalities directly under the central government; and (3) grave and complicated cases.

Article 20 of the Criminal Procedure Law (1996) provides that the intermediate court shall be the court of first instance in counterrevolutionary cases; cases punishable by death or life imprisonment; and cases in which foreigners have committed offenses or where Chinese citizens have committed offenses against foreigners. Note that whereas the Law of Civil Procedure provides that intermediate courts have jurisdiction over major civil cases, all criminal cases involving foreigners are to be tried in the first instance in the intermediate courts.

c. High People's Courts

Under Article 28 of the OLPC, the high people's courts have jurisdiction over cases of first instance assigned by laws to their jurisdiction; cases of first instance transferred from lower courts; appeals and protests against judgments and orders of lower courts; and protests lodged by the people's procuratorates in accordance with their duties of judicial supervision, further discussed below. Article 20 of the Law of Civil Procedure further provides that the high people's courts have jurisdiction over major cases within their area of jurisdiction. Similarly, Article 21 of the Criminal Procedure Law provides that the high people's courts have jurisdiction of first instance over major criminal cases that pertain to an entire province, autonomous region, or municipality directly under the central government. Under Article 15 of the Administrative Litigation Law, high people's courts have jurisdiction of first instance over administrative law cases that are grave and complicated involving the entire province.

d. The Supreme People's Court

Under Article 32 of the OLPC, the Supreme People's Court has jurisdiction of first instance over cases assigned to it by laws and decrees and cases that the SPC considers it should try itself; over appeals and protests against judgments and orders of high people's courts and specialty courts; and over protests lodged by the Supreme People's Procuratorate in accordance with its duties of judicial supervision. The SPC also has original jurisdiction over administrative, civil, and criminal cases that affect the whole country. Note that the SPC in the exercise of its discretion can choose to assume jurisdiction of first instance over any case as it deems appropriate. As a practical matter, the SPC rarely tries cases in the first instance preferring to hear protests and appeals from decisions by high people's courts, specialty courts, and the Supreme People's Procuratorate. The SPC also supervises lower courts.

The SPC also has the authority to issue interpretations concerning the application of laws in judicial proceedings. As noted earlier in Chapter 5, the SPC has assumed a leading role in legal interpretation, although its authority to do so remains questionable. Aside from its adjudicatory and interpretative functions, the SPC also plays a considerable role as a legislative and administrative organ.

5.　THE PROCESS OF THE COURTS IN DECIDING CASES

Cases in China are decided by a collegiate bench consisting of an odd number of judges with the exception of simple civil and minor criminal cases, which can be heard through a summary procedure before a single judge. In lower courts, a collegiate panel will generally consist of three judges with the size of the panel increasing with the level of the court. A collegiate bench can consist of judges and people's assessors or lay judges only. For cases on appeal or of second instance, however, the collegiate panel will not include people's assessors. In criminal cases, an investigation by the public security organs, the procuratorate, and judicial personnel precedes the trial of first instance. The trial will involve the interrogation of the defendant, questioning of witnesses, presentation of evidence, and court debate. The court then adjourns and prepares to announce its judgment. In criminal cases, the court must announce its judgment within one month and cannot exceed one and one-half months. Civil cases follow a similar pattern of questioning, presentation of evidence, and court debate by the parties. In civil cases, courts may attempt to persuade the parties to resolve the case by mediation prior to and even after the trial. Judgment is rendered within six months of the date that the case was put on the trial docket; in the case of expedited procedures provided for simple cases involving a single judge, judgment must be rendered within three months of the time the case was put on the court's docket. Appeals lie in the court of the next higher level and there is only one appeal as of right in all cases. In criminal cases only, the procuratorate, the prosecuting organ, also has a right of protest by way of appeal against the judgment of the court. The right of protest allows the procuratorate to seek a new trial from a higher court when the original court has committed some serious error. Appeals and protests in criminal cases must be decided within one and one-half months, appeals in civil cases must be decided within three months, and in administrative cases within two months from the day of receiving the appeal.

In addition to the panel or the judges, the president and the adjudication committee of a court also play important roles in the work of the court. Although there are indications that the practice is now changing, judgments of a court are not normally valid without the signature of the president of the court or the chief judge of a division of the court. The president or chief judge in most instances would not have been part of the collegiate bench that heard the case. Before endorsement, the president may refer the case to the court's adjudication committee. Article 11 of the OLPC provides that each court is to establish an adjudication committee consisting of the president and judges appointed by the standing committee at the corresponding level of the court with the recommendation of the court's president. While the composition of a collegiate panel may vary from case to case, the membership of the adjudication committee is permanent. The president of the court presides over the adjudication committee and the chief procurator of the people's procuratorate of the corresponding level have the right to attend meetings of the adjudication committee without voting rights. The purpose of the adjudication committee is to review difficult or controversial cases heard by a collegiate bench; a judge from the bench will normally make a brief report to the adjudication committee that may instruct the collegiate bench on how to decide the case.

Adjudication committees may decide a case based only upon a brief presentation by a judge without reviewing the papers or hearing from the parties. In a typical court, the adjudication committee may meet two or three times per month for half or a full day without any advanced preparation. At each meeting as many as twenty cases will be considered so it would be difficult for the adjudication committee to give significant attention to any case and the time spent on any case is limited. In some situations, depending upon schedules, a case may go before the adjudication committee before the trial itself begins so that in effect the case has already been decided before the public trial, rendering the trial itself meaningless.

6. LAW REPORTS

China follows a continental legal system model in which court decisions did not have binding precedential value as in a common law system such as that of the United States. In many cases, a court will decide a case by issuing an order that is no more than one or two sentences in length with no legal reasoning or analysis. There is no comprehensive national reporting system in China in which all court opinions are officially recorded. Since 1985, the Supreme People's Court has published the *Gazette of the Supreme People's Court of the People's Republic of China* for the purpose of providing instruction and guidance to lower courts and lower level procuratorates. The *Gazette* is published four times each year and contains notable cases decided by the SPC in addition to important national legislation, official documents, and judicial interpretations. The editorial committee of the *Gazette* has compiled *A Complete Collection of Leading Cases From the Gazette of the Supreme People's Court, 1985–1999* (Police Officer Press 1999), which contains about 300 cases that have appeared in the *Gazette* from 1985–1999. In recent years, some provincial level courts have also compiled collections of cases for the purpose of instructing lower courts. The most notable collection among lower courts is *Selected Cases Adjudicated in the Courts of Shanghai* (Shanghai People's Press, 1994–present), which is published annually and contains about 100 cases culled from all levels of courts in Shanghai. The recently instituted *Judicial Document Selections of the People's Court* (Law Press, 2001–present) is an official publication that contains the selected full text of written judgments, awards, and mediation documents.

7.   REOPENING FINAL JUDGMENTS BY ADJUDICATION SUPERVISION

One feature of the PRC court system that distinguishes it from legal systems such as that of the United States is the practice of adjudication supervision. The various laws of procedure allow the parties, the president of the court, the Supreme People's Court, and the procuratorate to reopen a final judgment and have the case retried where there was some serious error involved in the original proceeding. Adjudication supervision should be distinguished from the process of filing appeals or protests discussed in the previous section above. All appeals or protests must be filed within strict time limits. In civil and administrative cases, appeals must be filed within fifteen days and appeals of court orders must be filed within ten days from the time the judgment or order is received. In criminal cases, all appeals and protests from orders must be filed within ten and five days respectively from the time that the judgment or order is received. Once these time periods lapse, the automatic right to an appeal or protest is terminated and the judgment becomes final. In addition, after the appeal has resulted in a trial of second instance, the judgment of the second trial is final and cannot be challenged by further appeal. By contrast, the process of adjudication supervision permits the various parties to potentially reopen a judgment of first or second instance long after all time limits for appeals have expired and the judgment has become "final." In the case of civil cases, Article 181 of the Law of Civil Procedure provides for two-year statute of limitations for a party to apply for a retrial under adjudication supervision. Because Article 181 refers to "a party," it is unclear whether this time limitation also applies to the courts and procuratorates, which also have the right to seek a retrial. If the courts and procuratorates are not "parties" and outside the two-year statute of limitations of Article 181, then civil judgments are potentially subject to being reopened at any time. There is no statute of limitations in criminal cases and every year the president of the Supreme People's Court states that the process of adjudication supervision is used to correct cases "since the founding of the Republic." The Administrative Litigation Law also does not contain a statute of limitations for applications for adjudication supervision.

The process of adjudication supervision appears to be unique to the Chinese. The concept that legally effective and final judgments are subject to being revisited years after entry stands in stark contrast to the practice in the United States and other countries where the finality and permanence of the results of judicial proceedings is considered to be a hallmark of the legal system. Foreign litigants in China are often taken aback by the notion that a final judgment may be reopened years later. In China, however, the process of adjudication supervision is viewed as necessary to correct errors and to ensure quality and competence in a legal system that still lacks sufficient numbers of qualified judges. Adjudication supervision is also necessary in a legal system to monitor and control widespread abuses such as various forms of corruption and local protectionism among judges. China also believes that adjudication supervision can be used to rectify the injustices and errors made during the many turbulent eras in China's modern history, including the Cultural Revolution, which ended in 1976.

B. THE ROLE OF THE PROCURATORATE

Under the PRC Constitution, the procuratorate along with the courts and public security organs comprise the three major judicial organs that administer criminal justice. The procuratorate, modeled on the institution of the procuracy in the former Soviet Union, performs the tasks of approving arrests by the public security organs and prosecuting criminal cases, as further discussed in Chapter 8 of this volume. Under the constitutional scheme, the procuratorate and the courts are of an equivalent rank and report, along with the public security organs, to the people's congresses at various levels. While the procuratorate is equivalent in some respects to government organs that prosecute criminal cases in other legal systems, the procuratorate in the PRC is also an organ of legal supervision. Among its responsibilities, the procuratorate is to supervise the work of the courts and the public security organs to ensure that no errors are made in the administration of justice. This supervisory role over the courts distinguishes the procuratorate from government prosecuting organs in many other legal systems.

In supervising the work of the courts in criminal cases, the procuratorate exercises this power by protesting by way of appeal against cases of first instance and through the procedure of adjudication supervision against final judgments. Exercising its power of adjudication supervision, the procuratorate can also challenge civil and administrative cases even though it was not a party to those proceedings. (The procuratorate has no right to protest civil or administrative judgments through the ordinary appeals process.) Protests by way of adjudication supervision normally result in a retrial of the case. Article 186 of the Civil Procedure Law provides that "cases in which protest was made by the people's procuratorate shall be retried by the people's court." Similarly, Article 306 of the Criminal Procedure Law provides that after a protest by the procuratorate under judicial supervision, "a new collegiate panel shall be formed for the retrial of a case by a people's court." In 2000, some 21,098 were the subject of protests by the procuratorate. Of these, 4,697 cases were "corrected" and 7,440 were upheld. The other cases were withdrawn or settled by the parties on a voluntary basis through mediation.

The process of legal supervision of courts by the procuratorate is based upon the same rationale for adjudication supervision in general but also highlights another feature of the PRC legal system. Courts do not have a special stature in the PRC system of justice; they are viewed as one part of the administrative machinery used for the dispensation of justice and, like the other parts, their work is subject to review by the supervisory organs of the state.

C. ISSUES WITH THE CURRENT JUDICIAL SYSTEM

The preceding discussion has raised a number of issues and problems with the current PRC judicial system that merit further examination. Among these issues are judicial independence, professionalism, and local protectionism.

1. JUDICIAL INDEPENDENCE AND RELATED ISSUES

The modern concept of judicial independence is a basic and firmly established feature of the United States legal system and many other modern legal systems. The discussion of the inner workings of the PRC court system above and the earlier discussion of the influence of other government organs and the Party on the people's courts raise the issue of whether judicial independence, though to some extent recognized in the PRC Constitution and laws, is an established practice within the PRC system.

Chinese scholars note that judicial independence in the Chinese context differs from the concept as elaborated in western legal systems. In the PRC, judicial independence does not refer to the independence of a particular collegiate bench or individual judges but to the independence of the court as a whole from the outside influence of other state organs and Party pressures. This position was set forth early in the PRC's history to explain Article 78 of the 1954 Constitution regarding judicial independence. China's developing legal system lacked experienced adjudicators and, as a result, the more qualified and experienced judges, such as the president of the court and other senior officials, assisted the less qualified judges by giving guidance either directly or through serving on adjudication committees. So long as judges sought advice or counsel from others within the court system, courts were functioning independently. In addition, under China's state bureaucracy, it is natural for lower level bureaucrats to seek guidance and leadership from higher-level bureaucrats. In the other judicial organs, the public security bureaus and procuratorates, the practice of seeking guidance from higher-level officials and more experienced colleagues is commonplace. This bureaucratic culture also exists in China's courts. Most judges are civil servants in China and are viewed no differently from other civil servants and courts do not have a special status apart from the other judicial organs.

Whether the use of adjudication committees is consistent with an expanded notion of judicial independence followed by Chinese courts remains unclear, but such use raises other issues concerning procedural fairness and the rule of law. The type of cursory review of individual cases and the practice of adjudication committees of deciding some cases before the public trial raise the question of whether cases are decided after a fair process and a full consideration of the evidence and the positions of the parties. A decision made by an adjudication committee before trial outside of the presence of the parties renders the trial nugatory and meaningless. Recent changes contained in Article 149 of the 1996 Criminal Procedure Law now provide that courts are to come to a decision after hearings and deliberation and are to forward only difficult cases to the adjudication committee. Whether this new rule has significantly limited the use of adjudication committees in the criminal process is unclear. There is no similar rule for civil and administrative cases.

A similar issue of fairness is raised by the practice of lower courts in seeking instructions from higher courts on how to decide particular cases in the first instance. Alternatively, a lower court may seek approval from a higher court of a proposed method of resolving a case. Higher courts have also been known to act on their own initiative in instructing lower courts on how to decide cases. These practices would appear to compromise the rights of parties to have their cases decided by two trials, one of first instance and a second trial on appeal. Where lower courts get instructions from higher courts, an appeal from the trial of first instance is pointless as the case has in effect already been decided on appeal before or at the same time as the decision in the trial in the case of first instance.

Even under an expanded notion of judicial independence advocated by the Chinese, interference in the work of the courts by other government organs and the Communist Party is prohibited by both the Constitution and Organic Law of the People's Courts. As the earlier discussion indicated, however, the Communist Party had a practice of instructing courts on specific cases in the past. In a number of discussions with PRC judges, the author has been told that with the development of a more professional cadre of judges, party committees and adjudication committees now rarely instruct courts on how to decide individual cases. Whether and the extent to which some of the practices that appear to undermine judicial independence have been changed are, like many other internal features of the PRC legal system, not readily ascertainable. Even if some of the more direct forms of outside intervention in the judicial process are now being gradually phased out, judges are still beholden to local people's congresses for their wages, promotions, and dismissals. Indeed, the influence of local officials on courts in China is notorious and one of the primary reasons why China has a serious problem with local protectionism. Moreover, even if the Party no longer instructs courts on specific cases, presidents and other top court leaders continue to serve on Party political-legal committees that report directly to the Party committee. The leadership of the Communist Party is also a basic principle contained in the Constitution. Every year when the president of the Supreme People's Court presents its work report before the National People's Congress, the president acknowledges that the SPC carries out its work under the leadership of the Party Central Committee. These conditions operate to create constraints on judges acting independently even if specific instructions are no longer given on how to decide individual cases.

2. LOCAL PROTECTIONISM AND RELATED ISSUES

A serious problem in the PRC court system involves local protectionism. As noted earlier, courts are beholden to local people's congresses and governments for funding, salaries, and continuing employment. Some local governments and legislatures put pressure on courts to protect local economic interests. Local protectionism is manifested in court proceedings in usually one of two ways. First, parties from foreign locations that seek relief in a local court against a local defendant may find the court to be unsympathetic to their claims. This may occur when a multi-national enterprise with a sino-foreign joint venture in China brings an action against a domestic company or individual; when Chinese parties from one province travel to another province to bring an action against a local defendant; or even where parties from one city, town, or village within a single province travel to another area within the same province. Where the defendant is a state-owned enterprise or private enterprise that is important to the local economy, the plaintiff may find that local courts will favor the defendant at the expense of the law. Second, a party may have obtained a judgment against a defendant from a court in one location and now must travel to the defendant's home in another location in order to enforce the judgment. The plaintiff and enforcement authorities from the issuing court may find that local authorities have no interest in cooperating in the enforcement of the judgment. To the contrary, local authorities may ignore the foreign judgment or obstruct and oppose its enforcement.

Local protectionism is one widespread form of corruption but there are many others. Judicial misconduct in the form of accepting bribes and improper contact with the parties has also been a widespread problem with courts in the PRC. As further discussed in the next chapter, some of these problems can be traced to the low level of training and lack of professional ethics of the growing cadre of young PRC lawyers who engage in aggressive and questionable tactics in order to earn fees and achieve results for their clients. Parties who have pending cases have been known to lavish bribes, gifts, and to have ex parte contacts with judges outside of the courts in social settings. The Judges Law (1995) and the Supreme People's Court's enactment of the Basic Code of Professional and Ethical Conduct for Judges (2001) are recent attempts to set clear ethical boundaries for judges and judicial personnel. Law enforcement officials have also intensified efforts to punish judicial corruption. According to the Supreme People's Court, law enforcement officials investigated and punished 218 judges and judicial personnel for corruption in 2007. Those who are caught and punished most likely represent only a small minority of all judges and judicial personnel who have engaged in inappropriate conduct.

3. ENFORCEMENT OF JUDGMENTS AND RELATED ISSUES

The development of China's court system is of little use if court judgments and orders are not respected and obeyed. Problems in the enforcement of judgments and orders continue to plague the courts. The preceding section discussed the problems of enforcing foreign judgments in China but the adequate enforcement of all judgments is a broader issue affecting all courts. Although parties are required by law to abide by all court judgments, a persistent problem has been the lack of enforcement of civil judgments particularly in economic cases where recent reports indicate that 25–35% of all judgments are not enforced. While courts have the authority to freeze bank accounts and garnish wages, PRC courts do not currently have a general contempt power that can result in criminal sanctions. Courts also have no recourse to effective sanctions against other state or government organs that do not obey court orders and it is unclear whether a state-owned enterprise would obey a court order to suspend wages for one of its well-regarded employees. The author has been told by some government organs that they are of equal or greater bureaucratic rank to courts and see no reason to obey court orders. This position seems logical in China's bureaucratic system in which entities consider themselves to be bound only by orders issued by entities above them in the chain of command of the bureaucratic hierarchy.

Courts generally rely upon enforcement officers of the court to compel recalcitrant parties to perform. Court orders in China do not command the same level of respect and authority as they do in the United States and many parties are known to flaunt court orders. The problem has caused the Supreme People's Court to strengthen its division of enforcement and other courts to train more enforcement personnel and enact new measures supporting enforcement. Still problems in the enforcement of judgments persist as local protectionism continues to create serious obstacles in the enforcement of foreign judgments and as enforcement officers fail to perform their duties due to lack of funding, lack of professional training, lack of interest in their work, and corruption. One telling indication of the general level of low esteem for the court system is the numerous acts of violence against judicial personnel. In its work report to the National People's Congress in 2002, the Supreme People's Court indicated that in 2001 there were over 760 incidents of violence targeting law enforcement officials resulting in injuries to more than 800 judges and court personnel and in the deaths of several judges.

CHAPTER SEVEN

LAWYERS AND THE LEGAL PROFESSION

This chapter examines the role of lawyers and the regulation of the legal profession in the PRC by the Ministry of Justice. Traditional China did not hold either the law or lawyers in high esteem. Under a Confucian society, social harmony is the highest virtue and lawyers were held in low esteem because they assisted litigants in asserting individual rights and selfish interests that caused conflict and upset the social balance. Lawyers were not officially recognized in Imperial China as a valid profession. Called litigation masters (*songshi*) and knife-pen men (*daobi xiansheng*), lawyers helped litigants draft papers and gave advice but were never allowed to officially represent clients or to speak on their behalf in court. To the contrary, lawyers were sometimes despised, maligned, and even outlawed. In 1820, the Qing Emperor issued an edict calling for the punishment of any "litigation tricksters" who drafted papers for others in groundless lawsuits. A legal profession was never able to overcome widespread antipathy and to develop in Imperial China; only after several attempts at modernization and reform with the advent of the twentieth century as the last imperial dynasty was near collapse did a legal profession finally begin to emerge. During the brief tenure of Republican China (1912–49), a legal profession began to develop under the Nationalist government, but lawyers were poorly trained and were subject to lax professional and ethical standards.

A. LAWYERS IN THE PRC, 1949–1982

The history of the legal profession from the founding of the PRC in 1949 to the advent of economic reforms in 1979 is marked by several aborted attempts to develop a professional cadre of lawyers. In the early 1950s, a number of state legal advisory offices were established on a trial basis in a number of cities to advise citizens on the newly enacted laws governing marriage, land reform, and corruption. The 1954 Constitution and the newly enacted Organic Law of the People's Courts expressly recognized the right of an accused to present a defense in criminal proceedings. In 1956, the State Council approved the first regulations issued by the Ministry of Justice concerning the responsibilities and duties of lawyers and the legal profession.

Beginning in 1957 with the Anti–Rightist Campaign and through the end of the Cultural Revolution in 1976, the legal profession suffered a series of attacks as China lurched through a lost twenty-year period of political upheaval and chaos. Law and lawyers were vilified as standing in the way of the persecution of enemies of the revolution and the fledgling legal profession, like the institution of law itself, disappeared from the scene. The Ministry of Justice itself was abolished in 1959.

After the end of the Cultural Revolution as China embarked on its ambitious economic reforms, China's Party elders realized that a strong legal profession was necessary to draft the many laws that would be necessary to support the transformation of China's centrally planned economy into a socialist market economy. The ranks of the legal profession had been decimated by the ravages of the Cultural Revolution and a focused effort was needed to recruit a new generation of lawyers. The resuscitation of the legal system began in 1979, when the Ministry of Justice was formally reestablished after a twenty-year hiatus. In 1980, the National People's Congress began the long process of reviving China's moribund legal profession by enacting the Provisional Regulations on Lawyers, which became effective in 1982. The new PRC Constitution enacted in 1982 was a direct repudiation of the lawlessness of the Cultural Revolution and recognized for the first time a principle of the rule of law.

B. LAWYERS IN THE PRC, 1982–1996

Although the 1980 Provisional Regulations on Lawyers were drafted with the goal of developing a legal profession to support China's economic reforms, the Regulations were drafted with a centrally planned economy in mind. Economic reforms were just beginning and the drafters of the Regulations worked within the legal and political framework that they were accustomed to and could not have anticipated the changes that would occur in the next two decades. In order to address the pressing need for lawyers, the Provisional Regulations set minimal professional qualifications for lawyers that were flexible and pragmatic. No college or university degree or formal training was required to work as a lawyer. The Regulations did require that in order to be qualified as a lawyer by the local justice bureau, a candidate had to be a person who loved the PRC, supported the socialist system, and had the right to vote and to be elected to public office. In the first years after the promulgation of the Provisional Regulations, lawyers could be qualified without having passed any bar examination as the Ministry of Justice did not prescribe China's first national qualifying examination until 1986.

Not surprisingly many of China's first group of post-reform lawyers were of marginal competence. However, at the same time, the demands made on these lawyers were not very great by today's standards. Lawyers were defined as state workers and worked in state-owned legal advisory offices. The state bore all costs in establishing these offices and determined the numbers of lawyers. The fees charged for legal work were very low. For example, according to guidelines jointly issued by the Ministry of Justice and the Ministry of Finance in 1990, lawyers were to be paid RMB 30–150 ($4.38 to $21.90) for handling a criminal trial of first instance and one to five RMB ($0.14 to $0.73) for advising on all matters not related to property. Even by China's standards, these fee guidelines were unrealistically low. Moreover, all revenues earned by lawyers were turned over to the state. Lawyers were state workers who were paid a small government salary and expected to provide legal assistance to government organs, state-owned enterprises, work units, social groups, and agricultural communes. The work of most lawyers in the 1980s was limited to preparing the simple contracts for state-owned enterprises and administrative units that were characteristic of the centrally planned economy. Lawyers also performed some limited defense work but the PRC criminal laws and criminal procedure laws in effect at the time allowed access to counsel just seven days before the trial and severely limited the ability of lawyers to provide an effective defense.

As China moved into the decade of the 1990s and the pace of reform began to accelerate, the Provisional Regulations became increasingly out of step with the work that lawyers were being asked to do in China's changing economy. In 1981, there were 1,465 law offices and 5,500 lawyers. By 1989, there were 3,600 firms and 43,600 lawyers (23,800 were full-time). After Deng Xiaoping's southern tour in 1992 cemented the policies of economic reform and of opening of the nation to foreign investment, the period of the early to mid–1990s saw a dramatic influx of foreign investment of all kinds and a surge in the number of lawyers in the PRC. By 1997, there were 8,300 law firms and over 110,000 lawyers and in 2001, there were 9,691 law firms and 117,600 lawyers for a population of 1.2 billion people. By 2006, the number of lawyers reached 153,-

846. (China had a goal of 150,000 lawyers by the year 2000 under its Eighth Five–Year Plan.) While the number of lawyers in the PRC has risen sharply, the number of lawyers is still low by comparison to the United States, which has 950,000 lawyers for a population of 285 million. As the range of professional activities of lawyers expanded rapidly reflecting the rise in foreign investment, commercial, and business activity, it was already apparent by the mid–1990s that the Provisional Regulations were outdated and that a modern law reflecting the work of lawyers in China's new economy needed to be enacted to regulate a changing legal profession in the PRC.

C. THE LAWYERS LAW, 2007

On October 28, 2007, the Law on Lawyers of the People's Republic of China (originally enacted on May 15, 1996) was amended and adopted at the 30th Session of the Standing Committee of the Tenth National People's Congress of the PRC. The amended Lawyers Law became effective on June 1, 2008. With sixty articles in seven chapters, the Lawyers Law seeks to strengthen and modernize the legal profession by recasting their role, with some limitations, from state workers to professionals providing services to clients. The Lawyers Law also seeks to create higher standards of qualification and to establish stricter standards of ethical conduct to address the many abuses within the profession and to create a disciplinary body to enforce those standards.

Under the Lawyers Law, all candidates must undergo a two-step process: qualification and obtaining a practice certificate. The Lawyers Law provides for two routes to qualification as a lawyer in the PRC. Under the regulations of Ministry of Justice those with at least three years of legal education at an institution of higher learning or who have "attained an equivalent professional level" or who have obtained a college degree in another discipline and who have passed the bar examination may be qualified by the local justice bureau. The Lawyers Law does not require a law degree from a law school or law department to sit for the bar. Given that only a small elite can attend the limited number of formal colleges and universities in China and that only a few of these institutions have law schools or law departments, the drafters believed that requiring a law degree would be too restrictive to meet China's need for lawyers. Candidates who meet these educational requirements are then allowed to sit for the bar examination, which follows a format that exists in many other countries. The exam takes place over two days and consists of four sections; three of the sections are multiple choice and one requires an essay. The topics covered include administrative law, administrative procedure, criminal law, criminal procedure, civil law, civil procedure, company law, contracts, enterprise law, inheritance law, intellectual property, land law, labor law, marriage law, private international law, and professional responsibility and ethics for lawyers. The passage rate for the bar examination in

China is low by international standards. In 1998, 120,000 sat for the bar and 15,102 passed. In 2007, 294,000 sat for the bar and 64,680 passed. The low passage rate is intended to ensure quality in the legal profession.

Applicants can also be qualified without passing the bar exam upon an approval process. Under Ministry of Justice regulations interpreting the Lawyers Law, applicants for qualification by approval must have obtained at least a college degree in law, have work experience in legal education or legal research or other professional legal work, and have a senior professional title or equivalent professional level. This type of qualification was designed mainly to accommodate law school faculty but may also be used to qualify members of the judiciary or procuratorate.

After passing the bar examination and receiving qualification as a lawyer, the applicant must then obtain a practicing certificate in order to practice law in the PRC. Article 5 of the Lawyers Law provides that in addition to qualification, an applicant must uphold the Constitution, have practical training at a law firm for a full year, and be a person of good character and conduct. A practicing certificate will not be issued if the applicant has no capacity for civil acts or only a limited capacity (because of some disability or legal problem), has been subjected to criminal punishment (except for a crime of negligence), has been discharged from public employment, or has previously had his practicing certificate revoked.

1. REGULATION AND DISCIPLINING OF LAWYERS

As the previous section indicated, the legal profession in the PRC is subject to heavy government regulation in both the qualifying and licensing process. This substantial degree of government regulation in the PRC stands in contrast to the minimal degree of government regulation of the legal profession in the United States, which is largely self-regulating. The Lawyers Law may foreshadow a greater degree of self-regulation by creating a dual administrative structure in which the Ministry of Justice is primarily responsible for regulating and disciplining lawyers but in which various PRC bar associations may also reward and punish lawyers pursuant to their articles of association. The bar associations are non-state organizations formed at the national, provincial, and municipal levels under the guidance, but not regulation, of the corresponding justice bureau. The national level organization, the All–China Lawyers Association, was formed in 1986 and all PRC lawyers are members; all bar associations at the municipal and provincial level are corporate members. As bar associations gain in stature and prestige, they may take over more of the discipline process, but for now the Ministry of Justice remains the primary regulatory authority.

Under Articles 47–50 of the Lawyers Law, the Ministry of Justice and its local organs can discipline lawyers by ordering the cessation of the offending conduct, giving a warning, confiscating all illegal gains, suspending or revoking the lawyer's license to practice, and referring the case to judicial authorities for criminal prosecution where a crime is suspected of having been committed. Law firms may be disciplined by being required to disgorge any illegal gains and to pay a fine of up to five times the amount of illegal gains. Law firms are also subject to having their business licenses suspended or revoked. *See* Lawyers Law, Art. 50.

2. LAW FIRMS

Under Article 14 of the Lawyers Law, a law firm must have its own name, address, articles of association, and assets of at least RMB 100,000 (about $14,600). To form a partnership law firm, there must be three or more partners, and a promoter who must be a lawyer with practicing experience for three or more years. A partnership law firm may be formed as a general partnership or a limited liability partnership. The partners of a general partnership law firm are individually liable for the debts of the law firm. To form a sole proprietorship law firm, the promoter must be a lawyer with practicing experience of five or more years. The promoter has unlimited personal liability for the debts of a sole proprietorship law firm.

An application to establish a law firm must be approved by the judicial administration department of the people's government at or above the provincial level before the firm can legally open for business. If the judicial administration department approves the application, it will issue a law firm practice certificate or business license within thirty days of receiving the application. As with most other applications for business licenses in China, the application for a law firm business license usually involves a long vetting process in which judicial authorities are approached informally well before the formal application is submitted. Firms must renew their licenses on an annual basis by submitting a work report for the year, a copy of the law firm's practicing certificate, an audited financial statement, tax receipts and other materials as required. The renewal process is generally routine for most law firms and issues do not arise unless some impropriety has occurred. Subject to approval by judicial administration authorities, a partnership law firm that has been formed for three years and has 20 or more practicing lawyers is allowed to establish branch offices around the PRC. *See* Lawyers Law, Art. 19. Some PRC law firms have established foreign branches, including branch offices in the United States.

Articles 14–16 and 20 of the Lawyers Law recognize four types of law firms: state-funded, cooperatives, partnerships, and sole proprietorships. In state-funded law firms, the state provides the assets and also often provides continuing funding. Cooperatives and partnerships are voluntary associations between parties who provide their own assets and receive no state support. Liability in state-funded and cooperative law firms is limited to the assets of the firm whereas the partners in partnerships bear unlimited joint and several liability. As of 2004, there were 11,691 law firms, of which 1,742 were state-funded, 1,746 were cooperatives, and 8,024 were partnerships. The trend is toward an increase in partnerships.

Many state-funded firms are now financially independent and no longer receive state funds for their daily operations. The Lawyers Law also provides that a state-funded firm is to be independent in its practice, although as a practical matter a state-funded law firm continues to be beholden to a state organ that is its benefactor. From a client's perspective, there continues to be some significant differences between state-funded firms and partnerships and cooperatives even though the lawyer's fees charged by state-funded firms may not differ significantly in most cases. Whereas lawyers in cooperative and partnership firms stand to benefit directly from the fees and revenues generated in the form of profits, lawyers in state-funded law firms are paid a small salary and must turn over their revenues to the state. The compensation structure in state-funded law firms raises the issue of whether lawyers have sufficient incentives to perform at their highest level and to achieve the best results for their clients. The compensation of lawyers in state-funded law firms is not directly affected by the amount of fees generated and they stand to earn roughly the same compensation no matter how successful they are in representing their clients. In addition, lawyers at state-funded law firms earn only a tiny fraction of what partners at some elite PRC law firms now earn. The compensation and incentive structure means that the most capable lawyers and the lawyers with the best credentials, including those who have studied abroad and have obtained a U.S. law degree, will tend to eschew state-funded law firms and opt for private firms and much higher compensation.

a. Compensation and Billing Rates in PRC Law Firms

Information on billing rates and compensation for associates and partners in PRC law firms is closely guarded, difficult to verify, and rapidly changing. Anecdotal information indicates that third-year associates at top local law firms in Beijing can earn between RMB 180,000 to 200,000 ($26,354 to $29,283) per year based upon a billing rate of $50 to $100 per hour. Partners in top firms in Beijing can earn over $200,000 per year with some partners at a handful of ultra elite firms earning $1,000,000 and above (although these figures often include income that may be of questionable legality). Lawyers in local law firm do not bill local clients (PRC companies or individuals) on an hourly basis but usually agree on a fixed fee for a case. Local firms do bill multinational clients on an hourly basis. As of 2008, a handful of elite PRC lawyers are able to bill out at $500 to $700 per hour or more. By comparison, lawyers in foreign law firms in China or Hong Kong bill out at between $150–250 for a junior associate, $400 to $500 for a senior associate, and $600 to $1,000 for a partner. These figures for fees and compensation should be compared against the compensation for lawyers outside of private law firm practice. Lawyers in state-funded law firms, judges, and law professors earn about RMB 24,000–36,000 ($3,500 to $5,256) per year. Recent increases in salary now allow law professors at some elite law schools to earn RMB 120,000 per year ($17,520), but this is still a tiny fraction of what can be earned in a lucrative private law firm practice. (However, law professors in China have many sources of outside income from consulting, business interests, and government grants.) The disparity in compensation, which continues to grow, may explain why many judges and academics have recently departed for private practice. There is also significant disparity in the legal profession as a whole. It is said in China that 20% of all lawyers earn 80% of all annual revenue from legal services while 80% of lawyers share the remaining 20%.

Compensation at foreign law firms in the PRC tends to be significantly higher than in local firms. Legally trained professionals hired as legal consultants by foreign law firm branches can earn RMB 150,000 to 180,000 ($21,958 to $26,350) per year. PRC lawyers who have studied abroad and who are hired on as associates by foreign law firms can earn from $20,000 to $55,000. By far the highest levels of compensation are those available to PRC lawyers who have earned a JD degree from abroad and who have acquired foreign citizenship or permanent resident status. A PRC lawyer who has earned a JD from a U.S. law school and who has acquired at least permanent resident status is generally treated for compensation purposes like all other expatriate

U.S. citizens. A first year associate in the Beijing branch of a top U.S. law firm can earn $160,000 per year plus a housing allowance and other expenses, including an annual round-trip to the United States.

The billing rates and levels of compensation discussed above reflect the lucrative practice of top tier firms that have a client base of foreign companies. Most law firms, local or foreign, pursue a small list of multinational companies that are doing business in China because they have the resources to pay premium rates. Many if not most Chinese enterprises are not willing to pay for legal services. Many multinational enterprises are astonished to discover throughout the course of negotiations on a joint venture that could involve many months of meetings, reviewing documents, and tens of millions of dollars of investment that the Chinese partner never retains a lawyer on its behalf for the negotiations or to review the many complex legal documents that are necessary to consummate the project. Most Chinese enterprises will ask a senior manager such as a general manager or deputy general manager with no legal training to handle the negotiations and to review and draft documents. This practice reflects the general attitude on the part of PRC enterprises that any value that lawyers may add to the negotiation process is simply not worth the cost of their fees. The attitude also reflects a general lack of esteem for lawyers and the legal system. The result is that law firms, domestic and foreign, avidly pursue a short list of multinational enterprises as the premium client base necessary for any lucrative practice.

D. PRC LAWYERS WITH FOREIGN DEGREES

A recent trend is an increase in the number of PRC lawyers who have earned a Masters in Law (LLM) or a JD degree in U.S. law schools. Most of the earliest group of PRC students who arrived in the United States in the 1980s enrolled in LLM programs, which are usually one-year programs at the end of which the student is awarded the LLM degree. PRC Lawyers who seek the LLM degree can apply to U.S. law schools directly from China. Most law schools do not require the law school admissions test for the LLM program, but require instead a much less rigorous test of English as a second language. Students with a bachelor's degree in law, practicing lawyers, professors, and judges are among the typical group of PRC lawyers applying to LLM programs. Admission is usually not a difficult problem where the U.S. law school offers the LLM program and has slots available but financial aid is usually an obstacle as few U.S. law schools offer financial aid to foreign law students during the admissions process. Enterprising PRC students are often able to find scholarships and other forms of aid, however, once they arrive in the United States. Students who study for the LLM quickly discover that the JD is a far more useful degree for those who are interested in remaining in the United States to practice law. Some LLM students are able to transfer into the JD program directly as a result of good grades achieved in law school. Other students apply to JD programs while enrolled as LLM students. Students who are able to enter JD programs directly are usually those who have been in the United States for a number of years and who have studied in other programs such as history or economics and are able to achieve satisfactory results on the law school admissions test. Recently, however, some college students in China have been accepted directly into JD programs at some U.S. law schools.

The vast majority of the first wave of PRC lawyers studying in the United States did not return to China, but were able to gain U.S. citizenship or permanent resident status and remain in the United States. The benefits of U.S. citizenship are viewed as so compelling for PRC students who study in the United States that it is now considered to be an embarrassment if a student who studies in the United States returns to China without at least having obtained U.S. permanent residency, a status that will permit its holder to return to the U.S. from travel abroad and will lead eventually to U.S. citizenship. There is a common perception in China that PRC students who return to China without U.S. citizenship lack the ability of their more talented compatriots who are able to obtain U.S. citizenship. Most PRC students who study in the United States are able to remain as an entire industry using aggressive and sharp tactics to help secure U.S. citizenship has emerged. A common joke in the

PRC is that if the wife leaves first to go study abroad, a divorce is the certain result as remarriage to a U.S. citizen is the easiest path to United States citizenship.

A number of American law schools who accepted judges, government officials, and professors from China on the assumption that they would return to China and use their legal education in their original posts found that most opted to stay and work for law firms in the United States. Those who did return to China after a one-year stay were often middle-aged law professors with well-established careers in the PRC, but they were the exception. A recent trend is the increasing numbers of PRC lawyers with U.S. citizenship or permanent residency who are returning to work in China or Hong Kong in branches of foreign law firms or as in-house lawyers for multinational enterprises doing business in China. For many PRC lawyers, the reasons for returning to China can be compelling. Many U.S. law firms and U.S. based multinational enterprises continue to view China as a hardship assignment that requires additional incentives for their employees in the form of generous ex-patriate packages that include housing, cars, and schooling at an American or international school for their children. In addition to the daunting obstacle of the Chinese language, which can seem impenetrable, daily life in China can seem strange and alien. Those foreign employees who bring their families to China often find that they lead isolated lives that revolve around a small community of fellow ex-patriates. While many PRC lawyers do not view living in China to be a hardship, U.S. law firms and multinational enterprises offer the same ex-patriate packages to PRC lawyers who have acquired at least U.S. permanent residency. PRC lawyers trained in the United States will also be able to use their Chinese language skills, an advantage that is not always exploited when working in the United States. For many PRC lawyers, the ideal is to leave China for study abroad and to return to China armed with a U.S. degree and U.S. permanent residency or citizenship and to live under the conditions provided to ex-patriates among relatives, friends, and colleagues in a familiar culture and environment.

E.   FOREIGN LAW FIRMS AND FOREIGN LAWYERS

Foreign law firms have been allowed to establish branch offices in China since 1993 but are subject to a number of restrictions contained in the Tentative Provisions on Foreign Law Firms Establishing Offices in China jointly issued by the Ministry of Justice and the State Administration of Industry and Commerce. For example, in 1993 the PRC mandated that no more than forty foreign law firms would be issued a license to establish an office in China although many more than that number of firms sought access. The foreign firms that were able to acquire approval from the Ministry of Justice were then limited to one branch office in China that could be located in a list of approximately fifteen cities, including Beijing, Shanghai, and Guangzhou. The Tentative Provisions also prohibited foreign firms from interpreting Chinese laws and issuing opinions concerning those laws. In addition, foreign firms were prohibited from employing licensed Chinese lawyers. Those PRC lawyers hired by foreign firms could serve as consultants but would have to surrender their law licenses. Foreign lawyers were prohibited from taking the national qualifying examination for lawyers and could not obtain a practicing license. A number of other restrictions also appear in the Tentative Provisions, many of which appear to be designed to protect the fledgling local legal industry from competition by foreign firms.

Despite these restrictions, the PRC has turned away a rush of foreign firms seeking to establish foreign branches. A number of firms are anxious to establish offices in order to serve their multinational clients that are investing in China and to create a presence in what they believe will be an essential market for legal work. A number of well-known U.S. firms have offices in both China and in the more business friendly environment of Hong Kong, which is not subject to the jurisdiction of the Ministry of Justice. Some firms have also been able to establish consulting offices in other Chinese cities in order to circumvent the limit on having one branch office and have also created informal relationships with PRC law firms in order to perform legal work on issues of Chinese law.

China's entry into the World Trade Organization in 2001 should result in the lifting of some of these restrictions on the legal services field as part of China's WTO commitments although the commitments did not address some of the most severe restrictions. Among the restrictions that are expected to be lifted are the current limit on the number of law firms allowed to establish offices, the limit of one branch office, and the geographic restrictions on where branch offices can be established. Other restrictions are likely to gradually diminish over time with the continued development of the legal profession in China.

F. NOTARIES

Before concluding this chapter with an examination of current issues in the PRC legal profession, a brief discussion of the role of notaries in the PRC legal profession should be added. Notaries are state legal workers who provide the service of certifying that certain legal acts and legal documents have been properly executed and that certain facts have occurred. For example, a notarized contract certifies that the notary has witnessed the execution of the contract by the signature of the parties to the particular contract in question. A statement from a notary witnessing a particular event is also a state certification that the event has occurred. A notarization does not guarantee that the contract is not legally defective for some other reason unrelated to its execution or that the witnessed event has some particular legal significance.

The effect of a valid notarization is to create a strong evidentiary presumption in favor of the validity of the event or item that was notarized. Under Article 67 of the Law of Civil Procedure (1991), the people's courts are to accept notarized acts, documents, and facts as evidence unless the act of notarization itself was invalid. PRC law requires notarization for many different items. For example, the beneficiary under the laws of inheritance of a decedent's bank account must obtain a notarized certificate from the appropriate government department before the bank will release the funds to the beneficiary. A number of local jurisdictions have rules requiring notarization of contracts for the transfer, mortgage, and rental of land. Foreign and domestic parties to contracts relating to foreign investment often have the contracts and other documents notarized even if not mandated by law. The parties believe that notarization may help to reduce contract and other business disputes in the future. Other examples of documents that may be submitted for notarization include wills, gifts of property, proof of indebtedness, certificates of identity or relationship to another person, and adoption certificates, and succession. Notaries are also allowed to make suggestions and improvements to documents to ensure that they comply with all relevant laws.

The system of notaries was first established in the 1950s when courts and notarial offices performed most of this work. Notarial offices, along with other offices of judicial administration, were abolished in 1959 and not reestablished until 1980. The notary profession is governed by the Provisional Regulations on Notaries enacted by the State Council in 1982, the Provisional Measures on the Handling of Several Major Notarial Activities, and the Provisional Detailed Rules on Notarial Procedure promulgated by the Ministry of Justice in 1982 and 1986, respectively. In 2005, the Notarization Law of the PRC was adopted at the 17th meeting of the Standing Committee of the National People's Congress of the PRC. As previously noted, notaries are state legal workers and work in offices established by the Ministry of Justice and subject to its supervision. According to the 2006 Law Yearbook of China, there were 3,100 notarial offices employing 19,000 notaries. The qualifications for notaries require legal education and training but are slightly lower than those for lawyers.

G. CURRENT ISSUES WITH THE LEGAL PROFESSION

The rapidly changing nature of the legal profession in China raises a number of issues concerning the independence of the profession, competence, and professional ethics.

1. INDEPENDENCE OF LAWYERS

The Provisional Regulations on Lawyers enacted in 1980 considered lawyers to be state workers with the duty to protect the interests of the state, to promote the socialist legal order, and to remain faithful to the cause of socialism. Under this view of the role of the lawyer, where there is a conflict, the state's interests outweigh those of the client. By contrast, Article 2 of the 2007 Lawyers Law defines a lawyer as a practitioner who has acquired a lawyer's practice certificate and who provides services to the public in accordance with law. The Lawyers Law contains less of the heavy political rhetoric of the Provisional Regulations and is more consistent with the western view of the lawyer as a professional who provides services to clients as opposed to a servant of the state. Nevertheless, the Lawyers Law does contain enough vestiges of socialist rhetoric to raise some concerns about whether the duty of lawyers to serve clients is compromised or subjected to an overriding duty to serve the state. Lawyers are to abide by the Constitution, which contains numerous references to the leadership of the Communist Party and to the paramount duty of all citizens to uphold and protect the interests of the state. A Ministry of Justice notice issued subsequent to the Lawyers Law proclaimed that lawyers need to develop correct political thinking and must put the interests of society first. Law firms with three or more Party members need to set up a Party cell and firms with less than three members need to form Party cells in association with other firms. As in all other professions and walks of life, Party members are to lead the work of the legal profession. All lawyers are subject to regulation and discipline by the Ministry of Justice and its local justice bureaus.

The continuing use of political rhetoric may raise some concerns about the independence of lawyers, but while there are reasons for concern, zealous devotion to Party and state by China's professional elite should not be chief among them. In modern China, many young and ambitious professionals view the Communist Party and its ideals with resignation and cynicism. Many young people who recite the rhetoric of the Party will confess in private that the ideology it expresses is obsolete and devoid of any relevance to the lives of the young, ambitious, and educated class of professionals from which lawyers are drawn. Many young people even find the rhetoric and ideals of the Party and state to be ludicrous (in private) and completely out of touch with the realities of modern life in China. Most people of all ages in China view the Party itself as self-serving, corrupt, and lacking belief in its own ideals. The numbers of lawyers who serve business clients and who have developed lucrative law practices are not likely to subjugate the interests of their paying clients in favor of the state in the ordinary conduct of their law practices unless there is a clear and specific directive from a powerful state authority. To the contrary, as further discussed in a later section, they may serve their clients interests too zealously and for the wrong reasons.

Rather, more relevant in determining whether lawyers are independent is the type of law firm that they work for or the type of practice that they undertake. Those who are in administrative litigation against state organs or criminal defense work are more likely to be subjected to some pressure from government and Party organs because the interests of the state are directly involved and are adverse to the interest of their clients. State-funded law firms are beholden to the state organ that has invested the capital in the firm and that continues to provide funding for operating expenses. Those lawyers who work for partnership law firms, clearly the trend of the future, are not beholden to the state but are driven by the economic realities of a highly competitive marketplace for legal services for a small number of elite multinational clients.

2.   PROFESSIONAL COMPETENCE

Although the Lawyers Law and the Ministry of Justice have created higher professional standards in the legal profession, the issue of professional competence is still a serious one in China. As discussed in a previous section, a formal college or university education is not required to qualify as a lawyer. Lawyers can qualify by taking classes through correspondence courses, adult self-study programs, and television courses through technical colleges. Many of the technical schools that offer three-year specialized training in law have lax standards; government officials who seek qualifications as lawyers have been known to obtain a certificate from some of these technical colleges without ever attending a single class. Even the colleges and universities that offer law programs emphasize rote learning and memorization as opposed to legal reasoning and analysis.

By western standards, the work of many PRC lawyers, even those serving at some of the most successful firms, would be considered substandard. Letters or memoranda prepared for clients in English will contain misspellings of common words and typographical errors. Arguments are made and propositions of law are stated in meetings and court proceedings without any authority. Even the appearance of PRC law firms and lawyers would be considered to be unacceptable by western standards. Even some of the most successful PRC lawyers will appear in ill-fitting suits and in poorly constructed and unfinished offices with peeling paint and unkempt carpets.

From a foreign client's perspective, the more important issue may be a lack of substantive knowledge in certain key areas. Foreign clients interested in investing in China or in doing other forms of business need sophisticated local counsel. To be able to effectively serve the interests of foreign clients, however, a lawyer must understand and be competent in PRC law, the law of the client's home jurisdiction, and international commercial and business law. For example, a PRC lawyer who is advising a U.S. company that is establishing a joint venture in China needs to understand U.S. corporate law and the U.S. legal system in order to most effectively serve the client. The PRC lawyer must also at least be aware of U.S. tax issues and have access to competent tax counsel to assist on any technical tax issues. Local lawyers may also need to understand international treaties such as the Vienna Convention on Contracts for the International Sale of Goods (1980). With the exception of the PRC lawyers who have studied abroad and who have gained meaningful experience from practicing abroad for several years, few PRC lawyers have the required level of sophisticated knowledge and understanding of foreign and international commercial law.

One reason for the less than satisfactory level of professional competence among PRC lawyers is that competence is not emphasized among PRC lawyers themselves as an essential ingredient to a successful law practice. The author has sat in on numerous meetings between PRC lawyers and potential clients that follow a similar pattern. The client first explains the issue or problem at hand. If the matter is at all difficult, the PRC lawyer will first begin with a general admonition that the PRC legal and political system is opaque and mysterious even to local Chinese experts, implying that it is completely impossible for a foreigner to understand. The PRC lawyer may then proceed to an even more dire warning that the particular bureau, department, or groups of government officials that have authority over the matter of interest to the client are either indifferent or corrupt. Having alarmed the client with the bleakness of the situation, the PRC lawyer will then assure the client his firm has a special relationship with those key officials that hold dispositive authority over the matter at hand and that the firm, if retained, will use its influence to solve the client's problems or achieve its goals. PRC lawyers almost invariably emphasize their connections or *guanxi* with the brokers of power, not competence, expertise, or experience in handling similar cases, as the key to meeting the client's needs. The need to emphasize *guanxi* is understandable given the nature of the PRC legal and political system, as further discussed below, but it serves as a barrier to the further development of the legal profession.

3.   PROFESSIONAL ETHICS

The discussion of the importance of *guanxi* and influence peddling in the legal profession raises not only the issue of competence, but also the issue of professional ethics. Sharp practices and improper conduct among PRC lawyers constitute the most serious problem in the PRC legal profession today. The practice of law is among the most lucrative professions in the PRC today, offering the prospect of undreamed of riches for the successful lawyer. Compensation of over $100,000 per year is not unusual among the top group of practitioners and the elite earn even more in a country where the average salary for a mid-level manager in a large domestic company is less than RMB 5,000 ($730) per month. The Lawyers Law contains a number of provisions dealing with specific problems that were common in the profession. For example, Articles 39 and 40 of the Lawyers Law provide that lawyers are not to represent both parties in the same case; meet with judges, procurators, or arbitrators privately; entertain and give gifts to a judge, procurator, or arbitrator; or provide false evidence and conceal facts. Lawyers and law firms should not solicit business by slandering other lawyers or by paying middleman fees. Other provisions in the Lawyers Law, Measures for Punishing Illegal Activities (1997), Several Regulations to Oppose Unfair Competition in the Legal Profession (1995), the Lawyers Professional Responsibility and Practice Discipline Standards (1993) and the Lawyers Disciplinary Rules (1992) provide additional restrictions.

The contents of the various disciplinary laws in China do not differ significantly from those of professional codes in other countries except that they may be less detailed. As in other areas, the issue in China is not with having a lack of laws, but it is with the compliance with and enforcement of the law. Although reliable information is difficult to obtain, available sources indicate that since the enactment of the Lawyers Law in 1996, only a small number of lawyers have been disciplined by the Ministry of Justice. Although prohibited by the Lawyers Law, bribes of judges are commonplace and it is still a common practice for lawyers to arrange for private dinners with judges and their clients. Law firms and clients will invite judges to Hong Kong, Macau, or some other desirable locations for an all expenses paid seminar on some topic of law. The author knew of one instance where the judge trying a case was the student in an adult education program supervised by a professor who was acting as the plaintiff's lawyer.

The pursuit of a small number of elite clients and the undreamed of riches that can be earned through a lucrative law practice has created an intensively competitive marketplace where lawyers feel compelled to engage in sharp tactics to attract or retain valuable clients. Many foreign clients find that PRC lawyers seemed more motivated by pleasing them by obtaining exactly the result desired than by using independent judgment to offer candid and objective legal advice that may not always favor the client's interests. For example, in one instance when an in-house lawyer from a foreign company retained local counsel for an opinion letter on an internal corporate dispute, the local lawyer wrote an opinion letter that in every respect confirmed the positions taken by the in-house lawyer. Where a legal matter turns on a discretionary act of a government official, such as the approval of a long delayed joint venture application, the risk of some questionable and illegal conduct is especially high. In one instance, a lawyer guaranteed that a long delayed approval would be obtained if the client paid a $10,000 fee in addition to lawyer's fees. For many PRC lawyers, the goal is to achieve whatever the result desired by the client by whatever means necessary so as to retain the client's business. Using illegal tactics such as bribing a judge, procurator, or other government official without the client's knowledge is made easier in a legal environment that is often inaccessible to foreign clients. Many foreign clients have no means to verify or to check upon the work done by their local lawyers and the methods that are used. The client is pleased with the result and does not ask too many questions.

CHAPTER EIGHT

PROCEDURAL LAW

This chapter and Chapter 9 will provide an overview of the contents of the laws of the PRC. China divides its laws into procedural and substantive law. This chapter examines the law of procedure, which is contained in three major laws, the Criminal Procedure Law (1979, revised 1997), the Law of Civil Procedure (provisional in 1982, final in 1991, and revised 2007), and the Administrative Litigation Law (1990). The next chapter will provide an overview of the basic areas of substantive law.

Any review of the laws of an entire nation in the span of two chapters can provide only a general idea of the law, and the focus here is on highlighting some of the more salient features of Chinese law, especially those areas that may be unique to China, and on illustrating how some basic features of the Chinese legal and political system may diverge in some significant ways from legal concepts familiar to students of the law in the United States and other western legal systems. Following the discussion of procedural and substantive law, Chapters 10 and 11 will focus in more depth upon two areas of substantive law in China, the laws relating to foreign investment and intellectual property. These two areas have generated a great deal of interest

259

among foreign investors in China and are poised to assume even greater attention and significance as China becomes fully integrated into the World Trade Organization.

In both areas of procedural and substantive law, there are some significant gaps between the laws as written and as implemented in practice, between the ideals of the law and policy and the practice in action of the law and legal system. While a gap between written laws and laws in operation is not unusual in any legal system, the gap in China's legal system may be larger than in many developed legal systems. One explanation for this gap may be traced to the lack of adequately trained judges, lawyers, police, and a general lack of resources of the judicial and legal system necessary to support the proper implementation of written laws. For example, it is difficult to adequately implement complex business and commercial laws when China lacks a sufficient number of lawyers and judges who have adequate training to understand the complexities of the laws. Another explanation may be traced to a lack of political will. There is a tension between the desire of the Communist Party to legitimate its authority by promoting the rule of law and its fear that it will lose its power if it cannot assert sufficient control over government and society. This conflict may explain why many of the high ideals contained in the PRC Constitution and laws are not fully reflected in actual practice. Nevertheless, the laws in the PRC as written, even if not fully implemented, are not meaningless. They serve as an indication of the professed aspirations and ideals of a society; they may also provide a benchmark against which progress in the PRC legal system may be measured. As the legal system in the PRC develops, there may be a narrowing of the gap between the laws as written and as implemented.

A. THE CRIMINAL PROCEDURE LAW

The Criminal Procedure Law (CPL) was enacted by the NPC in 1979, thirty years after the PRC was founded in 1949, and revised extensively in 1996. (All references to the CPL below, unless otherwise indicated, refer to the 1996 CPL.) During the early years of the PRC, attempts to enact a code of criminal procedure were repeatedly interrupted by political upheaval and the legal system itself ground to a halt during the Cultural Revolution. The Criminal Procedure Law was one of the first major laws enacted as part of the nation's effort at rebuilding the legal system.

The 1979 CPL was based upon an inquisitorial model of the legal process associated with the civil law tradition of continental Europe as opposed to the adversarial model associated with the Anglo–American legal traditions of England and the United States. Under the adversarial model, the truth is discovered through a clash of conflicting positions espoused by two equal parties, the prosecution and defense counsel, in a contest before a passive and impartial judge who acts either as the fact-finder or as an arbiter for a fact-finding jury. Among the nations that currently use an adversarial criminal justice model are England, the United States, Canada, Denmark, and Italy.

Under the inquisitorial model, facts are discovered through a vigorous process of investigation led by legal professionals of the state. The inquisitorial model assumes that it is always in the interests of the parties to conceal facts and relevant evidence. Defense counsel plays little or no role in the investigation process as this task is left to various organs of the state, including the police, prosecutors, and the courts, all which are actively involved in a coordinated but theoretically impartial effort to discover the facts by investigation. In an inquisitorial model, the judge is not an impartial and passive arbiter but is also an active investigator. Both models emphasize discovering the facts and the truth, but inquisitorial models emphasize efficiency and crime control and assume that the judicial organs of the state will act in a fair and impartial manner in dealing with suspects. Among the nations that currently use an inquisitorial model are Japan, Thailand, Germany, and France.

The inquisitorial model of criminal justice as embodied in the 1979 CPL suffered from a number of deficiencies, further discussed below, and was extensively revised and amended in 1996. The revision amended seventy articles out of the original 164 in the 1979 CPL and added sixty-three new articles and deleted two articles. The revised CPL was enacted by the NPC on March 17, 1996 and became effective on January 1, 1997. The 1996 revision has tempered some of the harsher inquisitorial features of the 1979 Law and has added some important new protections for criminal suspects.

1.   THE CRIMINAL PROCESS IN THE PRC

The Criminal Procedure Law provides for five main stages in the PRC criminal legal process: (1) filing of a case; (2) investigation; (3) prosecution; (4) adjudication; and (5) execution of sentences. The public security organs are involved in the initiation and investigation stages of most cases. The procuratorate investigates some cases and handles the prosecution phase of all criminal cases. Courts are involved in the adjudication and execution phase of a criminal case.

a.   The Role of the Public Security Organs

The Ministry of Public Security, under the State Council, has overall responsibility for the police force of the PRC. At the local level, among other police functions, public security bureaus generally handle the first stages of the criminal process in the PRC. The first stage is the filing or initiation of a case (*li an*), which is the official commencement of the investigation phase. The police may discover facts upon their own or may be alerted by another government organ or by a report filed by a citizen. Once a decision is made to file a case, the police then begin the investigation phase. The police have the power to gather evidence by making an inquest of the site, interrogating witnesses, freezing accounts, and by demanding and seizing physical evidence that may prove guilt such as inventory, contraband, and records. If a suspect is identified, the police have five compulsory measures at its disposal under Article 50 of the CPL. These measures are compelling a suspect to attend an examination (*juchuan*), bail or awaiting trial under a guarantee provided by a third party (*qubao houshen*), surveillance of residence (*jianshi juzhu*), detention (*juliu*), and arrest (*daibu*). Awaiting trial under a guarantee and surveillance of residence are coercive measures designed to ensure that a suspect will appear for a trial but, unlike detention and arrest, do not involve taking the suspect into custody. An investigation can proceed without using any of these coercive measures, but the police generally resort to one or more of these coercive measures once a suspect has been identified as interrogation and confession are some of the most common and most effective techniques for gathering evidence of a crime. The 1996 revision has now added a provision limiting the period of awaiting trial under a guarantee to twelve months and the period of residential surveillance to six months. *See* CPL, Art. 58. Article 92 of the CPL, also added during the 1996 revision, provides that the period of interrogation under a compulsory summons for examination shall not exceed twelve hours and the police are prohibited from detaining suspects under the guise of repeated compulsory summons for interrogation. The revised CPL also gives suspects and their representatives the right to demand cancellation of all compulsory measures, including detention and arrest, that have exceeded their time limits under law, although the revised law does not provide for any procedures to challenge the lawfulness of any of the time limits of any of the compulsory measures.

All of the coercive measures for dealing with suspects can be exercised by the police upon its own recognizance with the exception of an arrest, which requires the prior approval of the procuratorate and the courts, and an arrest warrant must be produced at the time of the arrest. Under Article 60 of the CPL, the police can make an arrest when there is evidence of a crime, where a conviction would result in imprisonment, and where bail and surveillance of residence would be insufficient to prevent the occurrence of danger to society. After considering a request to approve an arrest by the police, the procuratorate can approve the arrest, or disapprove the arrest with an explanation of its reasons; if the procuratorate deems that a supplementary investigation is necessary, it shall at the same time notify the police of the need.

b. Detention

A detention, unlike an arrest, can be effected by the police upon the exercise of its own authority. Article 61 of the CPL enumerates seven categories of persons subject to detention, including persons preparing to commit a crime or in the process of committing a crime, persons identified as having committed a crime by victims or eyewitnesses, persons likely to escape or become fugitives after committing a crime, or persons who are like to destroy or falsify evidence.

After a suspect has been detained, the police are subject to a number of general time limits on how long the person can be held in custody under detention without formal arrest. Article 69 of the CPL permits detention of suspects without formal arrest for up to three days with an extension of one to four days for special circumstances during which period the police must request the procuratorate to approve the arrest; in special cases where a major criminal suspect is involved in repeated crimes or in criminal gang activity, the police have thirty days within which to request an approval of the arrest. The procuratorate has up to seven days to approve or disapprove the arrest. If the procuratorate does not approve the arrest, the police must immediately release the detainee. Under Article 9 of the new Police Law (1995), the police must interrogate the suspect within twenty-four hours of detention or within forty-eight hours in special cases upon approval of higher-level public security organs. In ordinary cases, a suspect can be held in custody without arrest for up to ten days. In special cases, the period of detention without arrest can be extended to fourteen days with a maximum period of thirty-seven days.

c. Custody After Arrest

Once the procuratorate has approved the arrest, the police and procuratorate are allowed to hold a criminal suspect in custody for two months, plus an additional month for complicated cases, subject to approval by the procuratorate at the next higher level. The revised CPL retains these original time limits contained in the 1979 CPL and adds a further extension of two months under Article 126 for detention after arrest for grave and complex cases in outlying areas where travel is difficult, grave cases that involve criminal gangs, grave and complex cases that involve people who commit crimes in various locations, and grave and complex cases that involve various locations and that present difficulties in the gathering of evidence. For cases that involve a sentence of imprisonment of at least ten years, Article 127 provides that the period of detention after arrest may be extended for another two months where the criminal investigation cannot be completed within the original two-month extension under Article 126, subject to the approval of the provincial level procuratorate. Article 125 provides for an indefinite period of detention after arrest subject to the approval of the NPC Standing Committee of a request submitted by the Supreme People's Procuratorate. Aside from the indefinite period of detention under Article 125, the maximum period of detention after arrest under the 1996 CPL is seven months.

d.   Other Changes in the 1996 Revision of the CPL Affecting the Police

One of the major changes in the 1996 revision is the elimination of the notorious "shelter for examination" procedure (*shourong shencha*) widely used by public security organs. First established in 1961, the shelter for examination procedure was considered to be an administrative practice and outside the procedures for detention and arrest in the 1979 CPL, although its precise nature was unclear and the practice remained controversial for many years. The procedure was established by the Ministry of Public Security and allowed persons to be held in detention where there was concern about a person's identity or where the suspect might be roaming around to commit crimes. While the 1979 CPL provided that in ordinary cases, suspects cannot be held in detention for more than ten days without an arrest approved by the procuratorate, a time limit retained in the 1996 CPL, under shelter for examination, a suspect could be held for one to three months without arrest. Faced with constant "strike hard" (*yanda*) campaigns initiated by the Party against crime, the police preferred to use the shelter for examination procedure in order to have more time to gather evidence in support of an arrest. It is estimated that at least 80% of all suspects arrested before the 1996 revision were first detained under this procedure. The shelter for examination procedure was not only subject to extensive international criticism but was also widely denounced among PRC legal institutions and legal scholars and its abolition is one indication of the PRC's increased attention to the rule of law.

While the shelter for examination practice has been abolished, the 1996 CPL did not affect another notorious administrative practice, the punishment of re-education through labor (*laodong jiaoyang*). Under the 1982 Re–Education through Labor Provisions, a person may be detained for between one to four years in prison-like conditions for enumerated violations, including activities considered to be counterrevolutionary or against the Party. The re-education through labor procedures are widely used against political dissidents who can be suddenly seized and locked up in a prison-like facility without any of the procedural safeguards of the CPL and forced to renounce their political beliefs. Recent reports from China indicate that members of the Falun Gong movement have been targeted for this type of punishment. The elimination of the shelter for examination administrative process intended for those suspected of committing common crimes while retaining the re-education through labor procedure used for political crimes may be an indication of the limits of the Party's commitment to the rule of law.

e. Public Perception of the Public Security Organs

The powers of the police to interrogate, detain, and arrest, although subject to greater restrictions under the 1996 revision, continue to be formidable and create considerable fear and apprehension of the police in the ordinary PRC citizen. Anyone who is a subject of a police action may face serious disruption of normal activities for months in isolation from family and friends in prison-like conditions. Because the police have significant powers and many seek to curry favor with the police, corruption and abuse of power have become serious problems. Most people in the PRC tolerate the myriad types of petty corruption engaged in by the police, who are known to eat in restaurants and take cabs without paying and to ask for false receipts for goods and services. One common problem encountered by foreign companies doing business in China that are the victims of economic crimes is that the police have discretion to proceed with a criminal investigation and if they do not, there is little or no recourse. The issue for foreign companies is that the police often expect inducements to act upon their complaints. For example, when contacted by foreign companies with a complaint, the police will often cite a lack of resources in asking for an advanced payment of several thousand dollars for expenses before filing a case and initiating any type of investigation. If the police investigation involves travel, the foreign company is expected to pay for airfare, hotels, meals, and entertainment for the police. Some public security organs have been known to ask for sizeable rewards for the capture and arrest of persons suspected of counterfeiting and pirating products manufactured by multinational enterprises in China.

The 1995 Police Law was intended to curb some of these excesses by promulgating standards of professional competence and behavior. It may be an indication of the seriousness of the problems of abuse by the police that the drafters of the Police Law found it necessary to explicitly provide in Article 22 that the police are prohibited from practicing fraud, covering up or conniving to commit illegal and criminal activities; from beating up individuals; from committing extortion and racketeering; and from demanding and accepting bribes, among other activities. Article 42 of the Police Law provides that the police shall accept the supervision of the people's procuratorate and administrative supervisory organs in accordance with law.

f. The Decision to Prosecute

Once the investigation phase is completed, if the police find clear, reliable, and sufficient evidence of a crime, the police are to forward the case to the procuratorate with a recommendation to prosecute. If during the course of the investigation, the police discover that the suspect has no criminal liability, the case must be dismissed and if the suspect is being held in custody under arrest, the police must immediately release the suspect. While most cases are investigated by the public security organs, Article 18 of the revised CPL provides that the procuratorate is to investigate crimes committed by state functionaries involving embezzlement, bribery, and dereliction of duty and crimes committed by state functionaries involving violations of a citizen's rights, such as illegal detention, extortion of confessions by torture, retaliation, frame-up, illegal search, and violations of a citizen's democratic rights. If the procuratorate believes that detention or arrest of the suspect is necessary in a case that it is investigating, the procuratorate will make a decision to arrest and the police will take the suspect into custody. A detainee in a case directly investigated by the procuratorate must be interrogated within twenty-four hours of being taken into custody. If the procuratorate decides that an arrest is necessary, a decision to arrest must be made within ten days of the detention with an extension in special circumstances of one to four days. These time limits on detention before interrogation and arrest are similar to the time limits imposed upon the police.

Once the investigation phase of the case is complete, the procuratorate must make a decision whether to initiate a public prosecution. The procuratorate must make a decision within one month of the completion of the investigation or within one and one-half months in difficult and complex cases. In deciding whether to prosecute the case, the procuratorate is required to interrogate the suspect. This means that the suspect is subject to a second interrogation by the procuratorate after the initial interrogation by the police. Note further that the maximum time limit of seven months set forth in Articles 124, 126, & 127 of the CPL discussed above for holding a suspect in custody during the investigation stage applies only for the period of investigation after arrest. This means that once the investigation is concluded the suspect can be held in custody for an additional one and one-half months while the procuratorate decides whether to initiate a public prosecution. If the procuratorate decides to go ahead with a prosecution, the defendant will continue to remain in custody during the course of the trial. If the procuratorate refuses to proceed with a prosecution, the case is dismissed and the suspect shall be immediately released. Under the CPL, the procuratorate also has a third option. The procuratorate can also decide that it does not have a sufficient basis to make a decision to prosecute and that a supplementary investigation is necessary. The procuratorate can remand the case to the police to conduct the supplementary investigation or the procuratorate can conduct the investigation itself. The supplementary investigation must be completed within one month. The 1996 CPL now stipulates that a supplementary investigation can be conducted no more than two times in any case, closing a loophole in the 1979 CPL, which allowed the police to detain a suspect indefinitely under the guise of repeated supplementary investigations.

g.   Limits on Prosecutorial Discretion

One of the major changes in the 1996 revision is the elimination of the power of the procuratorate to exempt defendants from prosecution, which was an option available to the procuratorate at the end of the investigation phase under the 1979 CPL. Exemption from prosecution implies that the suspect is guilty of the crime but is spared public prosecution and will not be subject to any criminal punishment. This practice was subject to intense criticism within China because it suffered from many glaring deficiencies; the practice raised serious fairness and rule of law concerns because the procuratorate had the power to find a suspect guilty without a trial and before the suspect had been granted legal counsel. The practice was also suspect because the procuratorate may have usurped the adjudicative power of the courts in violation of Article 5 of the 1979 CPL, which provides that the police, the procuratorate, and the courts are to divide responsibilities. PRC scholars and international observers have hailed the elimination of the exemption from prosecution as a major advance in the criminal justice system in the PRC.

h. Adjudication

The adjudication phase of the criminal case begins when the procuratorate forwards the materials of the case together with an indictment to a people's court that has jurisdiction over the case. As discussed in Chapter 6, all four levels of courts in the PRC have jurisdiction as courts of first instance over criminal matters, depending upon their seriousness, including the Supreme People's Court. While a single judge can try a simple case, most cases are tried by a collegiate bench consisting of three, five, and seven adjudicators. These panels in all four levels of courts may include people's assessors or lay judges who are appointed by people's congresses for a period of three years and who have equal status with a judge.

Under the 1979 CPL, a court had to review and examine a case thoroughly upon receipt of the case from the procuratorate in order to determine whether to accept the case for trial, send the case back for supplementary investigation, or to request the procuratorate to withdraw and dismiss the case.

The courts would often work closely with the procuratorate in reviewing cases; this process would often blur the line between prosecution and adjudication. In deciding whether to accept a case for trial, a court had to investigate whether the facts of the crime were clear and the evidence sufficient. This was essentially the same standard for determining guilt during trial so the decision to hold a trial meant that the court was predisposed to finding guilt. A number of observers in China called this process, "decision first, trial later" (*xianding houshen*). Under the 1979 CPL, the courts were also empowered to remand the case to the procuratorate for further investigation and were empowered to conduct inquests, interrogations, searches, seizures, and obtain expert evaluations in deciding whether to accept the case for trial. Under the 1996 CPL, judges are no longer required to engage in extensive pretrial consideration and investigation of a case. Under Article 150 of the 1996 CPL, in deciding whether to accept a case for trial, courts need to review the bill of prosecution to determine whether it contains clear facts of the crime accused, a description of the evidence, a list of witnesses, and photocopies of the major evidence in the case. In addition, the courts can no longer remand a case back to the procuratorate for supplementary investigation. Courts can also no longer engage in pretrial investigation of a case, although once a trial has begun, courts retain the power under Article 158 of the revised CPL to adjourn the proceedings in order to conduct investigations to verify evidence.

The trial begins with a reading of the bill of indictment by the procuratorate. The defendant and the victim of the crime are then allowed to present statements regarding the crime. The procuratorate is then allowed to interrogate the defendant. The victim, with the permission of the court, is also then allowed to question the defendant. After the interrogation of the defendant, witnesses give testimony and are subject to questioning by the procuratorate and the defendant. Under the 1979 CPL, judges were to take the leading role in the interrogation of the defendant. Under the 1996 revision, judges are now no longer required to lead the interrogation of the defendant, although judges retain the power to question the defendant and any witnesses. *See* CPL, Arts. 70 & 71. The procuratorate and the defendant then present all material evidence to the court, including affidavits of witnesses not in court, statements of experts, and records of inquests. Once the interrogation of the defendant, any witnesses, and presentation of the evidence is complete, the trial then enters into a phase called "court debate" in which the procuratorate and the defendant give speeches and debate with each other. At the conclusion of the debate, the defendant is allowed to present a final statement. The court then adjourns and renders a verdict of guilt or innocence. Courts are to render judgments within one month or one and one-half months after accepting a case, although a one-month extension is possible with the permission of the provincial level high people's court.

As previously discussed in Chapter 6, under prior practice the adjudication committee of the court, composed of the court president and other court leaders, sometimes instructed the collegiate panel on how to decide the case before the public trial even began. This practice was addressed by the 1996 revision to the CPL, which now provides under Article 149 that the collegiate panel is to issue a judgment after the hearing and deliberations and is to forward only difficult, complex, and major cases for consideration by the court's adjudication committee and only when the panel cannot come to a decision on its own. However, whether the 1996 revision has increased the independence of the collegiate panel in practice is unclear and the 1996 revision did not address the larger issue of the independence of the courts, the procuratorate, and police from the influence of other government organs and the Communist Party.

i. Procedure on Appeal

The defendant and the procuratorate have ten days to appeal a judgment from the time it is received and five days to appeal an order. Within five days from the time a judgment is received, the victim can request the procuratorate to file a protest or appeal. The procuratorate must decide whether to proceed with a protest within five days.

Under the 1979 CPL, a court of second instance was not required to hold an open hearing and many cases were decided on the basis of written documents without an opportunity for the defendant to be heard. Under Article 187 of the 1996 revision, it is still possible to decide an appeal without holding an open court session where the facts are clear, but the court of second instance must examine the case file, interrogate the defendant, and heed the opinions of the defendant and his representatives. If the court decides to hold an open hearing, the court of second instance will retry the case and is not limited by the scope of the appeal or protest. Cases on appeal must generally be concluded within one month or one and one-half months, except in grave and complex cases where one-month extensions are possible, subject to approval by a provincial level people's court. All death sentence cases must be verified and approved by the Supreme People's Court.

j. Adjudication Supervision in Criminal Cases

After the time period for the appeals process has been exhausted, the judgment or order becomes legally effective, but it is still possible to challenge the judgment under the adjudication supervision procedure, previously discussed in Chapter 6. As previously noted, the adjudication supervision procedure is not subject to a statute of limitations in criminal cases and, in theory, all cases decided since the founding of the PRC can be challenged under this procedure. Under Articles 203–205 of the revised CPL, there are four ways to initiate adjudication supervision in the event that there is some definite error in a court judgment. First, a party may present a petition to a court or a procuratorate for relief, although such relief will not suspend the operation of the judgment. Second, the president of the court may refer the case to the court's adjudication committee. Third, a higher level court, including the Supreme People's Court, may order a court at a lower level to retry the case or the higher level court may retry the case itself. Fourth, a higher-level procuratorate, including the Supreme People's Procuratorate, may file a protest with a court of the same level against a lower level court judgment. A case that is retried under adjudication supervision must be concluded within three months from the time the decision is made by a court to retry the case itself or to direct a lower court to retry the case.

k. Presumption of Innocence

Under the 1979 CPL, many judges were biased in favor of finding guilt once a case was brought to trial based upon the notion that if the police and procuratorate had completed their investigation and decided to bring a public prosecution, then the defendant must be guilty to some degree. Aggressive police and procuratorates were also known to intimidate witnesses into confessions of guilt in criminal investigations. Not only did a presumption of innocence not exist under the 1979 CPL, many observers in the PRC were known to remark that in reality the opposite was true: a criminal suspect was usually presumed guilty until proven innocent.

The 1996 revision has introduced a presumption of innocence, embodied in three separate articles, into the criminal process of the PRC for the first time in its history. Article 12 of the revised CPL now provides that no person shall be found guilty without being judged as such by a people's court according to law. Article 34 provides that before a public prosecution is initiated, the accused shall no longer be referred as the "defendant" but as the "criminal suspect." Article 162 provides that if the evidence is insufficient and the defendant cannot be found guilty, he shall be found innocent based upon the insufficiency of the evidence. Although the concept remains nebulous and weak, the presumption of innocence in the 1996 revision may help to create a more neutral stance on the part of judges, procuratorates, and police.

l. Right to Counsel and Role of Defense Lawyers

Both the 1982 Constitution and the 1979 CPL state that the defendant is entitled to a defense in a criminal proceeding, but, as a practical matter, lawyers were placed at a severe disadvantage in protecting their clients. The 1979 CPL provided that a people's court had to deliver a copy of the bill of prosecution to the defendant seven days before trial at which time the defendant would also be notified that he could appoint a lawyer or other representative to assist in his defense. By the time that defense counsel entered the proceedings, the police and the procuratorate had already completed their investigation of the case, had most likely interrogated the defendant at least twice, and were convinced that they had sufficient evidence of the defendant's guilt to proceed with a public prosecution. The court had also reviewed the file in the case and had discussed it extensively with the procuratorate. By the time that the court made a decision to hold a public trial and the bill of prosecution is delivered to the defendant, the whole criminal process had strongly biased the court in favor of finding the defendant guilty. Under these circumstances, a lawyer who mounted a vigorous defense could be viewed as attacking the credibility of the court itself. In 1983 the NPC Standing Committee created further obstacles to effective assistance of counsel by abolishing the seven-day notice period for particularly serious crimes, including those involving the death penalty. Moreover, while the defendant was entitled to consult a lawyer, the state had no obligation to provide a lawyer without expense for the defendant except in cases where the defendant was under a disability.

The 1996 revision now extends the right to a lawyer to the investigative stage of a criminal case. Under Article 96 of the 1996 CPL, the right to counsel attaches after the suspect is interrogated by an investigation organ for the first time or from the day on which compulsory measures are adopted against him. If the suspect is arrested, the lawyer may apply to find a guarantor before trial who provides a form of financial guarantee, similar to bail, on penalty of forfeiture that the defendant will appear at trial. The suspect's lawyer has the right to be informed of the charges against the suspect and may meet with the suspect in custody to discuss the case.

In cases where the suspect is not interrogated or where compulsory measures have not been adopted against the suspect, the right to counsel attaches when the case is transferred to the procuratorate for examination before prosecution. Under Article 33 of the 1996 CPL, the procuratorate must inform the suspect that he has the right to appoint counsel within three days of receipt of the case for examination. Article 36 now provides that from the date that the procuratorate begins to examine the case, defense counsel is allowed to meet with the suspect in custody and examine and duplicate judicial materials pertaining to the case. Defense lawyers are given the same access to materials and are allowed to meet with the defendant in custody when a court accepts a case for trial. Article 35 of the revised CPL allows defense counsel to present evidence along with the procuratorate during the trial whereas only the state could present evidence during the trial under the 1979 CPL. Under the revised CPL, victims and their relatives are allowed to bring private criminal prosecutions where the procuratorate refuses to initiate a public prosecution and are also allowed to file civil claims against the suspect ancillary to a criminal case. *See* CPL, Arts. 170 & 77.

Although the 1996 revision significantly expands a criminal suspect's right to counsel, there are still some significant limitations. Article 96 contains two important restrictions on the right to defense counsel. First, if a case involves state secrets, the suspect must obtain the approval of the investigating organ to appoint a lawyer. Second, where the investigating organ finds the crime to be sufficiently serious, it may insist on being present at the meeting between the suspect and defense counsel. As the 1996 revision contains no additional guidelines that clarify the meaning of the key terms of Article 96, it is within the discretion of the investigating organ to determine whether a state secret is involved or a serious crime has been committed. In addition, the right to counsel attaches only after the first interrogation and because the suspect does not have a right to remain silent, the police and the procuratorate are afforded an opportunity to elicit damaging statements or a coerced confession from the suspect during this first opportunity. An indigent defendant is still not guaranteed a state appointed lawyer although under the 1996 CPL, the state may decide to provide a lawyer. The appointment of counsel by the state is mandatory only if the defendant is deaf, mute, blind, a minor, or is facing a death penalty. Finally, the abuse of the criminal process by investigation authorities does not taint the evidence obtained through illegal means. Under the U.S. approach, evidence obtained by illegal means cannot be used against the defendant in criminal proceedings. The same is not true in China. While suspects have the right to file charges against the police, the procuratorate, or courts for abuses of the criminal process, such abuses do not result in the dismissal of the case or in the exclusion of evidence obtained as the result of illegal procedures.

m. Future Directions for the Criminal Justice Process in the PRC

The changes brought forth by the 1996 revision have shifted the PRC from an inquisitorial model of criminal justice to more of an adversarial model. The 1996 revision has also removed or diminished some of the overwhelming advantages of the state in the criminal process. Statistics show, however, that in practice the 1996 revision has not resulted in major changes in the results of the criminal process. Since January 1997, when the revised CPL took effect, the acquittal rate in criminal prosecutions rose from .34% in 1996 to .66% in 1997. In 1998, the acquittal rate rose to 1.03% but fell back to .97% in 1999 and to .90% in 2001. In 2001, of 729,958 suspects tried, only 6,597 were acquitted. In cases brought under the 1979 CPL in 1988 and 1992, the acquittal rates were .55% and .51% respectively, both only slightly lower than the 2001 acquittal rate. These acquittal rates alone do not indicate whether more guilty or innocent defendants are being acquitted since the specifics of each case will vary, but they indicate that no extraordinary changes have occurred in the PRC criminal justice system.

China is in the process of revising the Criminal Procedure Law in accordance with the spirit of the

2004 amendments to the Constitution that recognize human rights and the right to own and inherit property. Under the expected revisions, the Supreme People's Court will review death penalty cases by trying the case de novo instead of simply reviewing the paper records, which is the current practice. Other possible changes are limits on the ability of judicial authorities to detain suspects before arrest and to hold suspects in custody after arrest.

B.   THE LAW OF CIVIL PROCEDURE

In traditional China, law was chiefly criminal in nature and civil litigation was never considered a significant part of the legal system. The emphasis on social harmony and filial duty as well as the lack of a developed mercantile culture discouraged the development of a civil litigation system. Mediation and conciliation outside of the official court system were the preferred methods of dispute resolution and are still emphasized in the present civil procedure law. In the PRC, work on a system of civil procedure was begun shortly after the founding of the nation in 1949 but, like work on a law of criminal procedure, the enactment of a civil procedure law was interrupted by political upheaval and the drafting of such a law was not revived until the reform era beginning in 1979. Some of the traditional Chinese emphasis on criminal law, as opposed to civil litigation, is reflected in the sequence and enactment of the codes of procedure. While the Criminal Procedure Law was one of the seven major laws enacted in 1979 at the earliest stage of law rebuilding at the beginning of the reform era, the NPC Standing Committee did not adopt a provisional or trial civil procedure law until 1982. The provisional law was followed by various judicial interpretation documents issued by the Supreme People's Court and other major legal organs. The provisional law was replaced by the Law of Civil Procedure adopted by the National People's Congress in April 1991 and is still in effect today. The Law of Civil Procedure was revised by the Decision of the Standing Committee of the NPC on Amending the Civil Procedure Law of the PRC on October 28, 2007.

1. BASIC STRUCTURE OF THE LAW OF CIVIL PROCEDURE

The Law of Civil Procedure (LCP) is divided in four parts: (1) general provisions dealing with court jurisdiction and general requirements, a topic previously discussed in Chapter 6; (2) trial procedures, covering procedures for ordinary trials and summary procedures, appeals, and special provisions for particular types of actions; (3) execution procedures for the enforcement of judgments and orders; and (4) special procedures for foreign parties. Most major elements of the general framework for the criminal procedure law are also present in the civil procedure law. The court will use a collegiate panel of judges and people's assessors, except in summary procedure cases, which are tried by a single judge. The court will use facts as the basis and law as the criterion. The basic procedural framework for resolving a case is also the same: there is a trial of first instance with the stages of court investigation, court debate, judgment, and an appeals process, allowing for a trial of second instance. Court proceedings in civil cases are subject to adjudication supervision. As in criminal cases, the adjudication committee of the court may instruct the collegiate panel on how to decide difficult, complex, or controversial cases. All of these elements find parallels in the Criminal Procedure Law previously discussed in this chapter.

a. Initiating the Lawsuit

In initiating a lawsuit, the plaintiff has the choice between an ordinary procedure of first instance and a summary procedure of first instance. The latter procedure is appropriate where the facts and law are clear and is a less formal and simplified version of the former. In an ordinary procedure, the plaintiff files a written complaint or if the plaintiff has genuine difficulty in presenting a written claim, the plaintiff is permitted to state the claim orally, which is then transcribed by the court. *See* LCP, Art. 109. A complaint must identify the parties to the case, state the claims of the lawsuit and the facts and grounds on which it is based, and must state the evidence as well as identify any witnesses. *See* LCP, Art. 110. Within seven days of receiving the complaint, if the court finds that the complaint meets the requirements for acceptance, the court will place the case on its docket and notify the parties; if the court finds that the complaint does not meet the requirements for acceptance, the court will issue an order dismissing the complaint. The plaintiff can appeal the dismissal. *See* LCP, Art. 112. The court sends a copy of the complaint to the defendant within five days after docketing the case and the defendant has fifteen days to submit a defense. *See* LCP, Art. 113. Before the trial begins, the plaintiff is to collect all relevant evidence, but the court should also investigate and collect evidence that it considers necessary or that the plaintiff is unable to collect. This investigation process may require the judges to travel to the site in question in order to collect evidence.

Pre-trial discovery in civil litigation in China is minimal as compared with the United States. If a party seeks evidence that may be in the custody of the opposing party, the party would need to make a request to the court to direct the opposing party to turn over any relevant materials to ensure cooperation. In other cases, the court itself may conduct an investigation and gather evidence directly. There is little, if any, exchange of evidence between the parties and PRC litigants do not have access to coercive measures such as interrogatories, depositions, and document requests, which are generally used extensively during civil litigation in the United States.

b.   Pre–Trial Relief and Related Measures

Articles 92–96 of the LCP provide for a type of ex parte pre-trial provisional relief in the form of an order for property preservation similar to ex parte temporary restraining orders under U.S. practice. These provisions were designed to address the basic problem that all civil litigants in China (as elsewhere) face: the disappearance of the disputed property or funds in question during the course of the trial that would render any judgment unenforceable and meaningless. The LCP allows a party to file an ex parte application (without notice to the defendant and without the defendant's presence at any hearing) for a property preservation order prior to the filing of a complaint, thus permitting the party to preserve the element of surprise where the disputed property is in the hands of the defendant and may disappear once the defendant is notified of formal court proceedings. The applicant must provide security for the order. Within forty-eight hours, the court must decide whether to grant the order, which would entail sealing up, distraining, or freezing the property in question. The plaintiff then has fifteen days to bring an action in a people's court or the order is canceled. There is a similar procedure for property preservation once the trial has started and the parties are before the court.

The procedures under Articles 92–96 apply to the preservation of property only and a different procedure applies to the preservation of evidence. Civil litigants in China (as elsewhere) also face the problem of the destruction or disappearance of evidence in the custody of the defendant. In certain cases where the defendant is suspected of common economic crimes such as selling smuggled, counterfeit, or pirated goods, the seizure of evidence is critical to the success of the case and the inability to seize the contraband usually dooms the plaintiff's case to failure. Article 74 allows the parties to apply to a court for the preservation of evidence where there is a likelihood that the evidence may be destroyed or lost, but unlike the procedures for property preservation, evidence preservation is not an ex parte pretrial process, but is a procedure that can be used only after the trial has begun and after the defendant has already received notice of legal proceedings. The inability to proceed on an ex parte basis greatly diminishes the value of this procedure as the defendant may have disposed of relevant evidence upon receiving formal notification of the lawsuit.

Articles 97–99 provide for a procedure of advance execution of judgments while a trial is still in progress. This procedure is appropriate where there are exigent circumstances, such as where the plaintiff's continuing economic subsistence is at stake, e.g. claims for alimony, maintenance, and for remuneration for labor. The plaintiff may be required to provide security for the order of advanced execution. If the plaintiff ultimately loses the lawsuit, the plaintiff must compensate the person against whom the advanced execution was imposed for any resulting losses incurred.

c.   Trial Procedure

The court notifies the parties of the time and location of the trial three days before the trial is to begin. Article 121 allows the courts, whenever necessary, to travel and "hold trials on the spot." The first phase of the trial is "court investigation," which includes questioning of the parties and witnesses by the court, the reading of any statements of witnesses who are unable to attend the trial, the presentation of any documentary and material evidence, and the reading of any expert opinions. *See* LCP, Art. 124. With the permission of the court, the parties are also allowed to question the witnesses. The parties are also allowed to present any new evidence during the trial.

Once the stage of court investigation is completed, the next stage is court debate, which begins with a statement by the plaintiff or his agents or representatives followed by a statement from the defendant or his agents or representatives. If the trial involves third party defendants, the third party is also allowed to make a statement. Following the statements, the parties engage in a debate and are then allowed to make any final statements. *See* LCP, Art. 127. The court will then deliberate and enter a judgment. There is a general requirement that courts conclude cases within six months from the docketing of the case. *See* LCP, Art. 135.

Returning to the subject of mediation discussed earlier, there are several points in a civil case where the courts may conduct mediation among the parties in order to reach a voluntary settlement, regardless of whether the parties themselves may have already attempted mediation outside the court system. The first stage at which mediation is conducted is before the trial. The court acting through one adjudicator or as a collegiate bench may conduct mediation and invite relevant persons from other units to participate. *See* LCP, Art. 86. If this first effort is unsuccessful, the court may undertake a second attempt at mediation after the conclusion of the court debate and before the entry of a judgment. *See* LCP, Art. 128. A third attempt at mediation may be conducted during the appeals process, further discussed below.

For most types of cases if a settlement between the parties is reached at any stage of the proceedings, the court will draw up a mediation statement that is signed by the court, sealed, and served upon the parties at which point the statement becomes legally effective. *See* LCP, Art. 89. Some types of cases, such as divorce and adoption cases, which are reconciled do not even require a mediation statement. If the court conducting the mediation is a court of second instance, the mediation statement must be signed by officers of the higher level court and served on the parties at which point the judgment of the lower court shall be deemed set aside. *See* LCP, Art. 155. The emphasis on mediation within the PRC court system is one of its hallmarks. In recent years, approximately 99% of all civil actions were resolved by mediation.

d. Appeals and Adjudication Supervision

Under Articles 147–159 of the LCP, the procedures for appeals from decisions and orders by courts of first instance are similar to those under the Criminal Procedure Law. Except for trials of first instance in the Supreme People's Court, which are final, there is one appeal to a court at the next higher level. The appellate court will form a collegiate panel to consider the relevant facts and the law. After reviewing the case, making investigations, and questioning the parties, if the appellate court decides that it is not necessary to hold a trial, the court can render a decision on the basis of the written materials and its own investigations. Orders on appeal must be decided within thirty days and cases that are tried on appeal are to be decided within three months from docketing the case.

If a party does not appeal a judgment in a timely fashion or a court of second instance enters a judgment, the judgment is considered final, subject to the caveat that in China all final judgments in civil and criminal cases can be reopened through the procedure of adjudication supervision. Under Articles 177–190, the president of a court, a higher court, and the procuratorate all have the power to require a retrial of a civil case by the original court or by a higher court on the basis of some definite error in the original judgment. A party may also submit a request for adjudication supervision that may be granted if certain enumerated conditions are met, including new evidence warranting setting aside the original judgment, insufficiency of the evidence supporting the original judgment, and corruption, malfeasance, and embezzlement on the part of the judicial officers involved in the adjudication of the case. As part of its general supervisory authority over the courts, the procuratorate also has the power to require a retrial of a civil case, even though, unlike in a criminal case, the procuratorate may not have been involved in the original proceedings. Article 184 provides that parties must make a request for adjudication supervision within two years from the date that the judgment or ruling becomes legally effective or within two years from the date of any misconduct or illegal behavior on the part of the adjudicating personnel. A party is also required to make a request for adjudication supervision within three months after the party discovers or should have discovered that the judgment or ruling was defective. These time limits apply to "parties" and it is unclear whether judicial organs are "parties" and subject to these limits. If judicial organs are not "parties" then there is no time limit on their ability to reopen a judgment under adjudication supervision.

e. Enforcement of Judgments

Part 3 of the LCP concerns the execution and enforcement of judgments. Each court has an execution officer that is entrusted with carrying out court judgments and orders. Article 206 establishes a procedure for the enforcement of judgments in areas outside the locality of the court issuing the judgment. This provision is designed to deal with the problem of local protectionism where courts in different locations may protect a local defendant by refusing to recognize or enforce a court judgment. Under Article 206, a court in one locality can entrust a court in a different locality to carry out the execution. The entrusted court must begin to carry out the execution in fifteen days and must complete the execution within thirty days. If the entrusted court fails to enforce the judgment, the entrusting court may request a higher-level court to instruct the entrusted court to carry out the execution, but there is no recourse if the higher-level court refuses to so instruct or if the lower-level court disregards the instructions of the higher-level court.

Articles 217–231 provide for coercive measures to enforce court judgments. These measures include the freezing of bank accounts and distraining of property that can be sold to satisfy a court judgment. Courts in the PRC, however, have no general contempt power as a sanction against those who disobey court orders or judgments, although Articles 100–106 leave open the possibility that a perpetrator will be "investigated for criminal responsibility" if he obstructs civil proceedings by destroying or forging evidence, by threatening witnesses, by concealing or transferring property that has been frozen or sealed up, or by refusing to carry out legally effective judgments or orders of the court.

f.   Cases Involving Foreign Elements

Part 4 of the LCP is entitled "Special Provisions for Civil Proceedings involving Foreign Elements." Among the topics covered by this part are jurisdiction over foreign defendants, service of documents and time periods, preservation of property, and judicial assistance between PRC and foreign nations in the service of documents and in the enforcement of judgments, orders, and arbitral awards.

Regarding judicial assistance and cooperation with foreign nations, Article 260 of the LCP provides:

> In accordance with the international treaties concluded or acceded to by the People's Republic of China or in accordance with the principle of reciprocity, the People's Courts and foreign courts may request mutual assistance in the service of legal documents, investigation, taking of evidence, and other acts in connection with litigation, on each other's behalf.

China has entered into bilateral treaties concerning judicial assistance with a number of countries, including France, Italy, Belgium, Poland, Romania, and the United States. In 1991, China acceded to the Hague Convention on the Service Abroad of Judicial and Extra Judicial Documents in Civil and Commercial Matters. Under the Hague Convention, service of documents on foreign parties may be effected by a judicial officer or authority of the nation where the documents originate through a central authority of the state in which the party receiving the documents resides. In China, the Ministry of Justice serves as the central authority under the Hague Convention for receiving and transmitting judicial assistance requests, although the Supreme People's Court also plays a coordinating role when judicial assistance involves the work of the courts.

One area where judicial assistance involves the work of the courts is the enforcement of foreign court judgments. In most cases, the enforcement of a foreign court judgment in China will be resolved by resort to bilateral judicial assistance treaties and implemented in accordance with the LCP under the direction of the Supreme People's Court. In the absence of a treaty, China will enforce foreign court judgments based upon the principle of reciprocity, i.e. only if the foreign nation would enforce a similar judgment from a Chinese court. The party with the foreign court judgment will file an official copy of the judgment in a Chinese court and ask the court to enforce the foreign judgment by issuing a domestic law judgment that incorporates the contents of the foreign judgment. In typical cases, the Chinese court will examine the quality of the judgment, i.e. whether the process by which the judgment was obtained in the foreign court satisfies the general procedural requirements of Chinese law and then apply the test of reciprocity. Similarly, if a party who has obtained a judgment from a Chinese court seeks to enforce the judgment in a foreign nation, the party can apply directly to a foreign court or ask the Supreme People's Court to make the request on its behalf subject to treaty obligations where applicable or under the principle of reciprocity in other cases.

Enforcement of international arbitration awards takes place in accordance with the following process. First, under its obligations as a party to the 1958 New York Convention on the Recognition and

Enforcement of Foreign Arbitral awards, China will enforce foreign arbitral awards as provided in the Convention subject to China's reservation based upon reciprocity. Second, if the Convention is not applicable, China will enforce the award on the basis of any existing judicial assistance treaties with the foreign nation. Third, in the absence of a treaty, China will enforce the foreign arbitral award only if the foreign state would likewise enforce a Chinese arbitral award in its territory.

C. THE LAW OF ADMINISTRATIVE PROCEDURE

The basic procedural law in the area of administrative law is the Administrative Litigation Law (1990) (sometimes translated as the Administrative Procedure Law). Other major enactments are the Administrative Review Law (1999), the State Compensation Law (1994), and the Administrative Penalties Law (1996).

1. THE ADMINISTRATIVE LITIGATION LAW AND THE ADMINISTRATIVE REVIEW LAW

Prior to the Administrative Litigation Law (ALL), courts already had departments dealing with administrative disputes under the Security Administration Punishment Regulations of 1986. The ALL, however, was designed specifically to allow parties to challenge the legality of the actions of China's government organs of state administration. Although common in the United States and other developed legal systems, the concept that ordinary citizens have the right to challenge the legality of government actions in court did not exist in traditional China or in the prior history of the PRC. The explicit recognition of the right to challenge government authority in a public law and the right on the part of ordinary citizens to subject government organs to limits on their power has been hailed as a milestone in China's development of the rule of law. The discussion below examines the basic features of the ALL and the related Administrative Review Law adopted by the National People's Congress in April 1999.

Under the ALL, citizens, legal persons, and organizations can challenge the legality of a wide range of administrative actions within eight enumerated categories, including administrative sanctions such as detention, fines, cancellation of permits and licenses, and compulsory measures such as the sealing up and freezing of property. Other types of actions subject to challenge are interference with the operational autonomy of business enterprises, the refusal to grant permits and licenses, and the refusal to perform statutory duties. A catch-all category allows challenges where administrative organs have infringed "other personal or proprietary rights." *See* ALL, Art. 11. All administrative acts subject to challenge must be concrete acts directed against specific persons or entities; individuals or enterprises have no standing to challenge administrative decisions with general applicability under the ALL. Also excluded from challenge under the ALL are acts of the state in the areas of national defense and foreign affairs, administrative rules and regulations, certain decisions of an administrative organ regarding its own personnel, and specific administrative acts that are deemed to be within the final authority of the state organ as provided by law. *See* ALL, Art. 12.

The jurisdiction over most cases of first instance is in the basic level people's courts. Certain cases of first instance involving patents, customs, administrative acts undertaken by departments under the State Council or by the people's government of provinces, autonomous regions, or municipalities directly under the central government, and grave and complex cases within their areas are under the jurisdiction of the intermediate people's courts. *See* ALL, Art. 14. Grave and complex cases of first instance can be brought in the high people's courts where the case affects an entire province, or in the Supreme People's Court where the case affects the whole country. *See* ALL, Arts. 15–16. There is no requirement that administrative remedies must be exhausted in all cases before filing a suit in a people's court, except in those cases where some specific law or provision explicitly requires the plaintiff to first pursue channels of administrative review before bringing a suit in a people's court. *See* ALL, Art. 37.

Administrative review is governed by the Administrative Review Law (ARL), which came into effect on October 1, 1999. In general, the types of administrative actions that are subject to the system of internal administrative review are quite similar to those covered by the ALL. *See* ARL, Art. 6. The reviewing authority of the acts of an administrative organ is the people's government at the same level or the administrative organ at the next higher level of government. *See* ARL, Arts. 12 & 13. The scope of review is whether the facts clearly establish the act complained of, whether the evidence establishing the act is conclusive, whether the application of grounds by the administrative organ was correct, whether the procedures followed by the administrative organ were lawful, and whether the content of the act by the administrative organ is proper. *See* ARL, Art. 28. An inquiry into the appropriateness of the act complained of under administrative review may be broader than the review available under the ALL, which is limited to the legality of the act in question. An application for review should be brought within 60 days from receiving notice of the act in question. *See* ARL, Art. 9. Once administrative review is underway, the act cannot be brought before a court under the ALL and conversely an act that is challenged in court cannot be the subject of an administrative review. *See* ARL, Art. 16. The reviewing authority usually decides the matter based upon written submissions in accordance with relevant laws, administrative regulations, local regulations, rules, and other legally effective decisions and orders. *See* ARL, Art. 22. The reviewing authority should issue a decision within sixty days from the time the application is received unless other time limits are stipulated in relevant laws and regulations. *See* ARL, Art. 31. The reviewing authority has the power to sustain, quash, or modify the administrative act involved, to order the administrative organ issuing the act to perform its duties or undertake a new administrative act, and to order the payment of compensation in accordance with the law. *See* ARL, Art. 28. An applicant that is dissatisfied with the decision of the reviewing authority is entitled to bring a lawsuit in a people's court under the ALL except that the administrative decision, as provided for by law, is a final decision. *See* ARL, Art. 5.

In administrative litigation in the people's courts, the proceedings in administrative cases follow the general pattern of criminal and civil cases. The principles of judicial autonomy and deciding cases according to facts and law, discussed in connection with the codes of criminal and civil procedure, also apply to administrative cases. Similarly, the use of a collegiate panel to try a case with one appeal to a higher-level people's court and the procedure of adjudication supervision also track the general procedural framework of criminal and civil cases. Article 55 of the ALL provides that courts and other authorities must follow any existing international treaties and the principle of reciprocity.

Under Article 54 of the ALL, a court is to annul or partially annul an administrative act based upon any of the following circumstances: the inadequacy of essential evidence, erroneous application of the law or regulations, violation of legal procedure, exceeding authority, or abuse of powers. If an administrative organ has failed to perform its statutory duties, courts are also empowered to set a specific time for performance. If an administrative sanction is obviously unfair, courts are empowered to adjust the sanction. *See* ALL, Art. 54. Article 32 of the ALL provides that the defendant has the burden of proving the legality of the specific administrative act and is to provide evidence and the relevant documents in accordance with which the act was undertaken. Unlike in civil and minor criminal cases, mediation, except on the issue of compensation, is not conducted in administrative cases because the legality of administrative acts is not an issue on which the parties can bargain.

Compensation under the ALL is the subject of Articles 67–69, which generally provide that a citizen, legal person, or organization that has suffered an infringement of rights shall be entitled to compensation from the administrative organ that has committed the act. Mediation is expressly allowed on the issue of compensation only. Courts have various compulsory measures available to enforce judgments, including informing a bank to transfer funds from the administrative organ's account, imposing a fine for each day that the administrative organ refuses to comply with the judgment, and complaining to a higher level administrative organ with supervisory authority over the department in question. Where the dereliction in obeying the judgment is sufficiently egregious to constitute a crime, the court may seek a criminal investigation of the responsible persons in the administrative organ against which the judgment has been entered.

2.　THE STATE COMPENSATION LAW

The provisions concerning compensation in the ALL were drafted to be broad because there were some differences among the drafters and rather than delaying the adoption of the ALL, it was decided that the details concerning compensation would be worked out in a subsequent law on compensation. Work on such a law began almost immediately with the enactment of the ALL and in 1994, the Standing Committee of the National People's Congress adopted the State Compensation Law (SCL). Despite its title, the SCL is not a general compensation statute but deals only with two specific types of compensation: administrative and criminal compensation. Administrative compensation allows for compensation for infringement upon personal and property rights by administrative organs; criminal compensation allows for compensation when such infringement is caused by state organs involved in criminal investigation, prosecution, adjudication, and imprisonment. *See* SCL, Arts. 3, 4, 15, 16 & 17. The violation of personal rights includes illegal detention, arrest, or imprisonment and the wrongful infliction of bodily harm or death. Infringement of property rights includes losses incurred due to the unlawful cancellation of business licenses, illegal use of penalties and sanctions, wrongful confiscation of property, and losses caused by other illegal acts. Under the SCL, claims for compensation can be (1) filed directly with the organization liable for the infringement; (2) made as part of the request for administrative review; or

(3) included as part of the prayer for relief in administrative litigation. *See* SCL, Art. 19. Compensation occurs in the form of payment for direct financial losses, restoration or return of property, and lost wages. *See* SCL, Art. 25 & 26. The SCL does not recognize punitive damages or damages for emotional distress. In line with the ALL, damages caused by acts of general applicability and state acts involving sovereignty are excluded from the scope of the SCL. Infringements by legislative organs, military organizations, political parties, social organizations, and enterprises are not within the scope of the SCL.

3.   THE ADMINISTRATIVE PENALTIES LAW

An additional major legislative enactment in the area of administrative procedure is the Administrative Penalties Law (1996) (APL). The APL was designed to address the many abuses of powers by administrative organs. Since there was no law governing the imposition of administrative penalties and sanctions, administrative organs began to promulgate and enforce an increasing number of penalties even though they had no clear power to do so. A single offense could be subject to sanctions from several different administrative organs and enforcement was uneven and arbitrary, leaving aggrieved parties with no recourse. The APL does not itself contain penalties, but rather it is a procedural law governing how administrative organs may impose and enforce penalties, which will continue to be contained in laws and administrative regulations.

A basic principle of the APL is that administrative penalties must be contained in laws and administrative regulations and must be carried out in accordance with the procedures contained in the APL. *See* APL, Art. 3. Administrative penalties include warning, fines, and confiscation of property; orders for the cessation of business operations; suspension or revocation of licenses and permits; and administrative detention. *See* APL, Art. 8. As administrative penalties are specific acts, they are subject to review under the Administrative Review Regulations and challenge under the Administrative Litigation Law.

The APL imposes a number of restrictions on the enactment of penalties. Article 9 of the APL provides that restrictions on personal freedom as a type of administrative penalty can only be imposed in laws enacted by the National People's Congress or its Standing Committee. Once administrative organs have enacted penalties (other than those restricting personal freedoms), the scope of any detailed implementing rules must be strictly within the confines of the enabling laws. *See* APL, Art. 10. To deal with the problem of the widespread and uncontrolled proliferation of administrative penalties, the APL provides that central level legislative and government authorities are allocated the basic power to impose administrative penalties; local level authorities at the provincial level and ministries and commissions under the central level State Council are only allowed to supplement national legislation by issuing detailed rules within the scope of the centrally issued provisions. *See* APL, Art. 11–13.

Turning to the enforcement of penalties, the APL makes clear that only the administrative organ that has the power to impose penalties has the power to enforce or implement such penalties. *See* APL, Art. 15. Under the APL, the State Council or people's governments of provinces, autonomous regions, and municipalities under the direct control of the central government are to designate one administrative organ in charge of enforcing penalties (with the exception of restrictions of personal freedoms, which can be enforced only by the police). *See* APL, Art. 16. Among the authorities eligible to be designated as enforcement authorities are organizations authorized by law to manage public affairs. The entrusted organizations must meet a set of requirements, including familiarity with relevant laws and regulations and must have the capability to conduct technical inspections for compliance with the law. *See* APL, Art. 19.

The APL has incorporated some important procedural protections into the enforcement process. To begin with, the APL adopts a principle of fairness and openness, requiring all laws and regulations imposing penalties to be made public. *See* APL, Art. 4. This requirement is intended to eliminate the notorious practice by state organs of relying on internal documents to which aggrieved parties are not allowed access. The APL also requires the administrative personnel imposing penalties to reveal their identities and requires a public hearing in cases in which serious penalties such as the revocation of a business license or permit or the termination of a business operation is involved. *See* APL, Art. 42. A penalty decision must state the reasons and legal basis for the decision and a party has the right to explain its position and offer a defense. *See* APL, Arts. 31 & 32. Any decision that fails to state its reasons and legal basis is invalid; likewise, the failure to afford a party an opportunity to explain and defend its position will render a penalty decision invalid unless such rights are waived. *See* APL, Art. 41. Where a party is entitled to a hearing, the party must be informed of this right by administrative authorities. *See* APL, Art. 42. Other provisions in the APL are designed to ensure the impartiality of the administrative decision-makers, to eliminate the problem of one unlawful act being punished several times by different administrative organs, and to ensure predictability and fairness in imposing punishments through a principle of proportionality requiring that the punishment fit the wrongful act. *See* APL, Arts. 4, 24, 36, & 38.

While the APL has adopted a number of significant protections familiar to western legal systems, the APL is not without some major problems. Some of the administrative measures restricting personal freedoms, such as the Regulations Concerning Punishment for the Administration of Public Order (1986) and the Regulations Concerning Re–Education Through Labor (1957), allow for the deprivation of personal liberty for up to four years. Although these measures are now subject to the APL, so long as they are classified as administrative in nature, they fall outside the scope of the Criminal Procedure Law, which provides for far more extensive protections, such as the right to counsel, as previously discussed in this chapter. A second problem with the APL is that although many protections are now established in the written law, China continues to lack a culture in which affected citizens feel comfortable in challenging the state. Based upon the author's own experience in China, the protections in the APL, while impressive on paper, have not been actively asserted by parties against the state or faithfully followed by administrative organs.

D. MEDIATION AND ARBITRATION

In addition to laws of procedure governing litigation based dispute resolution procedures, China also has codes of procedure for mediation and arbitration, which are non-litigation based systems of dispute settlement. The topic of mediation has already been previously discussed in this chapter in the context of court directed mediation during the litigation process. Mediation is encouraged in civil cases, in minor criminal cases, and even in arbitration cases, as further discussed below. Only in administrative cases is mediation not available, except on the issue of compensation.

Mediation in these cases occurs in the context of a court action (except in arbitration cases), but China also has a system of non-judicial mediation through the people's mediation committees, which continue to undertake a major part of the burden of dispute resolution in China. This system was codified early in the history of the PRC in the 1954 Provisional General Rules for the Organization of People's Mediation Committees. The promulgation of the 1989 Organic Rules for People's Mediation Committees was designed to modernize the mediation system by providing more structure to the mediation process and by granting the system more autonomy from the influence of the Communist Party. The 1990 Measures for Handling Disputes among the People were designed to strengthen mediation within villages and urban areas. On September 11, 2002, Some Provisions Concerning the Work of People's Mediation was adopted by the Ministry of Justice. These provisions were designed to regulate some details concerning the People's Mediation Committees. In 2006, with over 4 million cases resolved through mediation and with over 850,000 mediation committees in place, China had the world's largest dispute resolution system.

Under the 1989 Rules, each urban neighborhood or village resident committee is entitled to establish a people's mediation committee. Workplaces such as government institutions, business enterprises, and schools were also able to establish mediation committees. Each mediation committee consists of three to nine members who are elected by the constituency that the committee serves. No specific legal knowledge is required although candidates should be impartial and have some basic knowledge of law and politics. The mediation committees are also subject to the guidance of the local people's governments and the local people's courts. Although the 1989 Rules impose a general obligation on the parties to honor the mediation agreement, there is no enforceable legal obligation to carry out the agreement, which is revocable at will. A party that revokes the mediation agreement may take the case to a government agency or to a people's court. In 2006, mediation committees settled 4 million cases in a wide variety of areas, including divorce, inheritance, parental and child support, property disputes, civil and economic disputes, and minor criminal matters.

Turning now to arbitration, China's laws of arbitration have evolved from the 1981 Law of Economic Contracts and the 1983 Regulations on Economic Contract Arbitration providing for dispute resolution of contracts by administrative organs in China's centrally planned economy to the 1995 Arbitration Law that now brings China's arbitration practices in line with world practices. Under the 1995 Law, jurisdiction of arbitral organs has been substantially enlarged. Non-arbitral subjects include disputes related to marriage, adoption, guardianship, support, and succession as well as administrative disputes that are to be handled by administrative organs as prescribed by law. Arbitration commissions are set up under government organs with higher qualifications for arbitrators, although there is no requirement that an arbitrator must be a lawyer. To ensure the impartiality of arbitrators, the 1995 Law provides a challenge system. Proceedings are conducted in an adversarial manner in which the parties may be represented by lawyers. A valid arbitration agreement is a prerequisite for jurisdiction in an arbitration commission and the award, once entered, is final and can be enforced through the courts, if necessary. There is recourse to set aside the award on certain enumerated grounds, such as where the arbitration commission exceeded its scope of authority or there was corruption in the process. As in court proceedings, mediation may be conducted prior to the entry of an arbitral award.

The 1995 Arbitration Law also provides for arbitration for cases with foreign elements, but the forums of choice for international business disputes among foreign parties are the China International Economic and Trade Arbitration Commission (CIETAC) and the China Maritime Arbitration Commission (CMAC), both of which are governed by substantially similar rules and have similar practices. Although there is some overlap between the jurisdiction of CIETAC and domestic arbitration commissions over international disputes, the 1994 and 1995 CIETAC rules provide that CIETAC's jurisdiction encompasses all types of cases involving international economic relations and trade and is broader than the jurisdiction conferred by the 1995 Arbitration Law. CIETAC arbitration also has a number of features that address common concerns that foreign parties have about international arbitration, including impartiality, expertise, and enforceability of awards. From the perspective of foreign parties, one of the major advantages of the CIETAC rules is that foreign arbitrators may be included in the arbitration panel and about one-third of all persons currently qualified as CIETAC arbitrators are foreign. A foreign party has the power to nominate one of the foreign arbitrators to the panel ensuring that at least one of the three arbitrators is foreign in any given arbitration. CIETAC arbitrators, as a group, are also more highly qualified to handle the increasingly complex and substantial commercial claims that are being arbitrated in China.

Among the other features of CIETAC procedures that appeal to foreign parties are that arbitration can be carried out in any language, including English, as agreed to by the parties, and foreign lawyers are permitted to represent parties before a CIETAC panel. CIETAC awards are final and are enforceable in China and in the over one hundred countries that are parties to the 1958 New York Convention on the Recognition and Enforcement of Foreign Arbitral Awards, which China joined in 1987. The number of cases handled by CIETAC has increased significantly in recent years. In 1989, CIETAC heard 300 cases. By 2007, the number of cases heard by CIETAC had almost tripled to 1,109.

E. PRC PROCEDURAL LAW AND INTERNATIONAL STANDARDS

The enactment of new or revised codes of procedure for criminal, civil, and administrative cases, along with codes for non-litigation methods of dispute settlement through mediation and arbitration, has created a general framework for dispute resolution in China that is consistent with modern international practice. There are a number of issues concerning the operation in practice of the system, which have been alluded to in this and other chapters, but a viable overall procedural legal system is now in place. The content of the substantive laws that are implemented through this general framework is the subject of the next several chapters.

CHAPTER NINE

SUBSTANTIVE LAW

Substantive law in the PRC is divided into the three major branches of criminal law, civil and economic law, and administrative law. Each of these areas of substantive law is implemented and enforced by the three major procedural laws previously discussed as supplemented by the non-litigation forms of dispute resolution of mediation and arbitration. With the exception of the area of administrative law, which is still developing, each of these areas has a fundamental substantive law and a series of additional laws. In the area of criminal law, the basic substantive law is the Criminal Law of 1979 as revised and amended in 1997. In the area of civil and economic law, the General Principles of Civil Law (1986) is the basic law, but as this branch is the most broad and diverse area of substantive law, there are many additional important laws that will need to be discussed below and in the next chapters, such as laws relating to contract, business enterprises, foreign investment, intellectual property, marriage, and succession. Constitutional law, discussed in Chapter 3, is considered to be a higher-level law (*mufa* or "mother law") and is usually treated separately by PRC scholars from the major branches of substantive law.

This chapter will provide a survey of the three major branches of substantive law. No attempt is made to cover all the specific disciplines of the substantive law and the discussion below will necessarily be highly selective. The purpose here is to give a brief overview and summary of the subject matter, the basic principles, and noteworthy features in each of the major branches of substantive law. This overview should provide the reader with a basic background in these areas that can serve as the basis for those who wish to engage in further research and analysis. The subject of reference tools for further research is covered in Chapter 12.

A. CRIMINAL LAW

Law in traditional China was associated with criminal law and viewed as an important instrument of social control. Reflecting its importance in the legal system, work on a criminal law was begun shortly after the establishment of the PRC and some of the earliest laws enacted in the PRC were laws on criminal punishment. Work on a comprehensive criminal law, like work on a law of criminal procedure, was interrupted in 1957 by the Anti–Rightist Campaign and then by the Cultural Revolution. Of the first seven basic laws to be passed in 1979 in the post-Mao reform era, two were laws related to criminal punishment, the Law of Criminal Procedure, as discussed in the previous chapter, and the Criminal Law enacted on July 1, 1979 and effective as of January 1, 1980. Over the years, the 1979 Criminal Law was supplemented by twenty-four regulations and acts enacted by the National People's Congress and the State Council before it was extensively amended and revised, along with the Criminal Procedure Law. Following the comprehensive revision of the Criminal Procedure Law in 1996, a major revision of the Criminal Law was adopted in March 1997. The changes in the 1997 Criminal Law reflect the significant economic and political changes that have occurred in China since 1979. Like its counterpart on criminal procedure, the 1997 Criminal Law has been viewed as addressing some major deficiencies in the 1979 Law. The discussion below focuses on some of the major changes and improvements contained in the 1997 revision.

1. LESS OVERTLY POLITICAL

Based upon drafts prepared in the 1960s and 1970s, the 1979 Criminal Law was a reflection of the times and was heavily political in nature. The 1979 Law explicitly adopted Marxist–Leninist–Mao Zedong thought as its guiding ideology and was replete with the political rhetoric of the Cultural Revolution. An example of the ideological nature of the 1979 Law is contained in its first Article, which provided:

The Criminal Law of the People's Republic of China adopts Marxism–Leninism–Mao Zedong thought as its guide and the Constitution as its basis. It has been drawn up according to the policy of combining punishment with leniency and integrates the concrete experiences and actual conditions of the various nationalities in our country in their practice of the people's democratic dictatorship, that is, the proletarian dictatorship led by the proletariat and based on the alliance of workers and peasants, in carrying out the social revolution and socialist construction.

The 1997 revision avoids the overtly political approach of the 1979 Law and signals an official repudiation of the class struggle nature of criminal law. By contrast with its counterpart in the 1979 Law quoted above, Article 1 of the 1997 Law now provides:

In order to punish crimes and protect people, this Law is formulated according to the Constitution and in light of the concrete experiences of fighting crime and the actual circumstances in our country.

As a consequence of the shift from the ideological nature of the 1979 Law to a more legalistic approach, the 1997 revision also abolished two of the 1979 Law's basic approaches to criminal liability: lack of equal treatment and adjusting punishment in accordance with political needs. Each of these elements is further discussed below.

2. EQUALITY BEFORE THE LAW

Mao Zedong had espoused a theory of using criminal law as a tool for class struggle and for attacking class enemies and counterrevolutionaries. Part of this ideology was to single out those persons with "bad" class backgrounds such as capitalists and landlords for harsh treatment as they were predisposed to become enemies of the state. As a consequence, the 1979 Criminal Law did not include a principle of equality of all before the law. Rather than equality before the law, explicit discrimination against certain "bad" elements of society was advocated as part of the continuing revolution. In the post-Mao era, as class struggle was replaced by economic reform as the primary mission of the nation, equality before the law re-emerged as an important principle that was included in the 1982 Constitution and the 1986 General Principles of Civil Law. By the early 1980s another major concern that supported a need for an equality principle was the need to prevent officials of all ranks from asserting the privilege to be above the law. Article 4 in the 1997 Criminal Law now provides: "All are equal in the application of law. No privilege whatsoever is permissible beyond the law." The emphasis in the current Criminal Law is on equal treatment before the law regardless of rank and on the elimination of privileges.

3. PROPORTIONALITY

Another consequence of the overtly political nature of the 1979 Law was the principle, embodied in Article 1 of the 1979 Criminal Law quoted above, of "combining punishment with leniency," which meant leniency to those who confessed and severity to those who resisted during the criminal process. As law was designed to vindicate the Party's ruling ideology, those who confessed and showed repentance to the state were to be treated better than those who defied the authority of the state. The 1979 Law did not provide specific criteria on what constituted aggravating or mitigating circumstances in adjusting punishment, but left it to the discretion of the courts to adapt sentences in accordance with political needs. This approach meant that there could be wide disparities in sentencing and also provided an escape for officials convicted of crimes to avoid severe punishment. The heavy emphasis placed upon confession was also thought to be inconsistent with a presumption of innocence.

The approach of combining punishment with leniency was abolished by Article 5 of the 1997 Criminal Law, which provides: "The severity or leniency of punishment shall be determined in accordance with the criminal acts and liability of the suspect."

4. ABOLITION OF CRIMES BY ANALOGY

Criminal law has long been viewed in China as a method of social control and it seemed natural for enforcement authorities in traditional China to provide for a catch-all type of offense called crime by analogy to punish acts that may have otherwise fallen into the gaps of any existing criminal code. The notion of crime by analogy was widely used in Imperial China and traceable to as early as the Han Dynasty (206–8 BC) and was finally abolished during the brief period of reform at the end of the Qing Dynasty during the last days of Imperial China. Crime by analogy was revived in the first criminal legislation issued by the Communist Party in the

1934 Chinese Soviet Republic's Act on Punishment of Counterrevolution and was reaffirmed in the first criminal law passed by the PRC in the 1951 Regulations on the Punishment of Counterrevolutionary Crimes. Crime by analogy was incorporated into the 1979 Criminal Code under Article 79, which provided:

> A crime not specifically prescribed under the specific provisions of the present law may be confirmed a crime and sentence rendered in light of the most analogous article under the special provisions of the present law; provided, however, that the case shall be submitted to the Supreme People's Court for its approval.

Under the 1979 Criminal Code, it was possible to convict and punish a person for a crime even though the specific act was not made illegal by a written law and the person committing the crime had no notice of its illegality at the time it was committed. This raises a host of due process and fairness issues since a basic tenet of most modern legal systems is that there can be no crime unless a written law already exists that criminalizes the specific act or conduct. Another concern is that the vagueness and broad scope of Article 79 would allow resourceful and clever judges to bring a wide array of behavior within the ambit of the Criminal Law by analogy. Nevertheless, the use of crime by analogy was justified under the 1979 Criminal Law because the law had a total of only 193 articles and only 103 of these articles were devoted to outlawing specific crimes. The drafters believed that the

sparseness of the 1979 Law needed to be supplemented by the catch-all crime by analogy provision
so as not to let offensive acts go unpunished due to
the oversight of the drafters. By contrast, the 1997
revision is far more comprehensive with 345 articles
specifying crimes. After a long debate in the preparation of the 1997 revision and strong opposition
from conservative forces, crime by analogy was
abolished by Article 3 of the 1997 revision, which
provides "Anyone who commits an act deemed a
crime by explicit stipulations of law shall be convicted and given punishment by law and no one shall be
convicted or punished for an act that is not deemed
to be a crime by an explicit provision of law."

5. SPECIFIC OFFENSES AND
NEW OFFENSES

While the previous section examined changes in
approach and orientation, this section turns to an
examination of changes in specific offenses and the
addition of new offenses under the 1997 Criminal
Law.

a. Crimes of Counterrevolution and Crimes
Against the State

The major purpose of all criminal laws in the
PRC has always been to target crimes against the
state. The 1979 Law contained a number of provisions on "counterrevolution" that were vague and
sweeping. In particular, Article 90 of the 1979 Law
contained a catch-all provision that defined "crimes
of counterrevolution" as "all acts endangering the

People's Republic of China committed with the goal of overthrowing the political power of the dictatorship of the proletariat and the socialist system." A number of other provisions in the 1979 Law prescribed severe penalties for crimes of counterrevolution with over 60% of the provisions prescribing the death penalty. The 1997 revision has deleted the catch-all provision of Article 90 and has replaced the terms "counterrevolutionary crimes," a political concept, with "crimes endangering state security," a legal concept, and has defined such crimes more concretely.

Articles 102–113 of Chapter 1, the first substantive provisions in the 1997 Criminal Law, enumerate twelve crimes of endangering national security. Article 102 of the 1997 Criminal Law retains the proscription against "colluding with a foreign state to jeopardize the sovereignty, territorial integrity and security of the motherland." New provisions have been added to specify crimes considered the most serious against national security, including disrupting the motherland (Article 103), armed rebellion (Article 104), subverting the government and overthrowing the socialist system (Article 105), collaboration with overseas groups, organizations, and persons to threaten national security (Article 106), and defection to the enemy and becoming a traitor (Article 108). A new Article 109 was added for a state functionary who defects to a foreign nation or becomes a defector while abroad on official business. This provision was apparently designed for those foreign officials who were sent by the state to go abroad to work or study and who did not return. Article 113 provides for severe penalties for the majority of the crimes against national security enumerated in Articles 102–113 with the death penalty applicable to a majority of these crimes "where the consequences of harming the state and the people are exceptionally serious and the circumstances are especially heinous."

It is important to emphasize that the 1997 revision does not reflect the Party's repudiation of its past actions and past prosecutions and convictions of persons under the 1979 Law. There will be no retrials or reviews of past convictions for crimes of counterrevolution. Nor does the shift indicate that the state will be less vigorous in prosecuting political dissidents who can fall into any number of the new 1997 provisions. The changes in the 1997 Criminal Law reflect the shift from an overtly political approach to a more legalistic approach to criminal justice, as described in the previous section, and the need to define crimes against the state with more specificity in light of China's recent economic development, but they do not represent a fundamental shift in government attitudes toward challenges to the authority of the state.

b. Other Categories of Crime

The remaining categories of crimes under the 1997 Criminal Law are Endangering Public Security (Articles 114–139), Undermining the Socialist Market Economic Order (Articles 140–231), Infringing Upon the Rights of the Person and Democratic

Rights of Citizens (Articles 232–262), Encroaching on Property Rights (Articles 263–276), Disrupting the Order of Social Administration (Articles 277–367), Endangering National Defense (Articles 368–381), Graft and Bribery (Articles 382–396), Dereliction of Duty (Articles 397–419), and Violation of Duties by Military Servicemen (Articles 420–451).

The 1979 Criminal Law contained about 110 offenses as compared with about 360 offenses under the 1997 revision. One major difference between the two laws is the significant increase in the number of economic crimes in the 1997 revision. Reflecting the changes in China's development are new economic crimes, including those relating to insider trading and price manipulation (Articles 180–182), financial fraud (Articles 192–198), and computer fraud and computer hacking (Articles 285–286). Articles 30–31 of the 1997 revision introduced the concept of corporate criminal responsibility for the first time into Chinese jurisprudence to address the problem of economic crimes being committed by business enterprises as a result of economic reforms. A number of new articles on intellectual property crimes (Articles 140–149, 213–220) are also new to the 1997 revision. The inclusion of intellectual property crimes was necessary to bring China into compliance with the requirements of the Agreement on Trade Related Intellectual Property Rights (TRIPS) of the World Trade Organization and was part of China's preparations for entry into the WTO. It also reflects the pervasiveness of commercial piracy in China.

The traditional crimes of murder, rape, assault, kidnapping, abducting and selling women and children are contained in Chapter 4 on Infringing Rights of the Persons and Democratic Rights. Among crimes that are unique to China is criminal defamation under Article 246, which prohibits publicly insulting a person or fabricating facts to defame a person. This provision reflects lessons from the Cultural Revolution and other periods of political upheaval where false accusations led to political persecution of many innocent victims. Other crimes relating to rights of the person that are new to the 1997 Criminal Law are organized terrorism (Article 120) and inciting racial hatred or discrimination (Article 249).

c. Elements of a Crime

To constitute a crime under the 1997 Criminal Law, four elements must be present. There must be (1) a criminal subject capable of bearing criminal liability; (2) the requisite mental element or condition; (3) an interest recognized and protected by the state that is infringed; and (4) substantial harm caused by the act or omission of the criminal subject to the interest protected by the state. With regards to a criminal subject, any person who has reached the age of sixteen and commits a crime shall bear criminal responsibility. A person between the ages of fourteen and sixteen will bear criminal responsibility only for serious crimes such as murder, rape, and robbery; otherwise there will be no criminal responsibility although the juvenile perpetrator may be subject to re-education under state supervision. Any person between the ages of fourteen and eighteen who commits a crime shall be given a lighter or mitigated punishment. In addition to a natural person, a legal person can also be a criminal subject under the 1997 Criminal Law. Under Article 30, a corporation, enterprise, institution, office, or unit is also capable of bearing criminal responsibility.

To be liable for a crime, the criminal subject must also have the requisite mental state of intent or negligence when the crime is committed. In addition to these general mental conditions, specific mental states are required for certain types of crimes. For example, under Article 152, the perpetrator must have disseminated obscene materials for the purpose of deriving profits to be guilty of smuggling obscene articles. To be guilty of the criminal sale of counterfeit products under Article 213, the seller must have knowledge that the goods were bearing a counterfeit trademark. There are many other examples of specific mental states in the 1997 Criminal Law.

The interests protected by the state are generally enumerated in Article 13 and further described in the many specific provisions describing individual crimes. Under Article 13, the types of interests that are enumerated include the sovereignty, territorial integrity, and security of the state; property owned by the state or collectively by the laboring masses; property owned by citizens; rights of the person or their democratic or other rights; and other rights. These rights are further described and developed in specific criminal provisions. For example, the interests of the state are further elaborated in Articles 102–113 dealing with Crimes Endangering National Security. Finally, a crime must generally involve substantially harmful consequences that are caused by the act of the criminal subject. Some offenses presume the existence of a harmful consequence, including most of the crimes of endangering national security and crimes of manufacturing and distributing fake and shoddy goods, among others.

d. Punishments

Punishments under the 1997 Criminal Law are divided into principal and supplementary punishments. Under Article 33, the principal punishments are (1) public surveillance; (2) criminal detention; (3) fixed-term imprisonment; (4) life imprisonment; and (5) the death penalty. Public surveillance appears to be unique to the PRC and can be compared to parole in other legal systems. Imposed only for minor offenses, public surveillance allows the subject to live in society under the supervision and surveillance of the local public security organ. Similarly, criminal detention is also for minor offenses and requires the subject to live in a detention house supervised by the local public security organ rather than in a prison or in an institution for re-education through labor. The subject is allowed to go home for one or two days per month and is paid for any work performed.

Principal punishments may be supplemented by additional punishments. Under Article 34 supplementary punishments are (1) fines; (2) deprivation of political rights; and (3) confiscation of property. In addition to other types of punishment, a foreigner who commits a crime may be deported as a supplementary punishment. Further, any person convicted of a crime may be required to compensate the victim for the economic losses caused by the crime. Finally, the court has the power to exempt a person convicted of a crime from punishment where the crime is minor but in such a case the person so exempted may, depending upon the circumstances, be reprimanded or ordered to make a statement of repentance, offer an apology, pay compensation for losses suffered by the victim, or be subject to administrative sanctions by the competent authority.

B. CIVIL AND ECONOMIC LAW

Unlike criminal law, civil law was not emphasized in traditional China and it is only with the advent of the twentieth century that civil law reforms began to take place in contemporary China. The enactment of the General Principles of Civil Law (GPCL) in 1986 now authoritatively defines civil law. Article 2 of the GPCL states that "the civil law of the PRC shall adjust property relationships and personal relationships between civil subjects with equal status, that is, between citizens, between legal persons, and between citizens and legal persons." Similar to the Criminal Law discussed in the previous section, the GPCL is the most basic and comprehensive law in its field. Other major pieces of civil law that will be discussed below are the Property Law (2007), the Unified Contract Law (1999), the Company Law (1993, revised in 2004 and 2005), the Marriage Law (2001), and the Succession Law (1985).

While civil law has always been recognized in the PRC as a separate branch of law, the recognition of a field of economic law began only after the advent of economic reforms in 1979. Over the years, there have been numerous attempts to define economic law and to distinguish it from civil law, but most of these attempts have been hampered by a reliance on abstract concepts that are difficult to implement in practice. At the outset of reforms, the basic idea was that China would move from an economy governed by administrative fiat to a market governed at least in part by economic principles and law. The role of law would be to regulate, enforce, and implement economic policies of the state that may be embodied in state economic plans or other state directives. With the enactment of the GPLC and its clarification of the role of civil law, further refinement of economic law was necessary as there was some overlap between these two concepts. So far no general code of economic law, similar to the GPLC, has been enacted and the debate on the scope of economic law has been carried out mostly in academic circles. A theory that has gained prominence views economic law as regulating vertical economic relations or economic management relations between higher level and lower levels of the planned sector of the economy as well as some horizontal relations that are closely related to vertical economic relations such as contracts entered into in furtherance of state plans. In addition, some internal structures of economic organizations as well as organizations related to foreign economic activities, such as sino-foreign joint ventures, also fall within the category of economic law. Such a definition of economic law is potentially very broad and can encompass numerous fields, leaving little room for civil law.

While the exact boundaries between economic and civil law may be unclear, significant consequences may result from the classification of a particular law as falling within one of these fields. Economic law has been viewed as enforcing and implementing the economic plans and policies of the state. Matters of economic law are subject to greater expectations of compliance with state economic plans or policies and are exposed to a greater degree of state intrusion and regulation than civil matters, which fall outside of state policies. The degree of compliance with state economic plans for matters of economic law has varied over time; early versions of the Economic Contract Law imposed rigid tests of compliance providing that all contracts in violation of state plans were void. Later revisions to the Economic Contract Law emphasized consistency with state economic policies. While scholars may continue to debate the exact nature and definition of economic law, they agree that economic law is a particularly important field and suggest that economic law comprised at least 70% of all items introduced in the National People's Congress, the NPC Standing Committee, and the State Council during the bulk of the crucial law-building decade of the 1980s. The next several sections will provide a survey of the major civil and economic laws.

1. THE GENERAL PRINCIPLES OF CIVIL LAW

The GPCL provides the foundation for all civil law in the PRC. The GPCL follows the tradition of civil law in continental Europe and the Soviet Union in dividing its subject matter into three central elements: (1) the subjects of civil law; (2) civil rights (including property rights and contracts); and (3) civil law obligations and liabilities. Chapter 1 of the GPCL sets forth basic principles, including the scope of civil law and provides that the basic principles of equality, fairness, voluntariness, fair compensation, honesty, and credibility apply in all civil activities.

a. The Subjects of Civil Law

Chapters 2 and 3 of the GPCL define the subjects of civil law as either natural persons or legal persons. Article 11 provides that a citizen of the PRC aged eighteen or over shall have full capacity for civil rights and civil obligations. A citizen between the ages of sixteen to eighteen may also be considered to be a person with full capacity for civil acts if his main source of income is derived from his own labor. See GPCL, Art. 11. Special rules apply for mentally ill persons and others of a limited capacity who may be represented by a guardian. See GPCL, Arts. 13–19. Article 8 provides that stipulations of the GPCL regarding citizens shall also apply to foreigners and stateless persons within the PRC. Chapter 2 on natural persons also includes individual industrial and commercial businesses, rural contracting households, i.e. those farm households that contract with the state to produce commodities, and partnerships of individuals. The inclusion of these entities in the chapter on natural persons appears to indicate that a privately owned business is excluded from obtaining the status of a legal person and that only the individuals who own or operate these businesses have civil capacity. This exclusion created a number of problems as private businesses sought to protect their corporate interests as distinct from the interests of the individuals who may have invested in these entities. It appears that the issue of how to treat these entities remains unresolved, but that the current practice is to treat the industrial and rural households as business entities for purposes of taxation, registration, and contracts but as individuals for liability purposes, i.e. individuals operating household businesses are subject to unlimited liability with their personal or family assets.

A legal person is defined as "an organization that has capacity for civil rights and capacity for civil conduct and independently enjoys civil rights and assumes civil obligations in accordance with the law." GPCL, Art. 36. These provisions, combined with Articles 30 and 31 of the 1997 Criminal Law, now provide for both civil and criminal corporate responsibility. Among the types of legal persons recognized by the GPCL are enterprises owned by the whole people, collectively-owned enterprises, sino-foreign equity joint ventures, sino-foreign contractual joint ventures, wholly foreign-owned enterprises, official organs, institutional units, social organizations, and economic associations (formed by associations between enterprises and institutions). When the GPCL was enacted in 1986, it did not explicitly accord legal person status to a business enterprise that was formed by wholly domestic (as opposed to foreign) capital. To the contrary, as previously discussed above, the GPCL seemed to exclude certain domestic private enterprises from legal person status by including them as natural persons. The Company Law, enacted in 1993, now makes explicit that certain enterprises that can be formed wholly with domestic private capital, the limited liability company and the joint stock company, are enterprise legal persons. *See* Company Law, Art. 3.

Chapter 4 of the GPCL deals with civil juristic acts and agency. Article 55 of Chapter 4 sets forth the conditions for a valid civil act, which requires civil capacity, intent, and an act that does not violate the law or public interests. Chapter 4 also states what types of civil acts are void and also sets forth principles of agency and the types of agency relationships recognized in the PRC: entrusted agency, statutory agency, and appointed agency.

b. Civil Rights

Chapter 5 of the GPCL is entitled "Civil Rights" and is divided into five separate sections for property rights, creditors' rights, intellectual property rights, and personal rights. The discussion below will focus on creditors' rights (including contracts), and personal rights. The sections in Chapter 5 of the GPCL relating to property rights have now been displaced as a primary authority by the 2007 Property Law, which will be discussed in a subsequent section of this chapter. Intellectual property rights will be discussed in a subsequent chapter.

(1) Creditors' Rights

Section 2 of the chapter on civil rights in the GPCL deals with creditors' rights. In keeping with the European civil law tradition, Article 84 defines a debt as a special relationship of rights and obligations established either by contract or through operation of law. The party entitled to rights in the relationship is the creditor and the party subject to obligations is the debtor. Three types of creditor-debtor relationships are recognized: those arising from contract (Articles 84 & 85), unjust enrichment in favor of the debtor causing a loss to the creditor (Article 92), and where one person acts as a manager or provides services to protect another person's interest when he is not legally obligated to do so (Article 93). Another notable feature of Section 2 is that it contains several articles relating to general contract rights, which were of greater significance prior to the enactment of the Unified Contract Law in 1999, as further discussed below. One departure from the European civil law tradition is that a tort, which is considered to be a fourth type of debt, is not included in Section 2 but is dealt with in Chapter 6 of the GPCL on civil liabilities.

(2) Personal Rights

The personal rights contained in Section 4 of the chapter on civil rights in the GPCL include the rights of all citizens to life and health (Article 98), the right to one's name (including the right to prohibit interference with one's name) (Article 99), the right of portrait, similar to a right of publicity, allowing a person the right to prohibit the unauthorized use of his image (Article 100), the right of reputation against insults, libel, or other types of defamation (Article 101), the right of honor preventing the divestment of honorary titles (Article 102), and the right to freedom of marriage (Article 103). Several of these rights are designed to protect personal dignity and reflect the need to provide legal protections against the abuses that occurred during the Cultural Revolution and other periods of political chaos and persecution. Article 103 on the freedom of marriage explicitly prohibits traditional Chinese practices of mercenary marriages and marriages based upon arbitrary decisions by third parties. Article 103 and Article 105, which provide that women have equal civil rights with men, are aimed at curbing some of the traditional practices of discrimination against women that continue to exert influence today.

Aside from the rights of citizens, Section 4 also recognizes the rights of legal persons to enjoy the right of name. The Anti–Unfair Competition Law enacted in 1993 also recognizes the right of legal persons or individuals engaged in business to be free from commercial defamation.

c.   Civil Obligations and Liabilities

Chapters 2 through 4 of the GPCL are devoted to subjects of civil law and Chapter 5 concerns civil rights. Chapter 6 of the GPCL concerns civil obligations and liabilities. Chapter 6 is divided into four sections: general provisions, breach of contract, infringement of rights (including torts), and methods of bearing civil liability and remedies.

Article 106 of the chapter's general provisions provides that a citizen or legal person is subject to civil liability based upon a breach of contract or some other obligation. Although civil liability is generally based upon fault, liability may be imposed in the absence of fault if the law so provides. Section 3 on infringement of rights is the section of the GPCL that deals with torts. In addition to general principles of tort liability for physical injury, Section 3 also sets forth a specific list of torts, including liability for substandard products (Article 122), engaging in operations that are greatly hazardous to the surroundings (Article 123), polluting the environment (Article 124), construction in public areas without the use of proper warnings and safety measures (Article 125), falling objects from buildings or construction (Article 126), and harm caused by a domesticated animal (Article 127). Other articles provide for joint liability where several tortfeasors are involved (Article 130), comparative negligence where the victim is also at fault (Article 131), and principles of vicarious liability where the tortfeasor has limited or no civil capacity (Article 133). As for remedies, Article 134 provides for various methods, including cessation of the wrongdoing; elimination of dangers; return of property; restoration of original condition; repair, reworking or replacement; compensation; contract damages; elimination of ill effects and restoration of reputation; and apology.

d. Limitations and Other Issues

The final three chapters of the GPCL deal with limitation of actions, civil relations with foreigners, and miscellaneous matters. Chapter 7 on limitations of actions provides for a general two-year statute of limitations with a special one-year period of limitations for claims involving compensation for bodily injury, sales of substandard goods, delays in paying rent, and damage to property left in the care of another person. Chapter 8 on cases involving foreigners contains a number of principles relating to treaty obligations, choice of law, and conflict of laws for dealing with foreign related matters. Chapter 9, the last chapter in the GPCL, contains a number of miscellaneous supplementary items, including provisions regarding the authority of national autonomous areas to formulate separate or supplementary items in accordance with the GPCL, definitions of terms such as "force majeure," and methods for calculating time periods.

2.   OTHER MAJOR ECONOMIC AND CIVIL LAWS

The following discussion will examine several other major areas of civil and economic law, including laws related to property rights, contracts, business enterprises, and family law.

a.   The Property Law

The Property Law of the People's Republic of China was adopted by the National People's Congress in 2007 and became effective on October 1, 2007. The Property Law replaces Section 1 of Chapter 5 of the GPCL as the primary law on property rights; however, Chapter 5 of the GPCL has never been withdrawn. Chapter 5 of the GPCL can be considered to have a supplementary role to the Property Law.

The 2007 Property Law recognizes three forms of ownership: state ownership, collective ownership, and private ownership. In the case of real property, the Property Law makes clear that there is no right of private ownership in the PRC. All land is subject to state ownership or, when allowed by the state, collective ownership by groups of farmers. This approach is made explicit in a number of provisions. Article 47 provides that the state owns all urban land and that the state and farming collectives own all rural lands. The state also owns all wildlife (Article 49), mineral rights, waters, and sea areas (Article 46). All other natural resources are owned by the state or by farmers' collectives (Article 48).

While ownership of all land is in the state, the PRC, like the United States, recognizes the distinction between ownership and possessory rights. While the state or collectives own all land, the right to use land can be transferred to private persons or enterprise legal persons. Land use rights and the ability to profit from them are protected by law (Article 117). Under this approach, it would be possible for a person or a company to have a legal right of possession to real property used as its site for 50 years or longer although, as a technical matter, ownership must remain in the state. Such a long period of possession of real property would provide a secure and stable environment for business.

The PRC maintains a registration system for all real property. Ownership and land use rights in real property are valid and effective only if they are officially registered with the appropriate land management authorities (Article 9).

Article 42 of the Property Law provides that all land or land use rights requisitioned by the state must be accompanied by the payment of full compensation and that suitable alternative housing must be provided for owners of houses that have been requisitioned. Payments for compensation shall not be embezzled, misappropriated, privately shared, or delayed. Article 42 was included to combat the perceived abuses by government officials in the requisition of privately held housing in both urban and rural areas for the development of new higher end housing, shopping malls, and commercial properties. Many owners of housing, especially in rural areas, believed that they were forced off their land by corrupt government officials and given inadequate payments. Government officials appeared to derive personal gain from the requisition of privately held property and the sale of the rights to develop those properties to builders of residential and commercial buildings.

The only form of private ownership of property that is recognized by the Property Law is ownership in chattel property. Individuals are entitled to own income, housing, household goods, production instruments, raw materials, and other chattel property (Article 64). Consistent with the spirit of the 2004 amendments to the Constitution that created a new emphasis on the protection of private property, Article 65 of the 2007 Property Law provides that a person's property rights shall not be encroached upon. These provisions are intended to protect personal wealth.

The 2007 Property Law stirred a great deal of controversy during its long period of drafting and debate. With the great expansion of personal wealth in China in the past two decades, there was a general sentiment both within the Party and the populace that a new law was necessary to recognize and protect the wealth generated by China's growing private sector. The 2004 amendments to the Constitution, with their greater emphasis on the protection of such rights, is a reflection of these same sentiments. However, many opponents of the 2007 Property Law believed that a law recognizing new rights in property might further exacerbate the growing gap between the rich and the poor and even destroy the basic premise of China's socialist system of state ownership of all real property. In the end, the 2007 Property Law did not break any new ground in the recognition and protection of property rights. The Property Law does reinforce and make explicit in much greater detail the rights of persons to own property and to be protected in their ownership of their personal wealth. However, the 2007 Property Law also maintains the basic socialist approach of state ownership of land with transferable possessory rights that can be owned by persons. This basic approach is the same approach that existed under the GPCL, which has been in effect since 1986.

b. Contract Law

The development of contract law in China serves as a useful barometer of recent changes in its legal system because autonomous contracts and transactions between economic actors are basic to a market economy. The extent to which autonomous contracts are allowed under PRC law will reflect the progress that China is making in its efforts to implement a legal system to support its transition from a planned economy to a mixed or transition economy with some free market features.

Contract law was already well established in the PRC prior to the enactment of the GPCL in 1986. China's first contract law, the Economic Contract Law (ECL), was enacted in 1981 and later revised in 1993. The ECL governed domestic Chinese contracts and was a major component of the new economic reform policies that represented a compromise between rigid state planning and increased autonomy for economic actors. While the ECL contained provisions recognizing the equal rights of the parties and the strict enforcement of contracts, the classification of contract law as economic law (as opposed to civil law) indicated that the basic role of the law was to enforce and implement state economic policies. Article 4 of the ECL prohibited the making of any contract that would violate state economic plans and Article 7 provided that all contracts in violation of the plan were void. As economic policy changes were made that sought to increase the autonomy of economic actors, the ECL was revised in 1993 by replacing references to state plans to state economic policies. These changes were to indicate that contracts were no longer subject to rigid tests of compliance against state plans, but the fundamental nature of the ECL as an economic law was not changed.

The ECL applied only to domestic Chinese contracts and an additional law, the Foreign Economic Contract Law (FECL), was enacted in 1985 to govern contracts between Chinese and foreign firms in areas of foreign trade and investment. The FECL offered contracting parties significant autonomy in selecting governing law, methods of dispute resolution, and commercial terms and conditions. Like the ECL, however, the FECL was fundamentally an economic law and, in keeping with this classification, all contracts under the FECL had to be approved by PRC authorities. The ECL and FECL were further supplemented by the Law on Technology Contracts, which was enacted in 1987 to deal with contracts for technology development, transfer, and consultancy services. Together the ECL, the FECL, and the Law on Technology Contracts were often referred to in the PRC as the three pillars of contract law.

The enactment of the General Principles of Civil Law in 1986 discussed above with its provisions relating to contracts on the capacity of parties, contract formation, and enforcement was a significant development in contract law in China. On a policy level, the incorporation of contract law into the GPCL raised the issue of whether contract law was economic law and essentially a tool of state economic policy or was civil law and outside of the mandate of state economic plans. While the GPCL required that contracts could not conflict with state policies, the inclusion of contract law within the category of civil law suggested that there should be a lesser degree of state regulation of contracts and greater autonomy in this field. The GPCL is also a basic law adopted by the full National People's Congress and is theoretically higher in the hierarchy of legal norms than any of the three individual contract laws. The primacy of the GPCL implied that it was not only a gap-filler but it also contained basic principles governing contract law that should override any inconsistent provisions in the individual contract laws. At the same time, the continuing existence of other laws emphasizing the economic nature of contracts also indicated that there was some debate and dissent within the various law-making organs of the PRC on the precise nature and function of contract law.

The enactment of the GPCL in 1986 and the Technology Contract Law in 1987 added to the fragmentation of contract law in the PRC, giving rise to the need for a unified law. Work on a unified law was actually begun in 1993 and went through several drafts before the Unified Contract Law (UCL) was passed by the Second Session of the Ninth NPC on March 15, 1999 with an effective date of October 1 of the same year. The UCL, which now replaces the ECL, the FECL, and the Technology Contract Law, represents the differing objectives and interests of the groups of scholars, government departments, and legislators that participated in its drafting. During the initial drafting stages of the UCL, legal scholars undertook a leading role and focused heavily on borrowing from foreign law sources. Much of the early scholarly debate was not on whether to rely on foreign law but whether to adopt continental or common law models of con-tract law. The drafters of the UCL undertook exten-sive study of contract law in the United States, Canada, Germany, the United Kingdom, Europe, and Australia. Extensive efforts were also made to study international treaties, especially the Vienna Convention on Contracts for the International Sale of Goods (1980) (CISG), a treaty founded by promi-nent industrialized countries such as the United States under the auspices of the United Nations

Commission on International Trade Law (UNCI-TRAL). The CISG purports to establish uniform standards for contracts for the international sale of goods and displaces domestic law, where applicable, in contracts between persons or entities located in different member countries, which now include the majority of industrialized states. The influence of the CISG, to which China acceded in 1998, is apparent in the UCL.

The influence of foreign norms of freedom of contract was particularly strong in the early drafts of the UCL. As the drafting process continued, however, and as drafts were circulated to broader local interests, the input of government departments began to limit contract autonomy and to reassert state control. The result of the drafting and legislative process is a law that contains a number of tensions that can be traced to policy compromises between the legal academics that sought to promote contract autonomy and government departments that sought to preserve state control over contracts.

c. The Unified Contract Law

Article 2 of the general provisions contained in Chapter 1 of the UCL provides that "a contract is an agreement reached by natural persons, legal persons, or other organizations that are in equal positions to create, change or terminate a relationship of civil rights and liabilities." Defining a contract as involving "civil rights and liabilities" apparently resolves the longstanding debate over the nature of contracts by providing that contracts are a matter of civil and not economic law and are thereby outside the mandate of state plans and state economic policy. Articles 3 and 5 of the UCL on the equality of the parties reinforce the autonomous nature of contracts. Article 4 on the freedom of contracts asserts that any party has the free will to enter a contract and that no unit or individual shall illegally interfere in contracts. The reassertion of state control over contract autonomy can be seen in Article 7, which provides that all parties entering into contracts shall obey "laws and administrative regulations and shall respect the public virtue of society. No party shall disturb social economic orders or damage the public interest of society." This provision creates a significant window for state intrusion into contracts as a number of existing laws and regulations allow state agencies to intervene in the formation and performance of contracts. The broad and vaguely worded limitations based upon social economic order and public interests also provide a potential avenue for invalidating or restricting contracts that conflict with government interests.

A more basic policy compromise on the scope and nature of the UCL is contained in the ancillary provisions of Chapter 8. Article 123 provides that "if other laws have different provisions on contracts, such laws shall prevail." The significance of this provision is that it relegates the UCL to the status of a gap-filler and a default law applicable only when other laws relating to contracts do not apply. Everywhere there is a conflict between the

UCL and other laws, those other laws are to prevail. It should be noted that the laws under Article 123 include administrative regulations that are issued with regularity and in large quantities by the various administrative organs of the state that seek to protect their domain and to govern their fields of authority. Article 123 preserves the power of state administrative organs to control contracts that fall within their scope of authority by issuing administrative regulations that supersede the UCL. In addition, Article 127 provides that government administrative departments are responsible, in accordance with their laws and regulations, for supervising and dealing with illegal activities involving contracts that harm the state's interest and the public interest. This provision is sufficiently broad to permit administrative entities to intrude into the formation and performance of contracts even where there were no existing laws or administrative regulations at the time that the contract was formed. It is imperative that foreign parties who enter into contracts in China be fully cognizant of the gap-filler nature of the UCL; they should undertake a thorough review of any existing laws, regulations, or other legally effective sources that may supersede the UCL or permit government intrusion into contract formation or performance.

Some official attempts have been made after the enactment of the UCL to limit the circumstances in which other laws will override the UCL. While the supremacy of other laws over the UCL remains clear, official interpretations of the UCL have attempted to harmonize the UCL with other laws and the Supreme People's Court has issued an interpretation of the UCL indicating that only national laws and administrative regulations relating to contracts issued by the central level law-making organs such as the NPC, the NPC Standing Committee, and the State Council prevail over the UCL. Nevertheless, the inclusion of Article 123 in the UCL that relegates it to a gap-filler was a significant victory for the government departments and administrative organs of the state because it preserves the supremacy of their regulatory power over their fields of authority over the autonomy of contracts under the UCL.

(1) Salient Provisions and Structure of the UCL

Following the general structure of the ECL and the FECL, the general provisions of the UCL contained in Chapter 1 are followed by chapters on contract formation (Chapter 2), validity (Chapter 3), performance (Chapter 4), modification and transfer of contracts (Chapter 5), termination (Chapter 6), liability for breach (Chapter 7), and ancillary provisions (Chapter 8). Part 2 of the UCL contains provisions on fifteen specific types of contracts, including sales; supply of electricity, gas, water, and heat; loans; leases; contractor's agreements; construction; transportation; technology development, transfer, and consulting; warehouse and storage; consignment; and brokerage. Each of the specific contracts has detailed rules contained in a separate chapter that apply in lieu of the general provisions contained in Part 1 of the UCL, which apply only to contracts that do not fall into any of the specific categories contained in Part 2. However, in keeping with the default character of the UCL, the specific provisions apply only if not in conflict with other laws and administrative regulations.

(2) Contract Formation

The formation of contracts under the UCL requires the parties to have civil capacity, which in turn is governed by the General Principles of the Civil Law on natural and legal persons previously discussed. Contracts can take oral, written, or other forms (Article 10), although certain contracts must be in writing, including technology transfer agreements (Article 342) and loan contracts (Article 197). Unlike its predecessors, the UCL does not stipulate content requirements and allows the parties the autonomy to determine the content of their contracts on their own, although Article 12 provides that all contracts should generally include the parties' names and addresses; subject matter; issues related to quantity and quality; prices or payments; performance deadlines, locations, and methods; liability for default; and methods of dispute resolution.

The provisions on the formation of contracts borrows heavily from foreign law and is based upon an offer and acceptance model that is in keeping with the increased emphasis on the autonomy of the parties. *See* UCL, Art. 13. An offer is an expressed intent to form a contract with another that is concrete and specific. *See* UCL, Art. 14. An acceptance is an expressed intent of the offeree to accept the offer. *See* UCL, Art. 21. Once the offeree accepts the offer, a contract is formed and no consideration is needed to form a valid contract, indicating that despite some borrowing from foreign law sources, Chinese contract law differs in some fundamental respects from common and civil law approaches to contract. Like some civil law approaches, the UCL uses a mirror-image rule requiring that the contents and terms of the acceptance mirror the offer or else the acceptance is considered to be a rejection and a counteroffer. *See* UCL, Art. 30.

(3) Validity of Contracts

A contract that is formed according to law becomes effective as soon as it is formed. *See* UCL, Art. 44. This represents a departure from prior practice where some contracts did not become effective until they were approved by PRC authorities. For example, foreign business contracts under the FECL were not valid until government approval of the contract was obtained and the contract was registered with PRC authorities. The problem that arose under this approach was that the approval and registration of contracts could take months, leaving the parties unsure of their rights and responsibilities in the interim. The parties also faced the possibility that the contract would not be approved at all or only with certain changes required by the approval authorities. The UCL now alleviates this problem by providing that the contracts are valid once formed and that approval and registration procedures "shall be followed." It should be noted, however, that in keeping with the gap-filler nature of the UCL, Article 44 does not apply in the case of some specific law or administrative regulation that requires approval and registration before the contract becomes legally effective. For example, many contracts involving sino-foreign joint ventures, including the joint venture contract itself, still require government approval under applicable laws before becoming legally effective. In these cases, parties continue to face the issues of uncertainty that characterized all contracts under the prior regime of the FECL.

In addition to the general limitations on the effectiveness of contracts contained in the general provisions in Chapter 1, Article 52 provides that a contract is invalid where (1) parties use fraud to enter a contract that harms the state's interests; (2) parties maliciously conspire to damage the interests of the state, collective interests, or a third party's interest; (3) parties use legitimate methods to form a contract for an illegal purpose; (4) social or public interests are harmed; and (5) mandatory provisions of laws or administrative regulations are violated.

(4) Performance, Modification, and Termination

Article 60 of the UCL provides that a party shall fulfill his obligations specified in the contract and shall fulfill the obligations of notification, assistance, and confidentiality. Articles 61–63 create default rules for contracts where specific terms concerning quality, price, reimbursement, and place of performance were not specified in the contract or where the products involved are subject to state pricing. Because third party performance of contract obligations in China is common, Articles 64–65 create rules on primary and secondary liability in the performance of such contracts. Articles 66–67 provide for the simultaneous performance of contracts where the parties are mutually liable to each other for debts and no order of performance has been specified. Article 68 provides for a justifiable suspension of performance by the party obligated under the contract to perform first if the party has accurate evidence indicating that the other party will be unable to perform its contract obligations because the other party (1) is facing a serious deterioration of his business operation; (2) has moved or withdrawn capital; (3) has suffered a loss of commercial credit; or (4) has experienced other circumstances showing a loss of ability to perform the contract.

Chapter 5 on the modification and transfer of contracts provides that parties may modify contracts by agreement. The modification of contracts encounters some of the same issues of legal effectiveness that were involved in the formation of contracts. Where the original contract had to go through an approval and registration process, modifications to the contract also need to undergo the same process but the modification is legally effective once an agreement is reached and these procedures simply need to be followed. *See* UCL, Art. 77. As in the case of the original contracts, however, some laws and administrative regulations specifically provide that no modifications to a contract shall be legally effective prior to government approval and registration. Foreign investment is one area where laws commonly require government approval for contracts and contract modifications before they become legally effective. In these cases, these laws and administrative regulations override the UCL and all approval and registration requirements must first be satisfied before any modification becomes legally effective. As for the transfer of rights, mutual agreement of the parties is not necessary for a transfer of rights by one party to a third party except where the transfer is prohibited by the nature of the contract, by an agreement of the parties, or by law. *See* UCL, Art. 79.

Termination of contracts occurs when (1) obligations have been fully performed as agreed upon; (2) the contract has been revoked; (3) obligations have been mutually terminated; (4) the obligor has lawfully received the contract goods; (5) the obligee has waived the right to the performance of the obligation; (6) all rights and obligations are merged; and (7) under other circumstances as provided by law. *See* UCL, Art. 91. Other circumstances that can lead to termination are agreement by the parties (Article 93), force majeure (Article 117), and clear indication of non-performance by one party to the contract (Article 108).

(5) Liability for Breach

Article 107 provides that remedies for breach of contract can consist of specific performance, remedial measures, and compensation. Where the non-performance relates to a payment obligation, the non-breaching party has the right to demand full payment or reimbursement. *See* UCL, Art. 109. In all other cases of non-performance of an obligation, the non-breaching party can demand specific performance unless the performance is in violation of law, the nature of the obligation is not suitable for specific performance or performance of the obligation will be too costly, or the non-breaching party fails to demand performance by the obligee within a reasonable period of time. *See* UCL, Art. 110. Remedial measures include repair, exchange, redo, return, and reduction of payment. *See* UCL, Art. 111. Compensation is calculated according to the damages suffered by the non-breaching party, including loss of profits but do not extend to unforeseen damages. *See* UCL, Art. 113. In addition to terminating a contract, force majeure will also excuse non-performance. *See* UCL, Art. 118. The non-breaching party has the general duty to mitigate damages. *See* UCL, Art. 119.

d.   The Company Law

Effective in 1994, and revised in 1999, 2004, and 2005, the Company Law (CL), like the Unified Contract Law, stands as one of the landmarks of PRC legal development and reform. While the UCL was concerned about transactions between economic actors, the Company Law was intended to create a uniform law for the reform era that would regulate the creation and structure of business enterprises, the most important group of economic actors in the PRC. Prior to economic reforms, there was no need for a uniform corporations law as all state-owned enterprises were essentially administrative units of the state under government departments that operated the enterprises according to state economic plans. The majority of these state-owned enterprises operated with chronic losses that were offset by state subsidies. The state tolerated these losses because state-owned enterprises provided housing, education, medical, and pension benefits for their many redundant workers and their families. As China entered the era of reforms, the Company Law was enacted to further two goals. The primary goal was to restructure state-owned enterprises into modern corporations in order to help resolve the problem of chronic losses that continues to be a major drain on the economy. A secondary goal was to support the development of private enterprises that would serve as a complement to the state-owned sector of the economy.

The western principles of corporate law embodied in the Company Law seemed particularly well suited to address the problems of state-owned enterprises. PRC authorities needed to maintain the fundamental socialist principle of state ownership of the means of production in China. At the same time, PRC authorities also needed state-owned enterprises to operate without the support of state subsidies and be responsible for their own profits and losses. Subjecting state-owned enterprises to market conditions would discipline them to avoid losses and relieve the economy of the massive burden of supporting these failing enterprises. For state-owned enterprises to have any chance of operating under market conditions, however, they needed to be free from the administrative intrusion and interference of their government supervisory departments. The western concept of a corporation suited these purposes because it is based upon the separation of ownership and management, allowing the state to maintain ownership of restructured state-owned enterprises but also allowing the enterprises the managerial autonomy necessary to operate their businesses effectively. Beginning in 1988 with the Law on Industrial Enterprises Owned by the Whole People, China adopted a number of reforms to address these problems, but the early legislation suffered from being piecemeal and narrow and also failed to provide meaningful enterprise autonomy or incentives for enterprise productivity and profitability. The Company Law was a comprehensive law designed to address these problems and to form the basis of a modern enterprise system. Although the Company Law was intended primarily as a vehicle to reform state-owned enterprises, it also served the secondary purpose of legitimating China's small private sector. Prior to the Company Law, enterprises formed entirely with domestic capital were not even recognized as legal persons under the General Principles of Civil Law. Under Article 3 of the Company Law, private enterprises that are limited liability companies or joint stock companies are enterprise legal persons.

(1) Business Forms under the Company Law

The Company Law provides for two forms of corporations, the limited liability company (LLC) and the joint stock company (JSC), which correspond to the U.S. distinction between the closely held corporation and the larger corporation, including those that are publicly listed on stock exchanges. The LLC is generally for smaller corporations, defined in terms of the number of investors and the amount of registered capital. In most cases, the LLC must have no more than fifty shareholders and a minimum capitalization of RMB 30,000 ($4,380). The minimum amount of registered capital of a one-person limited liability company must be at least RMB 100,000 ($14,600). The shareholders must pay the capital contribution in a lump sum as specified by law. In an LLC, each shareholder assumes liability to the extent of its capital contribution and the company assumes liability to the extent of all of its assets. *See* CL, Art. 3.

The JSC is typically larger than a LLC. The JSC can have any number of shareholders but it must have a minimum capitalization of RMB 5 million ($730,000). The JSC is entitled to offer stock through either the promotion or public issue method. Under the promotion method, the promoters themselves purchase all shares issued by the company. Under the public issue method, there must be 2 to 200 promoters who must purchase at least 20% of the shares and the remaining shares are offered to the public for general subscription. *See* CL, Arts. 79 & 81. To help prevent the issuance of risky securities, the CL provides that promoters cannot transfer their shares obtained under either method within one year after establishment of the company. *See* CL, Art. 142. Securities offered for public subscription may be listed on China's stock exchanges in Shanghai or Shenzhen with the approval of the State Council. *See* CL, Art. 121. The Securities Law (2005) was enacted to unify the disparate securities regulation regimes that had emerged after the establishment of the two exchanges in the mid–1980s. In a JSC, each shareholder assumes liability to the extent of the amount of shares held and the company assumes liability to the extent of all of its assets. *See* CL, Art. 3.

(2) Limited Liability and the Legal Representative

As noted above, both the LLC and the JSC adopt the principle of limited liability, a concept long familiar in western corporate law but relatively new to China. The adoption of a concept of limited liability was not, however, without some significant limitations created by the distinctive Chinese concept of a legal representative (*fading daibiao ren*), which is similar to an agent under U.S. law. The legal representative is the designated natural person that has authority to act on behalf of and to bind the company. *See* GPCL, Art. 38. The legal representative of the company is usually the chairman of the board of directors or in a small LLC that chooses not to have a board, the executive director. *See* CL, Arts. 45, 51, 68, & 113.

PRC authorities wanted to ensure that questions concerning the legal effectiveness of the acts of a company did not arise and therefore required that every company have a legal representative whose acts clearly bind the company. In addition, by exposing the legal representative to civil and criminal liability for the misdeeds of the corporation, PRC authorities sought to dilute the principle of limited liability in order to discourage corporate misbehavior. For example, the legal representative is personally subject to civil and criminal liability where the company conducts illegal operations beyond the range approved by registration authorities, commits fraud or conceals facts, secretly withdraws or transfers funds, or disposes of property without authorization after the company is dissolved, disbanded, or declared bankrupt. *See* GPCL, Art. 49.

(3) Foreign Investment Enterprises and the Company Law

Foreign investment enterprises (FIEs) such as sino-foreign joint ventures and wholly foreign-owned enterprises almost always take the corporate form but are generally subject to a different set of laws specific to foreign investment, such as the Equity Joint Venture Law (enacted 1979, revised 1990 & 2001), the Contractual Joint Venture Law (enacted 1988 and revised 2000), and the Wholly Foreign–Owned Enterprise Law (enacted in 1986 and revised 2000). Article 218 of the Company Law provides that the law applies to all companies within the PRC, including FIEs, but where FIE laws apply, FIE laws take precedence. Under this provision, the Company Law is a default regime and leaves open the possibility that the Company Law applies to FIEs where FIE legislation is silent on a certain matter that falls under a relevant provision in the Company Law.

Under current practice, most foreign investors establish FIEs under FIE laws and assume that the Company Law does not apply even in areas where FIE laws are silent. If the assumption that the Company Law does not apply to FIEs is erroneous, then FIEs established after the effective date of the Company Law may need to undergo some changes to accommodate the Company Law. So far these assumptions have not been challenged but the applicability of the Company Law to FIEs remains an uncertain area of the law and is in need of further clarification from government authorities. The applicable FIE laws and business forms are further discussed in detail in the next chapter.

(4) *Reform Objectives of the Company Law*

Both the limited liability company and the joint stock company under the Company Law are available to reorganize state-owned enterprises into the corporate form. It should be emphasized, however, that the Company Law is not intended as a means to privatize state-owned enterprises. In the case of the LLC, where the sole investor is a government department or a state authorized investment institution, the LLC is referred to as a "wholly state-owned company." *See* CL, Art. 65. A wholly state-

owned company is exempt from certain requirements normally applied to LLCs, such as holding
shareholder meetings. The wholly state-owned LLC
is in essence an administrative unit of government
that has been given the trappings of a corporate
form. In the case of the JSC, the state will retain
majority ownership of the shares issued by the
reorganized company thus maintaining the principle of state ownership. In order to further bolster
the position of the ownership rights of the state,
shareholders are given extensive rights under the
Company Law that exceed rights given to shareholders under U.S. law. For example, shareholders
of Chinese corporations have the power to determine business operation policies and investment
plans; to approve the annual financial plan, budget,
and final accounts; and to approve the distribution
of profits and dividends. *See* CL, Art. 38. These are
powers that are generally delegated to the corporation's directors under U.S. law. The extensive powers reserved to shareholders under Chinese law are
consistent with an overall approach that allows
management autonomy within an overall framework of state ownership and control. The purpose of
the Company Law is to remove the state from
intruding into the day-to-day management of enterprises, but not to relinquish state ownership or
control over state enterprises. By reserving extensive powers in shareholders, the state, as majority
shareholder, can choose to maintain as much or as
little control as it deems necessary.

While the Company Law was hailed as a milestone in China's legal development and has created the basis for a modern enterprise system, its usefulness as a vehicle of reform of state-owned enterprises has met with mixed results. The reform of the state sector requires a series of basic changes to the social system that extend beyond changes in enterprise legislation. In order to achieve meaningful reform of the troubled state sector, China must be willing to accept some painful consequences of reform, such as allowing some enterprises to go bankrupt with the attendant problems of unemployment and social dislocation that will follow. China must also create a viable alternative system of housing and social welfare services to replace the subsidies that were offered by state enterprises. While China has made some progress in instituting some of these wider social changes, the reform of the state sector remains a serious long-term problem.

e. Family Law

The 2001 Marriage Law (ML), first enacted in 1980 and revised in 2001, is the first modern marriage law of the PRC. While the first marriage law of the PRC, promulgated in 1950, sought to promote socialist ideology and modern family structure by eliminating the many inequities of the traditional Chinese family structure that recognized few rights in women, the 1980 Law had the much more pragmatic aim of developing marriage as a social institution creating the stability necessary for modernization and economic development. In addition to the basic principles also contained in the 1950 legislation such as freedom of marriage, equality of the sexes, monogamy, the prohibition of arranged and mercenary marriages and any other types of interference with the freedom of marriage, the 1980 Law included additional provisions protecting the rights of the elderly, children, and women. The 1980 Law also increased the marriageable age from twenty for men and eighteen for women to twenty-two and twenty respectively. In addition, the 1980 Law introduced birth control as a state policy and an explicit duty on the part of both spouses. Family planning would also later be included as a fundamental state policy in the 1982 Constitution. Under Article 16 of the 2001 Marriage Law, "both husband and wife have the obligation to practice family planning." The significance of creating an explicit obligation on married couples to practice family planning is that it legitimates the intervention of the state in preventing couples from having children in violation of the state's general one child per couple policy even if the couple is legally married.

The 1980 Law also added more detailed provisions on family property and the duty to support family members, including mandatory support obligations of grandparents for their grandchildren, brothers and sisters for their younger siblings, parents for their children, and children for their parents. These extended support obligations were designed to supplement China's poor public welfare system. To ease longstanding social stigmas attached to non-traditional families, children born out of wedlock were given equal rights to children born in wedlock. Adoption was also explicitly protected under the 1980 Law and a formal legal framework for adoption was later created in the Adoption Law (1991). Finally, the loss of mutual affection was introduced as a ground for divorce in order to give courts greater flexibility in deciding divorce cases.

The 2001 revision maintains the basic framework and approach of the 1980 Marriage Law but has added a number of detailed provisions on the division of property that reflect the modern nature of a marriage in the PRC as an economic partnership and the ability of women to accumulate property as a partner in the marriage. Detailed provisions on the division of property may also reflect the ability of some couples to accumulate property and wealth in China's new economy. For example, Articles 17 and 18 distinguish between jointly owned and separately owned property of married couples. Article 17 provides that joint property in the marriage consists of salary and bonuses, income from production and operation, income from intellectual property, inherited property, and other property under joint possession. The separate property of either spouse includes the prenuptial property of one party, medical expenses or living allowances acquired by one party as a result of personal injury, daily use articles, and other property owned by one party. *See* ML, Art. 18. Article 19 allows the parties to stipulate in writing which properties are owned jointly or separately by the parties. In the area of divorce, the 2001 revision has added a provision recognizing visitation rights to the children of the marriage in the non-custodial parent after divorce. *See* ML, Art. 38. The 2001 revision also adds a new Chapter 5 on compensation and legal liabilities allowing for compensation for the victims of family violence, maltreatment, and desertion. Other provisions added by Chapter 5 allow for compensation where divorce is caused by bigamy, illegal co-habitation with the spouse of another, or the fraudulent concealment or transfer of property at the time of divorce. The addition of these provisions reflects an unwanted by-product of China's economic development: the rise of an illegal sex industry and an increase in extra-marital liaisons. The 1994 Marriage Registration Regulations issued by the Ministry of Civil Affairs introduced pre-marriage health examinations to be implemented by local governments at the provincial level and imposed penalties to discourage the fraudulent registration of marriages.

The 1980 Marriage Law also recognized rights of inheritance by providing for reciprocal inheritance rights in husbands and wives and in parents and children. Although Communism is ideologically opposed to inheritance, China had to recognize inheritance rights as a practical matter to deal with the lack of a social welfare system and to accommodate the extended family support obligations imposed by law. As families began to accumulate wealth and property in China's new economy, the brief mention of inheritance rights in the 1980 Law and the subsequent decisions and opinions by the Supreme People's Court proved insufficient to create a suitable framework to regulate inheritance. In 1985, the Standing Committee of the NPC issued the Succession Law (SL), which was shortly followed by its implementation measures jointly issued by the Ministry of Justice and the Ministry of Civil Affairs.

Under the Succession Law, a citizen has the right to dispose of the following personal property at death: income, houses, savings, daily use articles, trees, livestock, cultural objects, books, reference materials, means of production lawfully owned by the decedent, and intellectual property rights. *See* SL, Art. 3. The Succession Law recognized three types of succession: statutory, testamentary, and through legacy agreements in exchange for support. *See* SL, Art. 5. Article 5 gives priority to a legacy agreement in return for support over testamentary and statutory (or intestate) succession, and to statutory succession over testamentary succession. Legacy agreements for support can exist between individuals or between an individual and a collective organization. The importance of legacy agreements again attests to the inadequacy of China's current social welfare system, as third party arrangements for support are common social arrangements. Note, however, that a legacy agreement between parents and their children is void as children have a pre-existing duty to support their parents. *See* ML, Art. 21. There are some limits in the Succession Law on the freedom of the decedent to dispose of property by will, including a provision reserving a portion of the estate for a successor without the capacity to work or without a source of income. The testator is also prohibited from disinheriting the under-aged or unborn, but there are no express limitations on the right of the testator to disinherit a surviving spouse or express recognition of the inheritance rights of women. These omissions may cause some problems for the inheritance rights of women given the traditional concept of male inheritance of property.

Statutory or intestate succession occurs when the entire estate or a portion is not disposed of under a will or through a legacy agreement or when persons entitled to an inheritance or legacy have died, disclaimed their inheritance, or have been disqualified from inheritance. *See* SL, Art. 27. The Succession Law then provides for intestate succession in two orders. The surviving spouse, children, and parents are in the first order who inherit to the exclusion of the second order, which consists of brothers, sisters, and grandparents. Children, siblings, and grandparents are defined to include those who are related to the decedent by law in order to eliminate the traditional Chinese practice of allowing inheritance only by blood relatives. *See* SL, Art. 10. Inheritance is to occur in equal shares with the right of representation, which allows lineal descendants of a child who predeceases the decedent to inherit in equal shares the share that the predeceased child would have otherwise inherited.

C. ADMINISTRATIVE LAW

The third major branch of substantive law in the PRC is administrative law, which has been defined as the area of law that deals with the jurisdiction, powers, and organization of the organs of state administration. Until recently, the development of administrative law has lagged behind that of other major fields such as constitutional law, criminal law, and civil and economic law. Administrative law was not included as a subject of legal education by the Ministry of Education until 1981 and did not become a mandatory subject until 1986. The first textbook on administrative law was not published until 1983. Even today, there is no basic substantive administrative law that corresponds to the Criminal Law or to the General Principles of Civil Law.

The underdevelopment of administrative law has been attributed to the traditional emphasis on policy and Party control rather than law in the area of state administration. During the early years of the PRC, the fusion of the Party and the state, the lack of a principle of checks and balances as a limit on government power, and the personality cult of Party leaders that led to the displacement of law by Party rhetoric left only a limited role for administrative law. Although a large number of laws of state administration were enacted in the period from 1949–56, administrative law documents were considered to be policy documents to be implemented through education and legal propaganda as opposed to being legal rules enforceable in a court of law. The intervention of political campaigns beginning in the late 1950s displaced the development of all law from the national agenda until the post-Mao era that began in the late 1970s. As the nation turned to the task of rebuilding the legal system in the period after economic reforms were launched in 1978, the focus was on criminal and civil and economic legislation. The need to develop administrative law, however, was officially recognized when the CPC Central Committee and the State Council included the topic of administrative management in their Seventh Five–Year Economic Plan (1986–1990). At the Thirteenth National Party Congress in 1987, the Communist Party recognized that the nation had to deal with some of the problems of a massive and inefficient state bureaucracy, over-concentration of powers, life tenure in leading posts, and privileges of various kinds. The CPC decided that it was necessary to promote greater government efficiency by enacting more laws on the organization of administrative organs, civil service regulations, and norms governing governmental activities. For the first time, the PRC also recognized the need for laws creating accountability on the part of state organs to the governed. This was an important shift in attitudes as administrative law was conceived as being mainly concerned with enhancing government efficiency through effective organization and proper allocation of powers and not as a constraint on the abuse of power.

As the subject of administrative law is mainly concerned with the processes of state administration, most of the major laws enacted in this area have been procedural in nature. Major steps in the development of administrative law in the PRC were the enactment of the Administrative Litigation Law (1990), the Administrative Review Law (1999), the

Administrative Supervision Regulations (1990), the State Compensation Law (1994), and the Administrative Penalties Law (1996). As the Administration Litigation Law, the Administrative Review Law, the State Compensation Law, and the Administrative Penalties Law have already been discussed as part of China's procedural law in the preceding chapter, the remainder of this section will briefly examine the Administrative Supervision Regulations (ASR). Administrative supervision is conducted by the state's supervisory administrative organs at all levels led by the Ministry of Supervision under the State Council. Under the ASR, supervisory organs are to supervise the activities of administrative organs of the local government at the same level and their personnel and personnel appointed by them in order to ensure the proper execution of laws, administrative regulations, policies, decisions, and orders. *See* ASR, Art. 2. The supervisory process is initiated once the supervisory organs receive complaints of violations. *See* ASR, 19. On the basis of the investigation, the supervisory organ is to put forward supervisory recommendations or certain supervisory decisions relating to sanctions such as warning, demotion, or corrections of violations of administrative rules and regulations. See ASR, Arts. 23 & 24.

Overall the supervisory system is a weak one for a number of reasons. The supervisory organs at local levels report to both their local governments and the supervisory organ at the next higher level. *See* ASR, Art. 3. The reporting structure raises the issue of whether the supervisory organ can be independent as it reports to the same entity—the local government—that it supervises. The independence and decision-making power of the supervisory organs appears to be further compromised by the requirement under the ASR that all major supervisory decisions must be approved by the local government at the same level and by the superior supervisory organ. *See* ASR, Art. 38. The local government or the superior supervisory organ can also overturn decisions by the supervisory organ. *See* ASR, Art. 40.

CHAPTER TEN

FOREIGN INVESTMENT

This chapter and the next focus on two topics of civil and economic law of importance to China's long term development and of great interest to foreign investors and multinational enterprises (MNEs) in China: foreign investment and intellectual property. As previously discussed in Chapter 1, foreign investment has played a significant, if not critical role, in China's development up to the present and is considered to be a national priority in supporting China's continued growth and modernization. The legal framework for foreign investment is the subject of this chapter. This chapter will turn first to an examination of foreign direct investment in China, the types of business vehicles available for foreign investment, and the legal and regulatory framework.

A. FORMS OF FOREIGN DIRECT INVESTMENT

A foreign direct investment (FDI) in China usually involves an equity ownership in one of three major foreign investment enterprises or business vehicles made available for FDI: the equity joint venture, the contractual joint venture, and the wholly foreign-owned enterprise. Each of these vehicles can usually be established as a legal person and a limited liability company. Forms of doing business that do not involve FDI are sales directly into China through the use of agents and distributors or manufacturing in China through licensing agreements. These subjects will not be covered in this chapter.

There are two other business forms that do not qualify as foreign investment enterprises that also need to be discussed. Foreign companies are allowed to establish a representative office in China to promote their businesses by facilitating contacts between businesses in China with the foreign company's main offices overseas and by serving as a clearing-house for information. *See* Tentative Provisions on the Administration of Resident Representative Offices of Foreign Enterprises, Art. 2. While the limitations imposed by law are not always observed, representative offices are not allowed to open a bank account for local currency transactions with a PRC bank and are not allowed to directly conduct any business such as issuing bills and invoices and receiving payments. One other option recently made available by the Company Law, discussed in Chapter 9, is the branch foreign office where a foreign company is able to set up what is essentially a department in China. *See* CL, Arts. 199–205. Unlike the representative office, the branch foreign office is permitted to conduct business in China but it has not proven to be a popular vehicle because of high entry barriers in the form of onerous capitalization requirements. Because the representative office is not subject to stringent capitalization requirements, it has proven to be the more popular of these two forms, although it is often used as a stepping-stone for further business expansion. Note that while FIEs are usually separate legal persons and limited liability companies, the representative office and the branch foreign office do not enjoy these advantages and their acts may be directly attributable to the foreign company for liability and jurisdiction purposes.

1.   THE JOINT VENTURE

A joint venture in the PRC is a business venture that is formed by a combination of two or more business entities into a third entity. A joint venture should be distinguished from other business agreements such as mergers or acquisitions. When Company A (the foreign investor) and Company B (a PRC company) form a joint venture Company C (a PRC company), the end result is three separate entities: A, B, and C. In a merger, Companies A and B combine to form Company C, but neither A nor B continues to exist as separate entities after the merger. In an acquisition, Company A would absorb Company B. Company A would be the sole surviving entity and Company B would cease to exist as a separate legal entity.

There is one variant of the joint venture form discussed above in the PRC. In some cases, the Chinese entity will be completely absorbed into the new joint venture. For instance, Company A (the foreign investor) may insist that Company B invest all of its assets into and be absorbed by the joint venture, Company C. This arrangement results in two surviving entities, Company C, the joint venture, and Company A, the foreign investor. This arrangement bears some similarities to an acquisition whereby Company A establishes a new company for the purpose of absorbing Company B. Note that where this arrangement occurs in China, Company B may be a subsidiary of a larger PRC corporate conglomerate. The foreign investor has essentially formed a joint venture with the PRC parent company by acquiring and absorbing one of its subsidiaries into the joint venture.

a. Equity and Contractual Joint Ventures

PRC law currently permits two types of joint ventures: contractual joint ventures and equity joint ventures. Each type of joint venture is subject to its own set of laws and regulations. Contractual joint ventures are governed by the Contractual Joint Venture Law (1988 and revised 2000) (CJVL) and by the Contractual Joint Venture Law Implementing Rules (1995) (CJVIR). Equity joint ventures are governed by the Equity Joint Venture Law (1979, revised 1990 & 2001) (EJVL) and by the Equity Joint Venture Law Implementing Regulations (1983, amended 1986, 1987 & 2001) (EJVIR). In general, the difference between the two forms is that the equity joint venture is more structured by law and the contractual joint venture is more flexible. For example, while an equity joint venture is required to distribute its profits in proportion to the capital contributions of each of the joint venture partners, the parties to a contractual joint venture are not subject to the same restrictions in the distribution of profits; the lack of such restrictions on the contractual joint venture permits more flexibility in the initial financing of the joint venture. *Cf.* EJVL, Art. 8 *and* CJVIR, Art. 43. Whereas the equity joint venture must take the form of a limited liability company, a contractual joint venture may take the form of a contractual relationship, partnership, or limited liability company. *Cf.* EJVL, Art. 4 *and* CJVIR, Art. 4. After a contractual joint venture has been established and is in operation a foreign investor may be able to recoup its initial capital investment in the joint venture in the form of a repayment of its capital contribution. In the case of an equity joint venture, a repayment of capital may be seen as a reduction in the capital of the joint venture, an action that cannot be taken without prior government approval.

While there are a number of differences between the equity and contractual joint venture, there are also many similarities. Both types of joint ventures are subject to similar requirements for set up and government approval. Both types of joint ventures also experience similar management and labor issues. Foreign investors, especially multinational enterprises, generally favor the equity joint venture because of some early confusion concerning the contractual joint venture and a perception that the equity joint venture provides for more predictability and certainty. For these reasons, the discussion below will focus on the equity joint venture.

b. Establishing the Joint Venture

All joint ventures, like all foreign investment enterprises, must undergo a multi-step approval process by the approval level of government authorities. Foreign investment in China is a privilege, not a right, and there is no recourse if government authorities do not approve an FIE. To increase the chances of approval, the foreign investor should carefully choose a joint venture partner, usually a state-owned enterprise, which enjoys strong connections with the appropriate approval authorities. The local partner can then vet the approval process by working closely with approval authorities throughout the entire process. The choice of a joint venture partner is also critical to the ultimate success or failure of the joint venture as a business operation and is usually the single most important decision that the foreign investor must make in establishing a joint venture. The choice of an inappropriate partner can lead to serious management problems that hamper the operations of the joint venture and, in extreme cases, can lead to the premature termination of the joint venture itself.

Turning to permitted fields of foreign investment, the Equity Joint Venture Implementing Regulations set forth the main industries in which equity joint ventures may be established:

(1) energy development, building materials, chemicals, and metallurgy;

(2) machine building, instruments and meters, offshore oil exploitation equipment manufacturing;

(3) electronics, computers, communications equipment manufacturing;

(4) light industry, textiles, food, medicine, medical apparatus, and packaging;

(5) agriculture, animal husbandry, aquaculture, and packaging; and

(6) tourism and services.

EJVR, Art. 3. In 1995, PRC authorities issued the Tentative Provisions on Guiding the Direction of Foreign Investment, which classify proposals for all FIEs (equity joint ventures, contractual joint ventures, and wholly foreign-owned enterprises) into four categories: encouraged, permitted, restricted, and prohibited. Under Article 5 of the Tentative Provisions, projects in the encouraged category are:

(1) comprehensive agricultural development projects and projects involving major raw materials for industrial construction;

(2) high technology projects;

(3) projects that meet international demand and are capable of upgrading existing products and that are export oriented;

(4) projects that involve environmental protection, pollution control, and the use of raw materials; and

(5) projects that involve manpower and resources in central and western regions of China.

These provisions were later supplemented by the comprehensive and detailed Foreign Investment Industrial Guidance Catalog, first promulgated by the State Development Planning Commission and the Ministry of Foreign Trade and Economic Cooperation in 1995 and extensively revised in 1997 and updated most recently in 2002 and 2007. The Guidance Catalog provides a detailed list of industries and areas where foreign investment is encouraged, restricted, and prohibited. As of 2007, the Guidance Catalog lists the following industries as among those industries prohibited to foreign investment: agriculture, forestry, animal husbandry, and fishery; mining; firearms and ammunition; production and supply of electric power, coal, gas, and water; warehousing; postal; education; culture and arts; broadcasting; and motion pictures.

Any category not listed in the Guidance Catalog is deemed to fall into the permitted category. As these guidelines and policies toward foreign investment are constantly being revised, the foreign investor should undertake a thorough review of these and any other investment guidelines before proceeding ahead. At the same time, it should be noted that while the guidelines set forth above apply generally to all FDI, the attitudes of any particular approval authority toward any particular FIE project may vary depending on the economic circumstances of the locality and the influence and stature of the local Chinese partner to the joint venture.

(1) The Approval Process and Approval Authorities

The approval process for a joint venture generally follows three steps: (1) preliminary approval by the supervising department of the Chinese partner and by the appropriate level approval authorities; (2) final approval by the approval authorities; and (3) issuance of a business license by administrative authorities.

Before examining each of these three steps, the role of the various approval entities will be briefly discussed. The appropriate entities can be divided into three groups: the supervising department, the foreign investment and economic planning authorities, and the industrial administrative authorities. Each of these groups is in charge of a different aspect of the joint venture project. The supervising department is the entity that is in charge of the Chinese partner to the joint venture. Before the Chinese partner, usually a state-owned enterprise, can proceed with the project, it must obtain the preliminary approval of its supervisory department. All economic and industrial sectors are subject to supervision by a particular supervision authority. For example, a local Chinese chemical or soap factory would be subject to the supervision by the local bureau of light industry, which regularly supervises the factory and reviews its financial performance, although, as previously discussed, SOEs are given greater managerial autonomy under recent reforms of the state sector. After the joint venture is established, the department in charge of the local partner becomes the department in charge of the joint venture, although joint ventures are given autonomy to conduct their business operations. *See* EJVR, Arts. 6 & 7.

A second set of approvals for all FIE projects will need to be obtained from the examining bodies with authority over economic planning and foreign investment. At the central level, the approval authorities are the State Development Planning Commission (SDPC), which approves project proposals and feasibility studies, and the State Development and Reform Commission (SDRC), which approves the joint venture application, the joint venture contract, the articles of association and ancillary documents. Local approvals are decided by provincial level or municipal level development and reform departments. Under the Interim Measures for the Administration of Examining and Approving Foreign Investment Projects issued by the State Development and Reform Commission on October 9, 2004, local approval authorities (i.e. those below SDRC) have jurisdiction to approve FIEs with a total investment that does not exceed $50 million in restricted industries and $100 million in encouraged and permitted industries (restricted, encouraged, and permitted industries are set forth in the Guidance Catalog discussed in the previous section above). All FIEs with total investment exceeding those amounts must be approved by SDRC. FIEs with a total investment of $500 million or more in encouraged and permitted industries and $100 million in restricted industries must be approved by SDRC and then reported to the State Council for verification.

As these guidelines are subject to frequent change and there are indications that additional revisions are being considered, the foreign investor would be well advised to check on all current changes before proceeding with the approval process. Once SDRC or its lower level counterpart gives its final approval of the project, it will issue an approval certificate.

The third entity involved in the approval process is the State Administration of Industry and Commerce (SAIC) at the central level or one of its local administrative units (AICs). The SAIC and its local departments regulate and supervise all industrial and commercial activity in the PRC and are authorized to issue business licenses to all lawful enterprises. No enterprise can lawfully commence business operations without a business license issued by the AICs. After approvals by SDRC or a lower level authority, the final step in the approval process is for the FIE to obtain a business license from the appropriate level AIC.

(A) Preliminary Approval Requirements and Procedures

The first step in the approval process is for the Chinese partner to obtain approval of a project proposal and a preliminary feasibility study from its supervising authority. *See* EJVIR, Art. 9. The project proposal and preliminary feasibility documents provide the supervising authority with a basis to decide whether there is a market for the joint venture products and whether the joint venture project will be economically viable. These preliminary documents also allow the supervising authority to assess whether the joint venture will be beneficial to the Chinese party and to the local economy. In most instances, the supervising authority either is actively involved in the preliminary negotiations between the Chinese and foreign parties to the joint venture or is kept informed by the Chinese party. By the time the project proposal and preliminary feasibility study is submitted for its approval, the supervising department will usually already be familiar with their contents because the local partner will have vetted the approval process. Once the supervising department has granted its approval, the documents are then forwarded to the appropriate level development and reform authorities for their initial review and approval.

(B) FINAL APPROVAL REQUIREMENTS AND PROCEDURES

Once all preliminary approvals have been obtained, the parties can then move onto the formal application and final approval by the appropriate level development and reform authority. Both parties are responsible for submitting the following documents on behalf of the joint venture:

(1) an application for the establishment of the joint venture;

(2) the feasibility study report jointly prepared by the parties to the joint venture;

(3) the joint venture agreement, the joint venture contract, and articles of association signed by the representatives authorized by the parties to the joint venture;

(4) a list of candidates for chairman and vice chairman of the board of directors nominated by the parties to the joint venture; and

(5) signed opinions concerning the establishment of the joint venture by the department in charge and by the people's government of the province, autonomous region, or municipality directly under the central government where the joint venture is located.

EJVIR, Art. 7.

The application for the establishment of the joint venture can be one page in length setting forth the names of the parties, the name of the new joint venture, and capitalization requirements. The feasibility study will be based upon the preliminary feasibility study that was part of the initial approvals. The feasibility study will go into further detail on how all economic requirements for the joint venture will be satisfied: the source of capital investment, technology, land, physical plant, personnel and labor force, equipment, supply of raw and auxiliary materials, components, transportation requirements, power, and utility. In addition, the feasibility study should also explain production plans, marketing plans and available markets for the products of the joint venture, sources of foreign exchange, availability of natural resources, and environmental and pollution considerations. In addition, the feasibility study should also include profitability analysis and targets, returns on investment, sources of working capital, and cash flow issues. In most cases, other than the degree of detail involved, there may not be significant differences between the preliminary feasibility study and the study that is then submitted for final project approval.

The parties can now move onto the two most important documents of any joint venture application, the joint venture contract and the articles of association. Although these two documents often contain similar language, they serve different functions. The joint venture contract contains the specific terms of agreement, the rights, and the obligations of the parties. Among the matters that need to be addressed in the joint venture contract are the capital contributions of each of the parties, division of management responsibilities, use of revenues, distribution and division of profits, and liabilities. By contrast, the articles of association create the basic constitution of the new business venture and should set forth matters such as the corporate structure of the joint venture, management structure and responsibilities, and issues relating to the governance and operation of the joint venture. PRC law sets forth content requirements for each of the joint venture contract and articles of association that are far more exacting and detailed than for similar business documents in western nations such as the United States. *See* EJVIR, Arts. 11 & 13. The amount of detail required allows the examining and approval authorities to review all of the operations of the joint venture in detail and to intervene and require changes if there are any conditions or terms that are clearly unfavorable to the local partner or to the local economy. It would not be unusual for the approval authorities to request detailed and specific changes of language and terms in the joint venture documents. In many cases, working through the Chinese partner, the parties are able to show drafts of all of these documents to the supervising department and to the approval authorities to obtain their input before final documents are submitted. Where changes to documents are required, the foreign investor, local partner, and the approval authorities will often meet in a negotiation session where various compromises and changes will be worked out. Once the final application is submitted, the approval authorities have three months to approve the application. *See* EJVIR, Art. 8. Where the parties have been able to involve the approval authorities in reviewing drafts and in the negotiations, the approval authorities will usually approve the application in a matter of days or within a week by issuing an approval certificate.

The discussion above may give the impression that the required documents for approval of the joint venture are negotiated in sequence and that the parties first complete the negotiations for one document before moving to the next. In practice, as soon as the parties agree to move forward with the joint venture project, the parties usually begin negotiations on all of the major joint venture documents, such as the preliminary feasibility study, the feasibility study, the joint venture contract, and articles of association. Agreement to move ahead with the joint venture is usually embodied in a letter of intent, which is a non-binding expression of the good faith of the parties to complete the joint venture deal. Because binding legal documents may take months to negotiate and complete, the parties want an indication that each side is negotiating in good faith before committing the time and resources to move ahead with negotiations. Although the letter of intent is not legally binding, most parties who sign a letter of intent take their commitments seriously and in good faith. The letter of intent is usually no longer than one page in length and will contain the basic elements of the joint venture project such as the name and business scope of the joint venture, the capital contributions of the parties, the size of the board of directors, and the number of directors that each side is allowed to nominate. The letter of intent is usually the first document signed by the parties and signals the start of serious negotiations.

(c) OBTAINING A BUSINESS LICENSE

The final step in the approval process is obtaining a business license from the appropriate level of the administration of industry and commerce. Within thirty days of receipt of the approval certificate, the parties must register the certificate with the AIC in order to obtain a business license. The business license is vital because no enterprise in China can lawfully operate without one. The date of the business license becomes the date of the formal establishment of the joint venture. Unless there have been some irregularities in the approval process, obtaining the business license is a routine matter that usually takes several days or a week. With the business license in hand, the joint venture is now ready to commence operations.

c. Management Structure of the Joint Venture

The management structure of the equity joint venture consists of a board of directors, which is the highest authority of the joint venture and decides all major issues, a general manager, and several deputy general managers. *See* EJVR, Art. 6. By law, the board of directors must consist of at least three directors (EJVIR, Art. 31), although most joint ventures have five to seven directors. The parties appoint directors to the board in proportion to their capital contribution, which also represents each party's share of the equity ownership of the joint venture. For example, where the foreign investor has contributed 60% of the capital and the Chinese partner has contributed 40%, the foreign investor would appoint three directors and the Chinese partner would appoint two directors in a five-member board. Under prior law, the Chinese partner was entitled to appoint the chairman of the board, but either party can now appoint the chairman, who also serves as the joint venture's legal representative. The party that does not nominate the chairman is entitled to nominate the vice-chairman. Note

that while the chairman has certain ceremonial
duties, such as convening the meetings of the board,
the position does not carry any additional powers
beyond those of the other directors, other than
those powers and duties derived from being the
legal representative of the joint venture. The board
is required by law to convene at least once a year at
a meeting presided over by the chairman. *See*
EJVIR, Art. 32.

Aside from the board of directors, the joint venture is to establish a management office, consisting
of a general manager and several deputy general
managers, that conducts the day-to-day business of
the joint venture. *See* EJVIR, Art. 35. Subject to
authorization by the board, the general manager
represents the joint venture in its external affairs
and can appoint or dismiss subordinate employees
of the joint venture. *See* EJVIR, Art. 36.

(1) Management Control Issues

Although foreign investors eagerly established
joint ventures during the first phase of investment
in China in the 1980s, many foreign investors discovered that conflicts with the local partner hampered the success of the new company. Some foreign
investors soon found that they did not share the
same goals, expectations, or management philosophies with their local partners. Many local partners
expected to earn profits and have dividends distributed immediately to satisfy their supervising departments whereas foreign investors generally had
a longer time horizon for profitability and sought to

reinvest dividends in the long-term development of the company. Other issues concerned price versus quality: while the foreign investor would seek to produce a higher quality product at a higher price, many local partners would opt for a lower quality product at a lower price as a result of many years of working in China's stagnant pre-reform economy. One area that proved poisonous to the relationship between the parties was competition between the joint venture and the local partner. In some cases, the local partner would use advanced technology from the joint venture to upgrade its own product to compete with the joint venture. These areas of conflict are examples of how many Chinese have come to describe working with foreigners: "Same bed, different dreams." Many foreign investors found that they spent a substantial amount of time and resources on managing conflicts with the local partner to the detriment of the overall success of the joint venture.

Differences in expectations and management philosophies have led some foreign investors to seek arrangements under which they can exercise the bulk of management control over the joint venture. The foreign investor should not assume that control of a bare majority of the board of directors will result in substantial control of the joint venture. For example, certain matters require unanimous board approval: (1) amendment of the articles of association; (2) termination and dissolution of the joint venture; (3) increase or assignment of the registered capital of the joint venture; and (4) merger of the joint venture with another economic organization. *See* EJVIR, Art. 33. Even in other matters that require only majority approval, the board of directors should act unanimously because no business organization can operate effectively for the long term if board decisions are regularly made by a majority imposing its will upon a dissenting minority. Rather, some foreign investors have found that management control can only be effectively achieved by contributing the vast bulk of the capital, controlling a strong majority of the board, and by appointing the general manager.

By contributing the vast bulk of the registered capital, such as 80 or 90%, the foreign investor should be able to appoint four directors in a five-member board. In addition, the expectations of the parties are that the foreign investor will have management control given the size of its investment and its stakes in the joint venture. The joint venture contract and articles of association can be drafted to reflect the control of the foreign investor.

A key to obtaining control of the joint venture is the ability to appoint the general manager. In many cases, the general manager is the single most important position within the joint venture. Although the board of directors is nominally the highest authority within the joint venture, most boards usually convene once or twice per year in half-day meetings that are largely ceremonial. Business reports are given at the meetings and votes on key issues are taken, but the directors are usually well aware of the contents of the reports and have already decided how to vote on particular issues. The infrequency and length of the meetings means that very little of substance is actually accomplished at the meetings. The result of this managerial structure is that the general manager conducts most of the affairs of the joint venture. While the board has supervisory power over the general manager, no business enterprise can operate effectively unless the board delegates broad authority to the general manager to conduct the day-to-day business of the company. If the general manager were required to obtain board approval of business issues on a regular basis, the management of the joint venture would be mired in constant delays, making effective management difficult and impracticable. Rather, most boards grant the general manager broad powers and only require major matters to be submitted for board approval.

In a foreign controlled joint venture, the articles of association can be written to require board approval for basic decisions affecting the joint venture and to delegate all other powers to the general manager. The foreign investor would then appoint a senior executive from its headquarters to serve as the general manager. In many instances, the general manager is also a member of the board of directors of the joint venture, increasing the importance and stature of the position.

2. THE WHOLLY FOREIGN–OWNED ENTERPRISE

As its name suggests, the wholly foreign-owned enterprise (WFOE) allows the foreign investor to maintain complete ownership of the business enterprise and to operate the business without the constraints of a partner that may not share the same goals, expectations, and values. For some types of enterprises, such as a research and development facility, the WFOE offers the additional advantage of allowing the foreign investor to maintain closer security and protection over its intellectual property and other proprietary information. For these reasons, although the joint venture was the investment vehicle of choice in the first wave of foreign investment in China in the 1980s, foreign investors have increasingly turned to the wholly foreign-owned enterprise in recent years. In 1997, the number of WFOEs approved jumped 26.5% over the previous year and for the first time actually exceeded the number of equity joint ventures approved in the same year. Total foreign investment in WFOEs since the beginning of reforms in 1978 is now second only to equity joint ventures. In 2007, the total number of WFOEs reached 29,543, exceeding the total number of equity joint ventures in China. WFOEs are now the fastest growing of all forms of FIEs.

a. Establishing the WFOE

WFOEs are governed by the Wholly Foreign–Owned Enterprise Law (1986, amended 2000), the Wholly Foreign–Owned Enterprise Law Implementing Rules (1990, revised 2001) (WFOE Rules), and the Interpretations of Various Provisions of the Wholly Foreign–Owned Enterprise Law Implementing Rules (1991). Because joint ventures are seen as better vehicles for the transfer of technology through the participation of the local partner, WFOEs have been subject to tighter restrictions than joint ventures, although recent changes in the laws have relaxed some of the more onerous restrictions. Prior to the 2001 revision of the WFOE Rules, relevant law provided that WFOE applications would be approved only if the WFOE committed to use advanced technology or export at least 50% of its products each year. Many foreign investors were able to convince approval authorities to adopt a flexible interpretation of the advanced technology requirement. Some examples of WFOEs satisfying the technology requirement in recent years include companies producing toys, laundry detergent, dishwashing liquid, cosmetics, paper products, and frozen food. Similarly, many foreign investors were able to convince approval authorities to accept vaguely worded and non-binding export goals as satisfying the export requirements.

The 2001 revision of the WFOE Rules has eliminated the technology and export requirements. Article 3 now provides that "the establishment of WFOEs must benefit the Chinese national economy" and that the PRC "encourages the establishment of technologically advanced WFOEs." These changes should result in the approval of a wider range of WFOEs in the future and Chinese officials have already indicated that they are willing to be flexible in order to attract foreign investment. Given the preference for exports and advanced technology, however, it remains unclear whether WFOE applications that do not meet either of these conditions will find more difficulty in obtaining approval.

PRC authorities frequently promulgate new guidelines and restrictions on WFOEs and other FIEs. As discussed in connection with the joint venture, the Foreign Investment Industrial Guidance Catalog sets forth general guidelines for all FIEs, including areas where all foreign investment is encouraged, permitted, and prohibited. The foreign investor would be well advised to review all up-to-date changes before moving forward with a WFOE project.

(1) The Approval Process and Approval Authorities

The approval process and approval guidelines for the WFOE are similar to those for the joint venture. Local authorities can approve WFOE projects with a total investment that does not exceed $100 million in encouraged and permitted industries and $50 million in restricted industries whereas projects exceeding those limits need central level approval. Projects exceeding $500 million in encouraged and permitted industries and $100 million in restricted industries need the approval of SDRC and then must be reported to the State Council for verification.

Unlike in the case of the joint venture, there is no local Chinese partner to assist the foreign investor in the application process. Some foreign investors engage local foreign investment service corporations to work with PRC authorities, but foreign investors should be aware that these corporations are for-profit subsidiaries of the approval authorities themselves and may not offer independent and objective advice. Other foreign investors engage PRC law firms to handle the application process, while some of the more experienced foreign investors handle the WFOE application through their internal legal departments.

Prior to the formal application process, the applicant must obtain preliminary approvals of a project report from the local level people's government where the WFOE will be located. The project report is similar to the preliminary feasibility study used in the joint venture application and allows local authorities to assess whether the project is economically viable and whether it will be beneficial to the economy. Once the preliminary approval is obtained, the applicant then submits a formal application to the approval authorities consisting of:

(1) an application for the establishment of a WFOE;

(2) a feasibility study;

(3) the articles of association of the WFOE;

(4) the name of the legal representative or the names of the board of directors of the WFOE;

(5) the legal certificate and a certificate of creditworthiness of the foreign investor;

(6) the approval by the local government of the intended place of establishment of the WFOE;

(7) a list of materials to be imported; and

(8) other documents to be submitted.

WFOE Rules, Art. 10.

Unlike the application for a joint venture, which can be a single page, the WFOE application requires a significant amount of detail. In the case of a joint venture, similar details would be required in the joint venture contract; as such a contract is missing in the case of a WFOE, PRC authorities require these details to be contained in the WFOE application. The application must include:

(1) name and address of the investor;

(2) name and address of the WFOE;

(3) amount of registered capital and total investment;

(4) scope of business, types of products, and scale of production;

(5) management structure and legal representative;

(6) technology and equipment to be used;

(7) target markets and ratio of export and domestic sales;

(8) foreign exchange balancing scheme;

(9) employee hiring, wages, and benefits;

(10) environmental impact assessment;

(11) land location and size;

(12) raw materials and energy requirements;

(13) project implementation schedule; and

(14) term of the WFOE.

WFOE Rules, Art. 14.

As in the case of a joint venture application, the feasibility study is an expanded and more detailed version of the preliminary application report and is intended to demonstrate the economic viability of the WFOE. The study should describe all inputs required, costs, projected revenues, and potential markets.

The articles of association of the WFOE are required by law to be highly detailed so as to allow the approval authorities a full opportunity to understand the operations of the enterprise. The foreign investor should be prepared for detailed comments and requests for specific changes in the articles and other application documents. As in the case of a joint venture application, the foreign investor would be well advised to submit draft documents to the approval authorities for comments early in the process. Note that unlike in the case of a joint venture, the WFOE laws are silent on the management structures and do not require a board of directors. The foreign investor may choose to adopt another management structure, such as a general manager without a board. Most foreign investors choose to establish a board of directors because they are familiar with this management structure. Where there is more than one foreign investor in the WFOE, a board of directors is almost universally adopted. Where a board of directors is established, the chairman of the board is the legal representative of the WFOE.

As the WFOE does not involve a local partner, the foreign investor will need to make arrangements with the appropriate authorities for a land site, road access, buildings, utilities, and other power requirements for the new company. In the case of a joint venture, the local partner will usually contribute land and buildings as part of its capital contribution and will divert a part of its utilities and power to the joint venture, which is usually located on lands owned by the local partner. The local partner will also transfer some of its employees to the joint venture. In the case of the WFOE, the foreign investor will also need to recruit its own employees.

Once the formal application is submitted, the approval authorities have ninety days from the date of the submission to grant or deny approval. *See* WFOE Rules, Art. 11. Once the project is approved, the approval authorities will issue an approval certificate that the applicant must register with the appropriate level industrial administrative authorities within thirty days of receipt in order to obtain a business license. *See* WFOE Rules, Art. 12. As in the case of the joint venture, the issuance of the business license is routine unless there have been some irregularities in the approval process. Once the business license has been obtained, the WFOE may lawfully commence operations.

b. Conversion and Reorganization of a Joint Venture into a WFOE

Until 1997, there was considerable uncertainty concerning whether joint ventures could be reorganized into WFOEs or whether the parties would have to first terminate the joint venture and submit a separate application for the establishment of a

WFOE. In 1997, the Ministry of Foreign Trade and Economic Cooperation (now renamed the Ministry of Commerce) and the State Administration of Industry and Commerce jointly promulgated the Several Provisions on Changes in Equity Interest of Investors in Foreign Enterprises. The provisions now provide for a set of procedures for converting and reorganizing a joint venture into a WFOE through a buy-out process whereby the departing joint venture partner voluntarily transfers its equity interest to the purchaser. The provisions also provide for other equity changes, such as where one joint venture partner may transfer a part of its equity interest to the other partner. While these provisions may have clarified the legal procedures involved in a joint venture reorganization, the legal and business issues associated with a buy-out can be complex and call for some careful planning. In most cases, the foreign investor is exposed to greater risks as it is the party that will buy out the interest of the local partner and continue the company as a WFOE. Once it receives payment, the local partner departs the scene and may be long gone before the foreign investor discovers problems concerning the transfer. *See* Daniel C.K. Chow, *A Primer on Foreign Investment Enterprises and Protection of Intellectual Property in China* 148–163 (2002). These new provisions and the growing preference on the part of foreign investors to strike out on their own indicate that the number of WFOEs in China should continue to increase in the near future.

3. THE HOLDING COMPANY

In the early phase of foreign investment in China, foreign investors established one or more manufacturing sites in the form of a joint venture or WFOE. As MNEs began to acquire a number of FIEs in China, many began to ponder the benefits of establishing a China holding company. The use of a holding company would allow the foreign investor to centralize ownership and management of a China corporate group in a single entity. The holding company would act as the equity holder and foreign investor in each of the MNE's joint ventures or WFOEs. In western legal systems, holding companies also perform a valuable treasury function by lending money and by originating or facilitating intra-company transfers and loans.

All FIEs in China are limited by the scope of their business licenses and many foreign investors found that their FIEs were generally limited to manufacturing and selling products. Beginning in the mid–1980s as their business operations expanded, foreign investors sought the economies of scale and efficiency that could be created through the use of a holding company and pressed PRC authorities to recognize this new entity. Although PRC law did not explicitly recognize holding companies, a few ambitious foreign investors were able to form holding companies on the basis of internal guidelines established by the Ministry of Commerce (MOFCOM was then known as the Ministry of Foreign Trade and Economic Cooperation or MOF-

TEC). On April 4, 1995, MOFCOM issued the Tentative Provisions on the Establishment of Companies with an Investment Nature (HC Tentative Provisions). The Tentative Provisions were further supplemented by MOFCOM with its issuance of the Explanation on Questions Relating to Tentative Provisions on the Establishment of Companies with an Investment Nature (1996) and the Opinion on Directing the Examination and Approvals of Foreign–Invested Enterprises (1996). In 1997, MOFCOM briefly suspended new approvals due to concerns that existing holding companies were exceeding their approved business scopes and not complying with reporting requirements. The suspension was short-lived but does indicate that MOFCOM has an on-going concern in subjecting holding companies to tight controls. In 2003, MOFCOM issued the Regulations on the Investment in and the Establishment of Holding Companies by Foreign Business Entities (revised in February and November 2004) (2004 Regulations), which integrated all of the existing provisions and instruments. However, the existing provisions and instruments were not formally withdrawn so they continue to have some supplementary value. The 2004 Regulations were further supplemented by MOFCOM with its issuance of the Supplementary Regulations on the Investment in and Establishment of Holding Companies by Foreign Business Entities in May 2006 (2006 Supplementary Regulations).

a. Prerequisites for Application

In order to be eligible to establish a holding company, the foreign investor must have:

(1) a total minimum asset value of at least U.S. $400 million in the year prior to the application; at least U.S. $10 million in registered capital already contributed to existing FIEs; or

(2) at least 10 FIEs already established engaged in production or infrastructure projects with total registered capital already contributed of at least U.S. $30 million.

2004 Regulations, Art. 3. Under either condition above, the foreign investor must also have good credit standing although PRC law does not further specify how such standing is established. Once established, the holding company must have at least $30 million in registered capital. *See* 2004 Regulations, Art. 3. The holding company can be formed as either a joint venture or as a WFOE. Where formed as a joint venture, the Chinese partner must have a total asset value of at least RMB 100 million (approximately $14.6 million) and have good credit standing. *See* 2004 Regulations, Art. 3. Because few foreign investors are likely to form a holding company as a joint venture, the discussion below is based upon the assumption that the holding company will be established as a WFOE.

The requirement that the foreign investor have at least a $400 million minimum asset value can be satisfied by a corporate group's assets when the foreign investor is part of that group. The HC Tentative Provisions do not further specify what constitutes a corporate group, but MOFCOM has indicated that a subsidiary of a multinational enterprise could use the assets of its parent and affiliates to satisfy the $400 million minimum asset requirement. *See* MOFCOM Opinion, Part 2. For many MNEs doing business in China, meeting the minimum asset value does not seem to be difficult. As of this writing, at least 245 holding companies have been established in the PRC and numerous applications for new holding companies are currently being considered by MOFCOM.

Although minimum asset value requirements have not been difficult for MNEs to meet, the other requirements that the foreign investor already have substantial existing foreign investments in operation have proved more troublesome. This requirement would appear to preclude foreign investors from establishing the holding company as its initial China FIE for the purpose of serving as an investor in FIEs that are established later. There does not appear to be a clear rationale for this requirement other than a general policy that the foreign investor seeking to establish a holding company must already have substantial existing business operations in China and concrete plans for future investment. In the past, some foreign investors have actually obtained preliminary approval for FIEs that they had no intention to establish in order to meet holding company requirements.

b. The Approval Process and Approval Authorities

All holding companies must be approved by MOF-COM. *See* 2004 Regulations, Art. 6. The foreign investor must first submit a holding company application to the local approval authorities where the company is to be established. Once local authorities approve the application, it is forwarded to MOF-COM for final approval. The application must include:

(1) application form, project proposal, feasibility study, and articles of association;

(2) supporting documents on the credit standing of the foreign investor, incorporation documents of the foreign investor, and documentation certifying the legal representative of the foreign investor;

(3) copies of the approval certificates, business licenses, and the capital verification reports issued by a PRC registered accountant of the enterprises invested in by the foreign investor;

(4) balance sheets of the foreign investor for the last three years; and

(5) other documents required by MOFCOM.

2004 Regulations, Art. 6. Once MOFCOM issues an approval certificate, the foreign investor must obtain a business license from the central level State Administration of Industry and Commerce. The foreign investor has two years in which to contribute the $30 million registered capital in foreign currency and is permitted to use RMB earned legally from its China business operations with relevant certificates verifying the sources of RMB issued by the Administration of Foreign Exchange. *See* Supplementary Regulations 2006, Art. 1. Some foreign investors have encountered difficulties in meeting this deadline. Where this occurs, the foreign investor can seek an extension from MOFCOM on the basis of special circumstances.

c. Permitted Scope of Business

PRC law now carefully circumscribes the business scope of holding companies. Under current law, a holding company is permitted to

(1) invest in sectors such as industry, agriculture, infrastructure, and energy that are encouraged by the state and in which foreign investment is permitted;

(2) provide the following services to its FIEs:

(a) assist or act as an agent for its FIEs (i) in the procuring of machinery, equipment, and office equipment and in the obtaining of raw materials, spare parts, and components required for production; (ii) in the sale of products inside or outside China; and (iii) in providing after sales services;

(b) balance foreign exchange services among its FIEs with the approval of the State Administration of Foreign Exchange;

(c) assist in the employment of staff for its FIEs and provide technical training, marketing, and consultancy services;

(d) assist its FIEs in the procurement of loans by providing guarantees; and

(3) establish scientific research and development centers, undertake to manufacture new products, develop advanced technology, transfer technology, and provide corresponding technical services;

(4) provide consultancy services to the holding company's investors; and

(5) contract with parent or affiliated companies to perform services.

2004 Regulations, Art. 10. Also, holding companies are allowed to perform services contracted for by an overseas company. *See* 2006 Supplementary Regulations, Art. 2. Prior to the enactment of the Tentative Provisions in 1995, some foreign investors were able to obtain a wider business scope for their holding companies, but MOFCOM has been consistent in holding new applicants strictly to the scope of business set forth above. While holding companies that were approved prior to 1995 are not affected by the Tentative Provisions, these companies have found that MOFCOM will require them to revise their business scope to adhere to the limitations set forth above as a condition of granting additional approvals such as for a capital increase. Some enterprising foreign investors have been able to obtain a slightly expanded business scope through heavy lobbying but MOFCOM is unlikely to deviate significantly from the 1995 requirements. Moreover, some foreign investors have found in the past that even when MOFCOM grants an expanded scope of business, the State Administration of Industry and Commerce will balk at issuing a business license for fear of acting outside of the law.

(1) The Holding Company as Investor in FIEs

The holding company scheme in the PRC allows the MNE to use the holding company as the foreign investor in a joint venture with a local Chinese partner. Note that the issue of the foreign invested status of the joint venture arises because it is a business arrangement between the holding company, a PRC legal person, and the local Chinese partner, also a PRC legal person. Under PRC law, however, the joint venture is treated as an FIE when one of the partners is a FIE holding company so long as its equity interest is at least 25% of the joint venture (all joint ventures must have at least 25% foreign ownership in order to maintain foreign invested status). *See* EJVL, Art. 4. Similarly, a wholly foreign-owned enterprise can be established under PRC law even though the sole investor is an FIE holding company and a Chinese legal person.

The advantage of using a holding company is that the MNE is able to have a single investor for all of its China FIEs. Some MNEs currently have a number of different corporate subsidiaries, affiliates, and divisions involved in different sectors of the MNE's business operations serving as the foreign investor with different local partners for separate joint ventures in China. Many of these different corporate entities within the same MNE may have little knowledge about the operations of their affiliated entities. The presence of a number of different entities can lead to a lack of coordination of business operations and to a loss of efficiency. The use of a holding company as a single investor has the advantage of presenting a single, unified presence to MOFCOM and other PRC authorities and may help to facilitate approvals and other matters. The holding company can also serve as a single source to receive dividends from all of the foreign investor's FIEs; these dividends can be used to pay for some of the holding companies' services and reinvested in research and development and in other unified business development plans for the China market.

MOFCOM's primary purpose in permitting the establishment of holding companies was to encourage additional foreign investment in China. MOFCOM has indicated that at least $30 million of a holding company's registered capital must be used as capital contributions to new or existing FIEs. *See* MOFCOM Opinion, Part 2. This requirement would suggest that in practice the holding company will need to exceed the $30 million minimum capitalization requirement under Article 2 of the Holding Company Tentative Provisions in order to have a sufficient amount of capital for its own operations once it has invested the required $30 million in its FIEs.

While the use of the holding company to invest in FIEs is clearly contemplated by MOFCOM, Article 10 of the 2004 Regulations set forth above is broad enough to suggest that a holding company can directly invest in a particular industry without establishing an FIE. Article 10 is also broad enough to permit the holding company to manufacture as well as invest and some MNEs have been able to receive approvals for their holding companies to manufacture. MNEs are interested in seeking the broadest use of holding companies and have continued to urge MOFCOM for flexibility in the interpretation of these guidelines.

(2) The Holding Company as a Management Center

Article 10 of the 2004 Regulations permits the holding company to assist its FIEs in the manufacture and sale of products and to provide consultancy services to foreign investors. This language has been interpreted to include management, personnel, advertising, legal, and financial services. Article 10(3) has also includes research and development and technical support. Under this structure, an MNE can establish a China center where all management and support functions for its FIEs can be located. The MNE can locate general managers for all of its strategic business units in the holding company. The general managers would supervise separate departments located in the holding company for advertising, sales, finance, human resources, in-house legal counsel, and corporate security. All of these central departments can provide services for all of the FIEs. The MNE can also channel the results of a research and development facility through the holding company for each of its FIEs. Although each of the FIEs will also have its own management structure, all important business decisions will be made by the holding company and the FIEs will function as manufacturing sites and instrumentalities of the holding company.

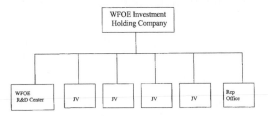

With the right structure and organization, the holding company can serve as the single investor in all of the foreign investor's FIEs and as a central management center. To further enhance and consolidate control, the foreign investor can establish a series of interlocking boards of directors. The WFOE holding company can be established with a three to five member board of directors with one or more of the directors also serving as general managers and directors on the boards of the FIEs. Such an approach would facilitate the development of a unified management and strategic approach for the foreign investor's China operations.

d. Current Issues with the Holding Company

Some of the benefits of the use of the holding company may be undermined by the pre-qualification requirements under Article 3 of the 2004 Regulations that the foreign investor must have already established FIEs in order to establish a holding company. The earlier discussion of the holding company suggested that there are advantages to the holding company serving as a single investor in all of the foreign investor's FIEs, but these advantages would be compromised if a prerequisite of establishing a holding company is to already have a number of existing FIEs. Yet, this appears to be precisely what PRC law requires. The present guidelines do not appear to permit the establishment of a holding company as an initial step for the foreign investor, but only as a later step as part of an expansion of an already established network of existing China FIEs.

While the holding company can still serve as the single investor in all existing FIEs if the foreign investor were to transfer all of its equity interests in its FIEs to the holding company, such transfers require the consent of the Chinese partner and approval of PRC authorities. The transfer process can be time consuming and complex because the foreign investor should not assume that such consents and approvals can be automatically obtained. Many MNEs have found almost universal initial resistance from their Chinese partners when they are approached for their consent to the transfer of the foreign investor's equity interests to the holding company. Local partners feel that they are losing a special status when the joint venture is grouped with other joint ventures with other Chinese partners. Local partners are also less sympathetic to the argument that use of a holding company will enhance the efficiency of the MNE's overall China operations as they are naturally most concerned with the performance of the particular joint venture in question. In addition, the consent of the FIE must be obtained before the holding company can lawfully provide the FIE with services such as advertising, accounting, and legal support. Where the FIE is a joint venture, the consent of the local partner will also be required. Many MNEs have found that in each case that the consent of the local partner is required, the local partner has considerable power to seek concessions on other issues or to even demand payment.

The holding company is also currently subject to other restrictions in the provision of services related to foreign trade, foreign exchange balancing, lending, and other financial services. Once the holding company is established, PRC law makes the dissolution of the holding company and the unwinding of a China corporate group complex and time consuming. Dissolving the holding company would involve a reassignment or sale of its equity ownership interests in each of its FIEs. Where the holding company is not the sole foreign investor in the FIEs, then this would involve the transfer of the equity interests to the other foreign investor and to the Chinese partner. Where the holding company is the sole foreign investor in the FIE, a transfer would involve the injection of a new entity to serve as the foreign investor in the FIE. Any of these changes would require obtaining numerous government approvals, the consent of the Chinese partner, and difficult valuation issues of equity interests and assets. The whole process of unwinding a holding company and a China corporate group could take several years to accomplish.

e.   The China Group or Conglomerate

While the types of investment vehicles in China remain limited, a foreign investor with substantial assets and a long-range business plan is able to build a corporate group through the use of the holding company, the joint venture, the WFOE, and the representative office. The use of the holding company, despite its present limitations, is a significant part of establishing a China corporate conglomerate. As China continues to undergo rapid changes, some of the existing restrictions on the holding company may be relaxed in order to attract a continuing influx of foreign investment and to meet the demands of foreign investors.

CHAPTER ELEVEN

INTELLECTUAL PROPERTY

This chapter will first briefly examine the history of intellectual property rights in China and then present an overview of China's current legal and regulatory regime, including the impact of China's entry into the WTO and its adherence to TRIPS. The chapter will then turn to an examination of commercial piracy and infringement of intellectual property rights, which continues to occur on a large scale despite the many efforts of intellectual property owners to control the problem.

A. INTELLECTUAL PROPERTY IN CHINESE HISTORY

In traditional China, copying was not condemned as improper but commended as a method of showing the proper deference to the past. Memorizing and repeating the Confucian classics during official examinations and copying the masters in painting and poetry helped to perpetuate the norms of the past and to replicate them in the present. Deference to the past is generally consistent with the conservative Confucian social philosophy that assumes that the norms established in the past by the masters of Chinese civilization were fundamental and constitutive of any Chinese society of any era. Only by understanding the past could a person attain the proper moral development and social training to become a good citizen in Chinese society. The indispensability of the past to attaining good citizenship meant that knowledge was not generally considered to be a form of private property but the common heritage of all Chinese as proper socialization required broad access to all past intellectual endeavors. The importance and vitality of the past is summed up by a passage in the *Analects*, one of the Confucian classics, in which Confucius himself says: "I transmit rather than create; I believe in and I love the Ancients."

As a result of the veneration of the past in traditional China, copying did not suffer from the same type of social stigma and condemnation that created the basis for intellectual property laws in western nations. This attitude existed at both the government and populace levels despite the introduction of intellectual property laws into China by the drafting of some intellectual property laws during the late Qing dynasty and by the Republican government after 1912. When the PRC was established in 1949, the Communist Party sought to abolish all forms of private property as China moved to a system of state ownership. The Party also specifically limited or denied protection for intellectual property as it rewarded individual creativity and private initiative during a period in which the Party stressed collective endeavor and common ownership. Until the advent of economic reforms in

1978, China never developed a tradition of viewing intellectual endeavors as creating property rights.

B. INTELLECTUAL PROPERTY IN MODERN CHINA

Although China did not have a tradition of intellectual property in its long history, China has enacted a comprehensive array of modern intellectual property laws and regulations in the span of just three decades beginning shortly after the commencement of the economic reform era in 1978. Much of the impetus for this swift development of intellectual property laws can be attributed to pressures exerted by foreign investors and foreign governments, particularly the United States. The situation for intellectual property protection in China has been described as the transplantation of a set of concepts from the west to a society that has long adhered to a set of values that is inconsistent with those concepts. This dynamic has led to a clash between China's intellectual property laws as written and its enduring cultural and political traditions that create tension and resistance in the full acceptance and full implementation of those laws. The pressures imposed by the United States have also triggered some resentment of foreign intrusion as the pressure tactics used by the United States are reminiscent of the gunboat diplomacy tactics used by foreign nations to pressure the Qing government into passing what became largely ineffective laws to address intellectual property protections in the late nineteenth century.

1. U.S.–CHINA BILATERAL NEGOTIATIONS

Under the 1979 Trade Agreement between China and the United States that was part of establishing diplomatic relations between the two nations, China agreed to provide protection for copyright, trademarks, and patents to American companies and persons on a reciprocal basis equal to the protections provided by U.S. law to Chinese parties. By 1989, both U.S. companies and the U.S. government believed that China's intellectual property protections were inadequate and the United States Trade Representative (USTR) placed China on the "priority watch list" of Special 301 of the Omnibus Trade and Competitiveness Act of 1988. Based upon Section 301 of the 1974 Trade Act (also known as "Super 301"), which was a general statute applicable to all areas of trade, Special 301 requires the USTR to notify Congress on a regular basis of "priority foreign countries" that fail to adequately protect U.S. intellectual property rights and to undertake all required remedial measures within a mandated period. A designation as a priority foreign country triggered a series of actions that could culminate in retaliatory trade sanctions imposed by the U.S. on the offending country. To increase the effectiveness of Special 301, the USTR created two other categories, a "priority watch list" and a "watch list" to put nations that had not quite crossed the "priority foreign country" threshold on notice that they might fall in that dreaded category if their protections did not improve. Special 301, like its predecessor Super 301, has been called the "nuclear bomb" of trade relations, better used as a threat than in practice because its use can escalate trade tensions into a trade war.

To avoid U.S. sanctions, China agreed in 1989 to a Memorandum of Understanding (MOU) that set out a series of steps that would improve China's intellectual property protection. Among other steps, China agreed to study the possibility of joining various international intellectual property treaties, to pass a copyright law by the end of the year and to amend its patent law by extending the period of protection to twenty years in accordance with international practice. In January 1992, China entered into a second MOU with the United States by which China agreed to accede to the Berne Convention for the Protection of Literary and Artistic Works by October 1992 and to make other changes to its existing copyright legislation. By 1994, the USTR determined that the situation in China had not improved and once again placed China on the Special 301 priority watch list. Although China had made significant progress in upgrading its laws, the USTR and U.S. companies felt that enforcement of the laws was inadequate. The USTR set a deadline by which China had to respond to U.S. demands or face retaliatory 100% tariffs on $1.1 billion of Chinese imports into the United States. China responded by threatening 100% tariffs on U.S. imports into China and also threatened to cut off negotiations with American automakers on joint ventures in China to build mini-vans and passenger cars. Just hours before the deadline, China and the United States signed the Agreement Regarding Intellectual Property, which included an action plan for enforcement of intellectual property rights calling for the creation of new enforcement bodies, including task forces, and special provisions for the protection of compact disks, laser disks, and CD ROMs. By May 1996, the United States was once again dissatisfied with China's efforts and again threatened China with retaliatory tariff sanctions on Chinese imports causing China to respond within the hour with its own threats of sanctions of a similar amount on American imports into China. The parties reached a new agreement, the 1996 Accord, just before the deadline.

Unlike the agreements reached in 1992 and 1995, the 1996 Accord did not specify new commitments that China had to undertake. Rather, the 1996 Accord mainly reaffirmed China's previous commitments to protect intellectual property rights. Since 1996, China has continued to upgrade its intellectual property laws in response to the 1996 Accord and to facilitate its accession to the WTO. By 1997, China had amended its criminal law to include a section on intellectual property crimes. China also upgraded the State Patent Office into the ministry level State Intellectual Property Office, charged with coordinating the work of the various government bodies that have responsibility over intellectual property rights and with overseeing the improvement of China's intellectual property legal regime.

2. CHINA'S CURRENT LEGAL FRAMEWORK

China's major intellectual property legislation includes the Trademark Law (1982, revised 1993 & 2001), the Patent Law (1984, revised 1992, 2000 & 2008), the Copyright Law (1991 revised 2001), the Administrative Regulations on the Protection of Computer Software (2002), the Anti–Unfair Competition Law (1993) protecting trade secrets, and related implementing regulations. The 1982 Constitution laid the basis for a legal regime protecting intellectual property with some general provisions recognizing the importance of the pursuit of artistic, cultural, literary, and scientific endeavors, although there is no explicit mention of copyright, patent, or trademarks. *See* PRC Const., Arts. 20 & 47. The 2004 amendments to the Constitution did not explicitly mention intellectual property rights but did provide that "citizens' legal personal property should be protected." In addition, the General Principles of Civil Law specifically provides that natural and legal persons are entitled to own trademarks, patents, and copyrights. *See* GPCL, Arts. 94–96.

China has also acceded to a number of major international intellectual property treaties, including the World Intellectual Property Organization Convention in 1980, the Paris Convention for the Protection of Industrial Property in 1984, the Berne Convention for the Protection of Literary and Artistic Works in 1992, and the Geneva Phonogram Convention in 1993. With the advent of China's entry into the WTO in 2001, China also acceded to one of the WTO's mandatory disciplines, TRIPS, which is the major driving force behind the harmonization of intellectual property laws around the world. TRIPS incorporates the major provisions of the 1967 Paris Convention on Industrial Property, the 1971 Berne Convention, and a number of other major international treaties. TRIPS is also the first international treaty to set forth minimal substantive standards for all of its members for seven major categories of rights: copyright, trademarks, geographical indications, industrial designs, patents, integrated circuit designs, and trade secrets. As an agreement of the WTO, TRIPS also incorporates the basic WTO (and GATT) principles of most favored nation treatment and national treatment. TRIPS also broke ground by including a section on enforcement, a topic that had not been covered in previous international agreements. Part 3 of TRIPS sets forth particular requirements on the types of judicial and administrative processes that all members must have in place for the enforcement of intellectual property rights, including the availability of ex parte injunctions and other pretrial provisional relief measures familiar to developed countries such as the United States. According to some observers, the adoption of TRIPS and its western intellectual property laws creates significant benefits for developed industrialized nations and does not give sufficient consideration to the interests of developing countries.

In the period leading to its accession to the WTO in 2001, China was actively drafting, revising, and enacting new legislation in preparation for the need to comply with TRIPS. These efforts have resulted in a current intellectual legal regime that, according to most observers, complies in all substantial respects with the requirements of TRIPS and other major international agreements. As further discussed in a subsequent section, the major issue for intellectual property owners in China is not with the substance or coverage of current laws, but with their enforcement.

a. Trademark Legislation

The first intellectual property legislation enacted by China after reforms was in the area of trademarks. In 1982, China adopted the Trademark Law (TL) that replaced the 1963 Regulations Governing Trademarks, which was primarily concerned with the control of product quality. Unlike its predecessor, the 1982 Law established a new administrative structure; set forth the rights associated with a registered trademark, including the right of exclusive use; clarified what actions constituted a trademark infringement; and provided additional sanctions and penalties. The Trademark Law Implementing Regulations (1983, revised 1988, 1993, 1995, 1999 & 2002) (TLIR) provided further detailed procedures for trademark protection and enforcement. The Trademark Law was revised in 1993 and in 2001 to bring the law into closer compliance with TRIPS.

(1) Eligibility for Trademark Protection

The 2001 Trademark Law has brought its definition of a trademark into conformity with Article 15 of TRIPS. Article 8 of the Trademark Law now provides: "Any visible symbols that may differentiate commodities of natural persons, legal persons, or other organizations from those of others, including words, figures, characters, graphics, three-dimensional symbols, and combinations of colors, and combinations of the aforesaid factors shall be eligible for registrations as trademarks." Product trademarks, service trademarks, collective marks, and certification marks are now all protected. *See* TL, Art. 3. China prohibits certain words or designs from use with a trademark, such as the state name, flag, or decorations of the PRC. There are also prohibitions for using a discriminatory reference in any trademark, making any detrimental references to socialist morals or customs of the country, and any geographical names of regions of the country. *See* TL, Art. 10.

Consistent with the Paris Convention and TRIPS, the 2001 Trademark Law now directly protects well-known trademarks, i.e. those trademarks with an international fame. Article 13 prohibits anyone from registering or using a trademark that copies, imitates, or translates well-known trademarks even if the marks are not already registered in China. Article 14 sets forth the criteria for determining a well-known mark.

(2) Registration System

China follows a first to file system for trademarks as contrasted with the first to use system in the United States. Under the first to file system, the person or entity that first registers the trademark acquires exclusive rights to use the trademark regardless of whether the person or entity first created and used the trademark. Once the trademark is approved by and registered with the Trademark Office of the State Administration of Industry and Commerce, the trademark will be entitled to protection under Chinese law. Although the first to file system can create some difficulties for those intellectual property owners from different legal systems, these difficulties were alleviated to some degree by the addition of new Articles 24 and 25 in the 2001 revision explicitly recognizing priority rights for certain trademarks. Article 24 grants a six-month priority in China for any trademark that is the subject of an application in a foreign country that is a participant with China in any bilateral or multilateral treaty recognizing priority rights or, in the absence of an applicable treaty, China will grant a six month priority on the basis of reciprocity. The six-month period of priority entitles the applicant of a trademark registration in China to claim priority over (and thus defeat) any competing trademark application in China for a six month period from the starting date, i.e. the filing date of an application in a qualifying foreign country. Article 25 provides that the display of a trademark for the first time in a Chinese government organization or sponsored international exposition will be automatically entitled to a six-month claim of priority for the mark in China.

The 2001 revision has also lifted restrictions on who may obtain a trademark. Under the prior Trademark Law, Chinese individuals had to register a privately owned company before they could obtain a trademark. The 2001 revision allows domestic, as well as foreign, individuals to obtain a trademark. In addition, Article 5 now allows for joint ownership of trademarks, providing flexibility for applications and a method for resolving disputes where marks have been used by more than one person or entity and the history of the mark is difficult to trace. The 2001 revision has retained the requirement that all foreigners or foreign enterprises must entrust a state qualified trademark agent to handle all matters dealing with the trademark including its registration. *See* TL, Art. 18. This special requirement for foreigners has created some difficulties as the number of qualified agents is still restricted and they enjoy the monopoly power from having a protected and exclusive right to represent foreign trademark owners in China.

The trademark application must specify the product or products to which it applies and the protection of the trademark will thereafter be limited only to those products. *See* TLIR, Art. 13. Once the application and copy of the trademark is filed with the Trademark Office, it will conduct a preliminary examination. Upon obtaining preliminary approval, the trademark is published for public review and comment allowing those who oppose the trademark to raise objections before the trademark receives final approval. If there is no justifiable opposition to the trademark, the Trademark Review and Adjudication Board will issue its final approval and the Trademark Office will issue a certificate of registration. Trademarks in China are valid for ten years from the date of registration, subject to renewals for an equal period of time. *See* TL, Art. 37. One of the most significant changes in the 2001 Trademark Law is the availability of judicial review for the relevant parties of all decisions of the Trademark Board, including the decision to reject a trademark application, the decision of the Trademark Board on an opposition petition, and the ruling of the Trademark Board on the maintenance or revocation of an existing registered mark. *See* TL, Arts. 32–33.

(3) Trademark Infringement

The owner of a registered trademark enjoys protection against infringement of the mark. Infringement is defined under the Trademark Law as using an identical or similar mark on identical or similar goods; selling commodities with an infringing trademark; copying or selling representations of a registered trademark without authorization; removing or changing a registered trademark from a product and replacing it with the infringer's own trademark and selling the product as the infringer's own (so-called "reverse counterfeiting"); or causing other harm to the exclusive rights of the trademark owner. *See* TL, Art. 52. The administrations of industry and commerce have the power to investigate and handle infringement cases although parties also have the option of proceeding directly in a people's court. *See* TL, Art. 53. Remedies available to the trademark owner are an order requiring the cessation of infringing activity, fines, and compensation. The 2001 revision now also explicitly provides that AICs have the power to confiscate and destroy products and equipment. *See* TL, Art. 55. A new article provides that trademark owners may seek a pretrial injunction and statutory damages of RMB 500,000 ($73,000) where the plaintiff's damages or the infringer's profits cannot be determined. *See* TL, Art. 56. The 2001 revision also provides that administrative authorities can transfer cases to judicial authorities for criminal prosecution where there is suspicion that a crime has occurred. *See* TL, Art. 54. The prior standard required proof, not merely suspicion, that a crime had been committed, which created a significant barrier to the transfer of cases for criminal prosecution. Whether this change results in a significant increase in criminal prosecutions in practice must await further experience; however, as of the current writing criminal prosecutions continue to be rare in the PRC. Other changes, such as the availability of pre-trial injunctions and statutory damages, have not proven to be readily obtainable in practice.

Although both the administrations of industry and commerce and the people's courts have jurisdiction to hear infringement cases, most trademark owners prefer using administrative authorities because of the simplicity and the speed of their response. Trademark owners are often able to obtain enforcement actions in the form of raids of suspected premises and seizures of suspected infringing goods on the same date that an application is made. An application usually consists of a complaint, the trademark registration certificate, and proof of suspected illegal activity, which can consist of sample infringing products, photographs, and written and oral statements. Most trademark owners have been satisfied with the initial response of enforcement authorities. Rather, as further discussed below, trademark owners believe that the penalties and sanctions that are the result of enforcement actions are not adequate to deter this highly lucrative illegal activity.

b. Patent Legislation

The Patent Law (PL) was passed by the NPC in 1982, revised in 1992, and revised again in 2000 to bring the law into closer conformity with TRIPS. At the end of 2008, the Standing Committee of NPC revised it again to increase punishments for patent infringements in order to provide greater protection to patent owners. The Patent Law Implementing Regulations (PLIR) were issued by the State Patent Office in 1992 and revised and reissued in 2001. These new laws strengthen patent protection for inventors and simplify patent examination and issuance procedures. Electronic submission of patent applications is now permitted in China.

(1) Eligibility for Patent

The Patent Law protects inventions, utility models, and exterior designs. *See* PL, Art. 2. An invention is any new technical solution relating to a product or process or improvement thereof, a utility model is any new technical solution relating to the shape or structure of a product that is fit for practical use, and an exterior design is any new shape, pattern, or color of a product that creates an aesthetic feeling and is fit for industrial application. *See* PL, Art. 2. An invention or utility model must exhibit novelty, inventiveness, and practical applicability in order to qualify for patent protection. In order to qualify for protection, an exterior design must not belong to an existing design, i.e. it cannot have been already publicly disclosed domestically or overseas. *See* PL, Art. 22 & 23. Certain discoveries and methods are excluded from patent, including scientific discoveries, rules and methods for mental activities, methods for the diagnosis or treatment of diseases, animal and plant breeds, and substances obtained by means of nuclear fission. *See* PL, Art. 25. The terms "novelty," "inventiveness," and "practical applicability" are generally equivalent to the concepts of "novelty," "non-obviousness," and "utility" required under U.S. law for a valid patent, although China applies different standards for different types of patent while the U.S. applies a single standard for all patents.

(2) Application Process

Owners of patent rights can be individuals or organizations. Foreign individuals and corporations will be granted patent rights in China in accordance with any bilateral or multilateral treaties that have been concluded by China and the foreign nation or on the basis of reciprocity. *See* PL, Art. 18. As in the case of trademarks, foreigners, foreign enterprises, and foreign organizations that seek to apply for a patent or need to handle other patent matters in China must engage one of the foreign patent agents designated by law. *See* PL, Art. 19. The new revisions also permit greater opportunity for inventors who create an invention in the course of employment for a work unit to obtain patent rights. *See* PL, Arts. 6–8. Rewards and compensation for inventors have also been increased. *See* PL, Art. 16; PLIR, Chap. 6.

After an application for a patent has been submitted, the Patent Office will conduct a preliminary examination of the application to determine whether all required documents have been submitted, whether the documents comply with legal requirements, and whether the application falls within any of the proscribed areas of the Patent Law. If the application passes this initial examination, the Patent Office will publish the application at the end of eighteen months from the filing date. Within three years from the filing date, the applicant may at any time request a substantive examination of the application; failure to make such a request within three years without proper reasons will result in the cancellation of the application. If there is no justified opposition to the application and it otherwise meets all of the requirements of the Patent Law, the patent will be approved. *See* PL, Arts. 34–39. The 2000 revision imposes new confidentiality obligations during the patent application and review process upon patent agents and state patent officials. *See* PL, Arts. 19 & 21.

Procedures are in place for internal review of decisions concerning invention patents by the Patent Re-examination Board and for judicial review by the people's courts. *See* PL, Art. 41. After the announcement of the patent by the State Patent Office, any person or entity may submit a request in writing to the Patent Office for the revocation of the patent. *See* PL, Art. 45. A decision on revocation is subject to judicial review in a people's court. *See* PL, Art. 46. The term of an invention patent is twenty years and the terms for utility model and design patents are ten years, starting from the filing date. *See* PL, Art. 42. However, the term of the patent can end sooner if annual fees are not paid as required or if the owner abandons the patent in writing. *See* PL, Art. 44.

(3) Patent Infringement

Patent infringement consists of any act exploiting the patent, including manufacture, sale, or use of the patent without the authorization of the patent owner. *See* PL, Art. 57. However, there are a number of uses that do not qualify as an infringement, such as use without knowledge that the product has been manufactured or sold without the authorization of the patentee or use for scientific research. *See.* PL, Art. 69.

When an infringement of a patent occurs, the 2008 Patent Law provides for a mediation procedure under Article 60. Where mediation is unsuccessful or the patent owner does not seek mediation, the patent owner can file a suit directly in a people's court or request the local patent administrative authority to handle the matter. The local patent authority is empowered to order the infringer to cease the infringing activity if a violation of the patent is found. *See* PL, Art. 60. New Article 65 provides that the patent owner can recover compensation based upon the economic loss caused by the infringement, the gain to the infringer, or, where the loss or gain is difficult to determine, based upon some reasonable multiple of the licensing fee for the patent. New Article 66 provides for pre-trial injunctions or property preservation before filing suit and Article 67 provides for the preservation of evidence. Article 63 provides for both civil and criminal liability for the counterfeiting of patents. As in the case of other intellectual property crimes, the public security organs must initiate all patent counterfeiting cases. Patent administrative authorities need to first transfer the case to the police before a criminal prosecution can begin.

c. Copyright Legislation

The Copyright Law (1990, revised 2001) (CL), Copyright Law Implementing Regulations (1991, revised 2002) (CLIR), and the Provisions on Implementing International Copyright Treaties (1992) are the basic copyright laws of the PRC. As with other intellectual property laws, the latest revisions to China's copyright legislation were intended to bring it more in line with TRIPS. Additional legislation, further discussed below, has been enacted to protect computer software.

(1) Copyright Eligibility and Rights

The 2001 revision brings the Copyright Law into compliance with the Berne Convention (the core of which is also incorporated into TRIPS) by providing for full copyright protection for works of literature, art, natural sciences, social sciences, engineering, and technology, among other fields, created in any of the following forms: written works, oral works, musical works, dramatic works, choreographic works, and acrobatic works; works of the fine arts and architectural works; photographic works; cinematographic works; engineering design drawings, product design drawings, maps, sketches, and other pictorial and graphic works; computer software; and other works as provided by relevant laws and administrative regulations. *See* CL, Art. 3. No copyright is available for laws, regulations, and other documents of a legislative, administrative, or judicial nature or for their official translations; news on current affairs; calendars; general numerical tables; and forms and formulas in general use. *See* CL, Art. 5. The term of copyright protection is the life of the author plus fifty years in the case of a natural person or fifty years in the case of a legal person, such as a business enterprise. *See* CL, Art. 21.

While prior law consolidated all rights into the single right of remuneration and exploitation, the 2001 revision adds twelve additional rights to bring the Copyright Law into conformity with the Berne Convention. Protected rights now include the exclusive right to copy, publish, rent, perform and alter a given work. Most of these rights can be exercised by others with permission. *See* CL, Art. 10. No permission or remuneration is required for certain types of uses, including private use for study, research, or amusement; quoting or publishing the work by the media for general circulation; or translating or copying the work in limited quantities for use in teaching or government. *See* CL, Art. 22. Uses beyond these permitted activities will usually require permission from the owner and may include the payment of remuneration. Note that consistent with the Berne Convention, China recognizes moral rights in addition to economic rights under Article 10. Among the moral rights are the right of authorship, alteration, and integrity. Unlike economic rights, moral rights are not assignable and are subject to an unlimited term of protection. *See* CL, Arts. 10 & 20.

For natural and legal persons in China, copyright adheres in the work at the time of its creation. For foreigners and stateless persons, copyright exists on the date that the work is first published in China. Foreigners and stateless persons will also enjoy copyright protection in accordance with any agreements that the foreign nation of their place of residence has entered into with China or in accordance with any multilateral treaties to which the foreign nation and China are parties. In accordance with the full national treatment principle of the Berne Convention, where the foreign work is first published in a third country that has entered into an international copyright agreement with China, the work will enjoy copyright protection in China even though the nation where the foreigner or stateless person resides has not entered into an international copyright agreement with China and the work would not be entitled to copyright protection in China if the work were first published in the nation of residence. *See* CL, Art. 2.

(2) Infringement

Infringement is defined under the Copyright Law to include publication or reproduction of another's work without permission or using the work without providing remuneration. *See* CL, Art. 46. Copyright administrative departments are now authorized to investigate infringement cases and are empowered to confiscate material, equipment, and instruments used in any infringing activity. Administrative authorities are also authorized to order the infringer to cease the infringing activity, make an apology, pay compensation, and pay fines. *See* CL, Art. 47. In appropriate cases, administrative authorities can also transfer cases to judicial authorities for criminal prosecution. Compensation can be based upon the actual economic losses of the copyright owner or on the illegal gains of the infringer. Where these amounts cannot be determined, a people's court is authorized to award statutory damages of up to RMB 500,000 ($73,000). *See* CL, Art. 48.

As in other areas of intellectual property, the people's courts have concurrent jurisdiction with the copyright administrative authorities and an owner can choose to proceed directly in court with a lawsuit. Consistent with new changes in patent and trademark law, Articles 49 and 50 of the 2001 Copyright Law now provide for pre-trial injunctions and orders for evidence preservation. Courts are also authorized to confiscate illegal gains, infringing products, and equipment used to produce infringing copies. *See* CL, Art. 51.

(3) Computer Software Legislation

The Copyright Law now expressly includes copyright software as a protected work, but the detailed rules for the protection of software are contained in separate legislation. Under the Administrative Regulations on the Protection of Computer Software (Decree No. 339) (ARCS) issued by the State Council in 2002, authors enjoy copyright in software developed by them whether the software is published or unpublished. *See* ARCS, Art. 5. Both moral and economic rights are recognized in computer software. Among the economic rights in software are reproduction rights, issuance rights, rental rights, and the right to provide software to the public through the Internet. *See* ARCS, Art. 8. The term of protection for computer software is consistent with general copyright protection, i.e. the life of the author plus fifty years or a flat fifty-year period where the author is a corporate person. *See* ARCS, Art. 14. Using standards consistent with the general Copyright Law, the new Regulations also provide for civil and criminal liability in software infringement cases as well as for pre-trial injunctions and property preservation orders. *See* ARCS, Arts. 24–27.

Authors are encouraged, but not required, to register their software under the Measures for the Registration of Computer Software Copyrights (2002). Registration is not a condition for obtaining copyright protection as copyright attaches upon the creation of the software. The major benefit of registration is that it provides evidence of ownership and, to some extent, of the content of the software and will facilitate resolution of competing claims of authorship and enforcement. Registration requires submission of the source code of the software but the applicant is now allowed to have the source code sealed to address concerns about confidentiality raised by authors under prior law.

d. Trade Secrets

Consistent with TRIPS, China protects business or trade secrets under the PRC Anti–Unfair Competition Law (1993). Article 10 of the Anti–Unfair Competition Law defines business secrets as undisclosed technical or business information that may be used for economic gain. Article 10 also prohibits the theft or unauthorized disclosure of business secrets and also imposes liability on third parties who profit from business secrets with actual or constructive knowledge that the secrets were procured illegally. In addition, Article 219 of the 1997 Criminal Law imposes criminal liability for certain thefts of business secrets. In China's intensely competitive marketplace, protection of proprietary business information is a serious problem, but as with other areas of intellectual property in China, the enforcement of laws against theft of business secrets is difficult to obtain in practice. Problems of enforcement are the subject of the discussion below.

C. PROBLEMS OF COMMERCIAL PIRACY

While China has made substantial progress in the enactment of intellectual property laws that meet the requirements of TRIPS and other international standards, the adequate enforcement of such laws remains a serious problem. The lack of adequate enforcement against violations of intellectual property rights in China has contributed to the rise of some of the world's most serious commercial piracy problems. Many foreign investors and local Chinese entrepreneurs point to commercial piracy as one of their most serious business problems in China today.

1. COPYRIGHT PIRACY

Large-scale problems of copyright piracy, which refers to the unauthorized copying of another's protected work, first began to occur in China in the 1980s leading the USTR to place China on the Special 301 priority watch list and to the first MOU between the United States and China in 1989. Under the pressure of additional agreements with the United States in 1992, 1995, and 1996, China has made some progress in the enforcement against copyright piracy but the problem remains severe. According to industry groups, losses from all forms of copyright piracy reached a peak of $2.8 billion in 1997 but declined slightly to $2.6 billion in 1998, and in 2005 the losses declined to $1.07 billion. There has also been an overall decline in the rate of piracy in all the major areas of piracy, such as motion pictures, music, and business and entertainment software, but China still has some of the highest piracy rates in the world. One industry group estimated that 82% of all software used in China at the end of 2006 was pirated, a piracy rate that is the second highest in the world after Vietnam. This figure actually represents a decline from 1995 when 99% of all entertainment software and 96% of all business software was pirated. Retail software revenues lost to piracy were estimated at $5.4 billion for 2006.

In the area of audio-visual products, China's enforcement authorities continue to seize massive quantities of pirated products. PRC authorities estimate that they seized more than 78.9 million illegal audio-visual products in 2005. China continues to hold highly publicized "destruction parties" of pirated products. On September 16, 2006, Beijing enforcement authorities destroyed over 1 million pirated CDs, DVDs, and VCDs in a public ceremony during "the hundred day anti-piracy campaign." In the area of books and journals, piracy has been linked to some of China's largest and best-known publishers. Over half of all copies of academic journals in all university libraries in China are unauthorized. Annual losses to U.S. publishers stemming from piracy of academic journals alone are estimated to be $100 million.

2.   TRADEMARK COUNTERFEITING

While there may have been an improvement in the area of copyright piracy in the past decade, the problem of trademark counterfeiting may have actually worsened in the same period. Trademark counterfeiting refers to the reproduction and use of another's trademark on identical or substantially similar goods. Counterfeiting should be distinguished from copyright piracy discussed in the preceding section. In the case of copyright piracy the object is to copy the content of a fixed medium of expression such as books, films, musical recordings, computer software, and audio-video products. There is not necessarily any attempt to convince the consumer that the pirated product was produced by the original copyright owner. By contrast, counterfeit products are often indistinguishable from the genuine product and will often bear the company name and address of the trademark owner. In some product categories, consumers are deceived into purchasing an inferior quality product disguised as a famous brand.

In the mid–1980s, there were virtually no counterfeits in China. In the early 1990s, the production of counterfeit goods for sale in China and for export abroad began to rise dramatically. The causes of counterfeiting can be attributed to the relaxation of constraints upon domestic companies, allowing them to manufacture and distribute the products of their choice, and to the influx of foreign companies into China with their well-known trademarks, creating a strong consumer demand for famous brands. By the mid–1990s, counterfeiting had far surpassed copyright piracy as the most serious intellectual property problem in China.

On June 30, 2000 the State Council Development and Research Center (DRC) issued a report highlighting the seriousness of trademark counterfeiting and its harmful impact on China's economy. The DRC report estimated that in 1998 counterfeiters flooded China with over $16 billion of fake products and indicated that the problem was getting worse. The DRC report expressly noted that its estimates of counterfeit goods in the Chinese market did not include fake cigarettes or pharmaceuticals, two areas notorious for high rates of counterfeiting so that the actual number of counterfeit products in China may far exceed the $16 billion figure. Some MNEs claim that their losses from counterfeiting equal 15 to 20% of total sales in China. One U.S. consumer products company claims that it loses $200 million per year to counterfeiting and others make similar claims. Based upon the DRC report, the information provided by individual companies, and additional research, industry groups claim that losses from trademark counterfeiting in China are in the tens of billions per year. Moreover, according to a survey of

152 foreign and Chinese enterprises conducted under the auspices of the DRC for its report, 75% of the companies surveyed believed that counterfeiting has worsened in the four-year period from 1997–2000 and that 30% of those surveyed believed that the problem has worsened considerably.

A rising concern for brand owners is that China has become a major exporter of counterfeit products to locations such as Russia, Europe, Africa, South America, and North America. While there are no reliable estimates on the size of this illegal export trade, what evidence that does exist suggests that the trade is massive. One consumer products company seized 52 million counterfeit products in 2000 and discovered that 16 million of these products were earmarked for export to countries as diverse as Chile, Indonesia, Nigeria, Paraguay, the Philippines, Russia, Spain, and the United States. In 2007, U.S. Customs seized $113 million in counterfeit and infringing goods at various U.S. ports of entry, an increase of 26% in domestic value in just one year. China was the single largest supplier of counterfeit and infringing products, accounting for 80% of the the value of the 14,775 shipments of counterfeit goods seized at U.S. ports in 2006. The amount of counterfeit and infringing goods seized by U.S. Customs can represent only a tiny fraction of what enters the U.S. market.

PRC authorities have taken a number of steps in response to the recent sustained lobbying efforts by industry groups in China. In August 2004 Vice Premier Wu Yi called on authorities from all levels of government and all departments to conduct a fierce anti-counterfeiting campaign that drew praise from industry groups. In response, the Ministry of Public Security of PRC conducted a one-year long anti-counterfeiting campaign nick named "Hawk". A new national anti-counterfeiting coordination committee was also established under the direction of Vice Premier Wu. The State Council circular announcing the anti-counterfeiting campaign stated that cases involving foreign invested enterprises should be a major target of the campaign.

3.   BARRIERS TO EFFECTIVE ENFORCEMENT AGAINST COUNTERFEITING

This section will briefly examine the major barriers that impede effective enforcement against counterfeiting. The discussion below, while focused on trademark counterfeiting, illustrates general problems that also plague enforcement efforts against copyright piracy and other forms of intellectual property violations.

a.   Local Protectionism

Efforts by both the U.S. government and industry lobbying groups have been largely directed at central level authorities in Beijing to make legislative changes and national commitments to combat counterfeiting. While it appears that central level leaders understand the importance of protecting intellectual property for promoting China's long-term economic development, central level authorities are legislative and policy-making bodies. Actual implementation and enforcement of the law occurs at the local level where there continue to be questionable commitments to suppressing counterfeiting, copyright piracy, and other forms of economic crimes.

Local level leaders are evaluated by the economic performance of their local political units and counterfeiting can be a boom to the local economy. The trade in counterfeit goods can absorb large numbers of unemployed workers, generate substantial revenues, provide tax revenues, and support other legitimate industries such as warehouses, hotels, restaurants, and nightclubs in the local economy. In the town of Yiwu in Zhejiang Province, well known as the center of commercial piracy in China, everyday at least 200,000 customers visit the over 33,000 wholesale stores and outlets selling over 100,000 varieties of products. Industry experts estimate that over 90% of the daily use and consumer products sold in Yiwu are counterfeit or infringing goods. Yiwu serves as a wholesale distribution center for products sold all over China. Yiwu also does a brisk export trade to countries in Africa, Asia, and South America. According to Yiwu government authorities, total sales of its wholesale business totaled $2.4 billion in 1997—the last year that figures were made publicly available—more than the total business revenues of most MNEs in China. These wholesale businesses also account for a substantial portion of the taxes paid to the local government supporting a host of public services. Most of the businesses that sell counterfeit and infringing goods in Yiwu negotiate a fixed amount of taxes to be paid to the local government in lieu of payment based upon graduated tax rates linked to revenue. It is no exaggeration to say that the entire local economy in Yiwu is built on the trade in counterfeit and pirated goods and that shutting down this illegal trade would be tantamount to shutting down the local economy. The trade in counterfeit and pirated goods has transformed Yiwu from a poor farming town into an economic model that other towns are seeking to emulate.

Not only are local leaders reluctant to shut down productive economic activity, local government entities often have a direct financial interest in the illegal trade itself. For example, in Yiwu, the local administration of industry and commerce has invested millions of dollars in the construction of the wholesale markets that sell counterfeit and infringing goods and charge monthly management fees to the businesses that sell these illegal goods. The AIC is also the same body that is in charge of enforcement against trademark counterfeiting and infringement. In Yiwu and in many other locations, the local AICs may have a financial interest in the very activity that they are supposed to suppress. In addition, the bulk of the wholesale and export of counterfeit products in Yiwu is owned and operated by a large corporate conglomerate that is owned by former and possibly some current government officials and Party leaders. These current or former government officials and Party leaders are able to exert enough influence on local enforcement authorities to protect the flourishing trade in counterfeit goods. Although Yiwu is an extreme example of the obstacles that are created by a local environment that is supported by counterfeiting, the same types of issues are present in many locations throughout China. In addition to having local officials that may have a direct or indirect financial interest in counterfeiting and piracy, local enforcement officials, prosecutors, and judges may be beholden to the local governments that appointed them and may face pressures to protect the local trade in counterfeit and pirated goods.

Overcoming local protectionism cannot be done simply through the drafting of new laws on intellectual property protection or the periodic "strike hard" campaigns initiated by central authorities against counterfeiting and piracy. While most of China's top leaders acknowledge that counterfeiting is a serious problem, China has a long list of problems of varying degrees of urgency. Any decision by central authorities to suppress local protectionism will involve significant political and social costs at a time when the PRC faces many difficult problems competing for the limited resources of the central government. Where local authorities are unwilling to shut down an economic activity that is perceived to be beneficial to their local economies, PRC central authorities will need to expend significant political resources to overcome the resistance of local authorities. Cracking down on counterfeiting may also result in serious social turmoil caused by the loss of employment, the shutting down of legitimate businesses, and other painful consequences. Faced with the significant costs involved in any serious nationwide campaign against counterfeiting, China's central authorities will naturally avoid incurring such costs, if possible. To date, it appears that China's central authorities lack the political resolve or commitment to launch a serious nationwide crackdown on counterfeiting.

b. Lack of Adequate Sanctions and Criminal Prosecutions

Local protectionism and the lack of mandatory guidelines for the imposition of serious fines and criminal sanctions have resulted in an enforcement system that does not adequately deter counterfeiting. Most brand owners in China are successful in using administrative authorities to bring raids and seizures, but many brand owners complain that counterfeiters and pirates are often back in business in a matter of weeks after an enforcement action has been completed. Set forth below are recent enforcement statistics reported by the State Administration of Industry and Commerce, the central level authority with primary authority over trademarks:

AIC TRADEMARK ENFORCEMENT ACTIVITY, 2002–2005

Year	Cases	Avg Fine	Avg Damages	Criminal Prosecutions
2002	23,539	$823	$22	59 total or 1 in 398 cases
2003	26,488	$1,059	$47	45 total or 1 in 588 cases
2004	40,171	$785	$51	96 total or 1 in 418 cases
2005	39,107	$1,056	$37	91 total or 1 in 429 cases

Source: State Administration of Industry and Commerce Annual Statistics

The average fine imposed on the counterfeiter or infringer in 2005 is $1,056, an increase of more than 55% over the 1997 figure but is still so low as to be considered a cost of doing business in a very lucrative trade. The amount of compensation awarded to brand owners in 2005 stands at $37, a negligible amount. Damages awarded by AICs seek to award the brand owner the profits earned by the counterfeiter after deducting all expenses (as represented by the counterfeiter) and are not based upon economic losses suffered.

Turning to the issue of criminal prosecutions, administrative authorities are to transfer cases that involve criminal liability to judicial authorities for criminal prosecution. The standards for criminal liability for counterfeiting are set forth in the Criminal Law of 1997. For example, under Article 140, a producer or distributor who has sales of inferior quality counterfeit goods exceeding RMB 50,000 ($7,300) but below RMB 200,000 ($29,200) must be sentenced to a term of imprisonment of up to two years and must also pay fines. As the level of sales increases, so does the severity of the criminal punishment. Other provisions in the Criminal Law use a similar approach based on sales of counterfeit or inferior quality goods. *See* Criminal Law, Arts. 141–148. As the statistics above indicate, however, the rate at which cases are being transferred by administrative authorities for criminal prosecutions actually fell from 1 in 398 cases (59 total cases transferred) in 2002 to 1 in 429 cases (91 total cases) in 2005. These levels of criminal prosecutions are too low to serve as a deterrent to wrongdoers.

One reason for such a low criminal prosecution rate is that administrative authorities are often reluctant to transfer cases to judicial authorities. Administrative authorities expend time and resources in conducting raids and seizures but are unable to collect fines from the perpetrator when a case is transferred. AICs will also have to transfer to judicial authorities confiscated products, machinery, and other evidence that might otherwise be sold at a public auction with the proceeds retained by the AICs. An additional reason is that the current practice in the PRC is to set a high evidentiary bar for criminal cases by requiring physical evidence of completed sales in the form of sales orders, sales receipts, ledger and account books, and tax documents. Counterfeit goods seized on the premises, packaging, or the equipment used in the manufacture of counterfeit goods, no matter how large the quantity, are not considered evidence of completed sales. Few if any counterfeiters keep such physical records of their illegal activities and gathering probative evidence has proven to be a difficult burden for most brand owners.

c. Problems in the Private Enforcement Industry

The enforcement of intellectual property rights in China relies heavily on the use of a flourishing private enforcement industry consisting of investigation companies, security firms, and law firms. PRC authorities do not have the resources to engage in protracted investigations of suspected counterfeiters and pirates who conduct clandestine operations in underground factories. Many brand owners will hire a private investigation company or law firm to conduct an investigation and collect evidence of illegal activity before approaching PRC authorities. With the evidence in hand, the brand owner, through its representatives, can present a complaint to authorities and also lead the authorities to the site of the suspected illegal factory or sales operation. Private investigation work is technically illegal in the PRC because it is considered to be a form of police work that is within the exclusive purview of the PRC government. However, because of a lack of resources and a high demand for enforcement, PRC authorities tolerate the existence of a private investigation industry and welcome its support. As a private investigation industry is not a recognized and lawful field of business in the PRC, the industry is unregulated by PRC authorities. Any one who seeks to establish such a business can do so. Those private investigation companies that have business licenses usually have market research listed as their business scope in their licenses obtained from PRC administrative authorities.

The unregulated nature of the private investigation business, the nature of the work, and the lucrative rewards of this flourishing industry can attract persons of questionable character and morals to this industry. In addition, investigation companies and law firms are in a fierce competition for the same multinational clients that have substantial budgets for intellectual property enforcement work in China. All of this combines to foster an atmosphere of fierce competition and sharp practices. One common questionable tactic is to pay "case fees" to officials for conducting enforcement actions. Since PRC authorities have discretionary authority on whether to accept a case, many officials ask for a case fee in exchange for proceeding with an enforcement action. Case fees generally range from RMB 1,000 to RMB 5,000 ($146—$730) per case but can be much higher. The author was present in one meeting with local public security bureau officials who asked for a "reward" of RMB 50,000 ($7,300) for each arrest of a suspect. For large-scale enforcement actions involving dozens of enforcement officials, payments of up to $100,000 have been demanded—and paid. Government officials have been known to buy apartments and cars using cash received from companies.

While this practice is of questionable legality under PRC law, it is a common practice for investigation companies to pay these fees and to pass on the costs to their often unsuspecting clients in the form of miscellaneous expenses. Companies from the United States are generally averse to making such payments in light of the Foreign Corrupt Practices Act of 1977, which prohibits certain payments to foreign government officials. As of this writing, some nations do not have similar laws so the domestic law of other countries may not prohibit foreign companies from making payments to foreign officials. By making such payments, investigation companies are able to report successful raids and seizures in order to keep their unsuspecting clients happy. Another common practice is for investigation companies to issue "trap" orders for products. Posing as a buyer of counterfeit goods, an agent of the investigation company will order the production of a large quantity of counterfeit goods and then arrange with enforcement authorities to conduct a raid to seize the very goods that were specifically manufactured at the behest of the investigation company. This tactic is also of questionable legality under PRC law. There are many other examples of bribes, gifts, and other questionable practices in this highly competitive industry. While making such payments by investigation companies may achieve the short-term objective of keeping their clients happy, such payments contribute to the further corruption of the PRC enforcement system to the long-term detriment to the rule of law in China.

Questionable and illegal practices also exist within the internal legal or security departments of foreign companies doing business in China. In many cases, an MNE will appoint one or more local employees to oversee the use of private investigation companies and law firms in the enforcement of intellectual property rights. In other cases, some companies will establish their own anti-piracy team that works directly in the field tracking down counterfeiters. In house anti-piracy teams have been known to seize and destroy property on the spot without any prior government authorization and make gifts and payments to government officials in exchange for enforcement activity. In addition, local employees have also been known to receive kickbacks for awarding work to private investigation companies and law firms. Many of these local employees are paid no more than RMB 10,000 per month ($1,460) but are authorized to hire or recommend private investigation companies and law firms that are paid from an enforcement budget that can be as high as several million dollars per year.

4.   THE EFFECT OF TRIPS ON COMMERCIAL PIRACY IN CHINA

After undergoing extensive revisions in anticipation of WTO accession, China's intellectual property laws were in substantial compliance with TRIPS when China formally acceded to the WTO in 2001 and China continues to review all of its laws to bring them into compliance with the WTO. Most observers do not believe that China's WTO accession will result in an immediate improvement in the enforcement of intellectual property rights. To the contrary, some observers argue that China's entry into the WTO will result in a short term rise in the domestic and international sales of counterfeit goods produced in China, although over the long term, as China's legal system develops, enforcement against counterfeiting and piracy should improve. For the short term, the same reforms that benefit the trade in genuine goods will also benefit the trade in counterfeit and pirated goods. As China undertakes the extensive reforms that will further lift restrictions upon its domestic markets, the production, distribution, and export of genuine and counterfeit goods alike should increase. To take one example, consider the growing export trade in counterfeit goods. Under China's pre-WTO system, export privileges were allocated only to a few types of companies, including certain state-licensed trading companies with export rights. Counterfeiters seeking to export their products generally had to secure the cooperation of a compliant state trading company. China has agreed to gradually lift these export restrictions as part of its WTO accession, allowing counterfeiters to export their products directly to locations around the world. The result has been a sharp short term rise in the export of counterfeit goods.

Nor should Part 3 of TRIPS, which includes specific enforcement obligations, result in an immediate improvement of intellectual property protection in China. Part 3 creates a general obligation to provide an enforcement system that is "effective" and serves as "a deterrent to further infringements." *See* TRIPS, Art. 41. A dispute on whether China meets this vague standard, however, will need to be resolved through the use of the WTO's dispute settlement procedures under its Dispute Settlement Understanding, another of the WTO's major disciplines. This dispute settlement process could take years and will require the complaining party to gather evidence, to build a case, and to allow China the opportunity to contest any allegations of breach of its obligations.

5.   LOBBYING BY BRAND OWNERS

In 1998, a group of MNEs formed the China Anti–Counterfeiting Coalition to lobby the PRC government to enact or revise legislation to address the counterfeiting problem. At the request of the PRC government, the name of the group was changed to the less threatening Quality Brands Protection Committee (QBPC). The QBPC includes over eighty of the largest and most well known MNEs doing business in China. The approach of the QBPC is to promote long term change in China's laws and improvement in enforcement results through a co-operative non-confrontational approach. Most MNEs and the QBPC do not wish to do anything to offend the Chinese government. It remains unclear whether this approach is achieving any tangible results. As of this writing in 2009, after more than a decade of intensive efforts by the QBPC and its predecessor entities, multinational companies, and foreign governments, the counterfeiting problem in China continues to be the most serious in world history.

CHAPTER TWELVE

REFERENCE TOOLS FOR FURTHER RESEARCH

This chapter provides references to a set of English language research tools and other resource materials for those interested in doing additional research on the PRC legal system.

A. INTERNET RESOURCES AND ELECTRONIC DATABASES

The following research guides point the reader to various sources in hardcopy and electronic sources for laws, cases, statutes, regulations, news, and policy statements of the PRC. These research guides are especially useful for the reader who is seeking information pertaining to PRC law but is uncertain about where relevant materials may be found.

(1) *A Complete Research Guide to the Laws of the People's Republic of China*, by Joan Liu and Wei Luo, Law Librarians: http://www.llrx.com/features/prc.htm

(2) *Guide to China Law Online*, published by the Library of Congress: http://www.loc.gov/law/help/guide/nations/china.html

(3) *Internet Chinese Legal Research Center* by Wei Luo of Washington St. Louis School of Law: http://ls.wustl.edu/Chinalaw/

(4) *Judicial Information of the People's Republic of China* by Zhai Jianxiong: http://www.llrx.com/features/chinajudicial.htm

The following websites contain current and comprehensive electronic databases containing cases, laws, and regulations. Some of these sites also contain commentary and articles about substantive areas of Chinese law. Most of the sites require a subscription.

(5) *Isinolaw*: http://www.isinolaw.com

(6) *Sinolaw*: http://www.sinolaw.com.cn

(7) *Westlaw China*: http://westlawchina.com

(8) *China Law Information* by Beijing University: http://www.lawinfoChina.com

(9) *China Law Reference Service Online*: http://www.cch.com.hk/HK/default.aspx

(10) *China Environmental Law*: http://www.chinaenvironmentallaw.com/

(11) *China Legislative Information:* http://www.chinalaw.gov.cn

(12) *Soshoo*: *http*://www.soshoo.com

(13) *China Foreign-related Commercial and Maritime Trial*: *http*://www.ccmt.org.cn/

(14) *Chinese Civil Law Network*: *http*://www.cclaw.net/

(15) *China Data Online*: http://chinadataonline.
     org/

The PRC Ministry of Commerce (MOFCOM) has its
own public website which contains official translations of selected laws and government policy documents in English: http://english.mofcom.gov.cn/.
Lexis has English translations of selected PRC laws
and regulations from 1950 to present and several
Chinese news sources, e.g., *China Law and Practice*
since 2001, and *Xinhua News*. Westlaw has news
and business articles in various databases, including: *China Daily* from 1995 to present, and *China
Business Review*, a business law periodical, since
2002.

Several official PRC government websites also
provide general news and information about China:

(16) *China Daily*, official newspaper of the
     PRC government: http://www.chinadaily.
     com.cn

(17) *People's Daily*, official newspaper of the
     Communist Party of China: http://english.
     peopledaily.com.cn

(18) *Xinhuanet News Agency*, official news
     agency of the PRC government: http://
     www.xinhuanet.com/english

(19) *China Gateway to News and Information*,
     official government gateway website with
     links to government agencies: http://www.
     china.org.cn/

The South China Morning Post, a privately
owned Hong Kong newspaper, has current news

and information about China at http://www.scmp.
com. The United States government also maintains
the following websites with current information and
statistics about China: *CIA's World Fact Book:
China*, https://www.cia.gov/library/publications/the-
world-factbook/geos/ch.html; *US Department of
State Country Information: China*, http://www.state.
gov/p/eap/ci/ch/.

B. TREATISES, LOOSELEAF REFERENCE
SERVICES, AND BOOKS

There are a number of useful treatises or loose-
leaf reference services that provide updated materials on Chinese law. *China Law Reference Service*
(Hong Kong: Asia Law & Practice, 1996–present) is
a multi-volume loose-leaf service that contains up-
to-date translations and digests of current laws,
circulars, notices, and orders. *China Law Reference
Service* has an accompanying on-line service mentioned in the previous section on electronic databases and a periodical service, *China Law and Practice,*
which provides monthly periodicals containing the
latest laws, regulations, digests of laws, and commentary. *Doing Business in China* (Freshfields, ed.,
Juris Publishing, 2d ed. 1999 to present) is a one
volume loose-leaf service that contains articles by
practitioners and authors, mostly based in Hong
Kong and China, on areas of Chinese business law.
*Corporate Counsel's Guide to Doing Business in
China* (Kenneth A. Cutshaw, ed., Business Laws,
Inc. 1999 to present) is also a one volume loose-leaf
service on areas of business law topics.

Sweet & Maxwell Asia, based in Hong Kong, publishes a series of scholarly treatises mostly by PRC and Hong Kong scholars on various topics of Chinese law, including volumes on Administrative Law, Banking Law, Constitutional Law, Company and Securities Law, Intellectual Property Law, International Trade, and Trusts. A list of these topics can be accessed through its website: http://www.sweetandmaxwell.com.hk/. Kluwer Law International publishes a large number of titles on Chinese law, a list of which can be accessed through its website: http://www.kluwerlaw.com/. Williams S. Hein & Co. publishes a Chinese law series in which US based scholars examine a certain law in the PRC with commentary, additional materials, and annotations of the laws in explanatory footnotes. So far the series has volumes on the Unified Contract Law, the law of SARS and other infectious diseases, the 1996 Criminal Procedure Law, the 1997 Criminal Law, among other laws. As of this writing, the author is aware of only several volumes of collected judicial cases published in English. One volume, *Protection of Intellectual Property Rights: Cases and Comments* (Law Press 1999), is compiled by the Shanghai High People's Court. Sweet & Maxwell publishes a volume on opinions of the Supreme People's Court as part of its China Law Series. Butterworths publishes the China Law Reports, spanning 1991–1995, with English translations of cases from various courts in China covering civil, criminal, administrative, and economic law. No doubt more English language editions of PRC cases will appear in the near future.

The following are some notable books on general aspects of the Chinese legal system: *A Guide to the Legal System of the PRC* (Peter Corne et al., eds., Asia Law & Practice 1997); *Basic Concepts of Chinese Law* (Tahirih V. Lee, ed., Garland Press 1997); Ronald C. Brown, *Understanding Chinese Courts and Legal Process* (Kluwer Law International 1997); Albert H.Y. Chen, *An Introduction to the Legal System of the People's Republic of China* (Butterworths Asia, rev. ed. 1998); Jianfu Chen, *From Administrative Authorization to Private Law* (Martinus Nijhoff Publishers 1995); Jianfu Chen, *Towards an Understanding of Chinese Law, its Nature, and Development* (Kluwer Law International 1999); *Chinese Law* (G. Wang & J. Mo., eds., Kluwer Law International 1999); *Chinese Law and Legal Theory* (Perry Keller, ed., Ashgate Publishing, Ltd. 2001); *Introduction to Chinese Law* (Chenguang Wang et al., eds., Sweet & Maxwell Asia 2001); Laszlo Ladany, *Law and Legality in China* (University of Hawaii 1992); *Limits of the Rule of Law in China* (Karen G. Turner et al., eds., University of Washington 2000); Stanley Lubman, *Bird in a Cage: Legal Reform in China after Mao* (Stanford University 1999); Pittman Potter, *The Chinese Legal System: Globalization and Local Legal Culture* (Routledge 2001).

The following are some notable books on specific areas of Chinese law: William P. Alford, *To Steal a Book is an Elegant Offense: Intellectual Property Law in Chinese Civilization* (Stanford University 1995); *China and Hong Kong in Legal Transition: Commercial and Humanitarian Issues* (Joseph Dellapenna et al., eds., American Bar Association 2000); *Chinese Intellectual Property, Law and Practice* (Mark A. Cohen et al., eds., Kluwer Law International 1999); Daniel C.K. Chow, *A Primer on Foreign Investment Enterprises and Protection of Intellectual Property in China* (Kluwer Law International 2002); Peter H. Corne, *Foreign Investment in China: The Administrative Legal System* (Hong Kong University 1997); Peter Feng, *Intellectual Property in China* (Sweet & Maxwell Asia 2003); Chaowu Jin, *Regulatory Environment of Chinese Taxation* (William S. Hein & Co. 2006): Chaowu Jin & Wei Luo, *Competition Law in China* (William S. Hein & Co. 2002); Feng Lin, *Constitutional Law in China* (Sweet & Maxwell Asia 2000); *Law-Making in the People's Republic of China* (Jan M. Otto et al., eds., Kluwer Law International 2000); Mary L. Riley, *Protecting Intellectual Property Rights in China* (Sweet & Maxwell Asia 1997); Peter Vout et al., *China Contracts Handbook* (Sweet & Maxwell Asia 2000); Kuihua Wang, *Chinese Commercial Law* (Oxford 2000); Westel W. Willoughby, *Constitutional Government in China: Present Conditions & Prospects* (William S. Hein & Co. 2000); Chaowu Jin, *Regulatory Environment of Chinese Taxation* (William S. Hein & Co. 2006); James M. Zimmerman, *China Law Deskbook: A Legal Guide for Foreign–Invested Enterprises* (American Bar Association 2005).

C. JOURNALS AND PERIODICALS

China Law and Practice (Asia Law & Practice, 1996–present) is a commercial periodical that is part of the *China Law Reference Service* multi-volume loose-leaf service on Chinese laws, regulations, orders, and circulars. *China Law and Practice* is published on a monthly basis and has the most up-to-date PRC laws and digests. *China Law* (China Legal Service, 1987 to present) is a Hong Kong based bi-monthly periodical published under the auspices of the PRC Ministry of Justice to provide commentary on contemporary legal issues, analyses of Chinese law, and translations of PRC laws. *Chinese Law and Government* (M.E. Sharpe, 1968 to present) provides English translations of scholarly works and policy documents.

There are also a number of academic journals that focus on Chinese law or regularly carry articles on Chinese law: *Chinese Journal of International Law*, Chinese Society for International Law in Beijing, 2002 to present; *Columbia Journal of Asian Law*, Columbia University School of Law, 1987–present (formerly *Journal of Chinese Law*); *Journal of Chinese and Comparative Law*, Centre for Chinese and Comparative Law of the University of Hong Kong, 1995 to present; *Pacific Rim Law & Policy Journal*, University of Washington, 1992 to present; and *UCLA Pacific Basin Law Journal*, University of California at Los Angeles School of Law, 1982 to present. There are also a large number of student-edited international law journals of general scope that regularly carry articles on Chinese law. These articles can be easily found by a search on Westlaw or Lexis.

*

INDEX

References are to Pages

467

CRIMINAL LAW—Cont'd

CULTURAL REVOLUTION

CURRENCY TRANSACTIONS

CUSTOMS

DEMOCRACY

DEMOCRATIC CENTRISM

†